CURSE OF THE BLACK BAMBINO

BASEBALL'S FAILURE TO ATTRACT AFRICAN-AMERICAN ATHLETES

By Anup Sinha

TABLE OF CONTENTS:

Note From the Author *4*

Prologue: The Black Bambino *9*

Chapter 1: RBI and the L.A. Story *12*

Chapter 2: The Saga of the All-Black Lineup *30*

Chapter 3: How Did Baseball Became So Slow and Unathletic? *39*

Chapter 4: Come On, Scouts! There's More to Dwight Gooden than Being Black and Righthanded *66*

Chapter 5: How Desire, Access, and Opportunity Made Football the African-American Dream *107*

Chapter 6: The Unfinished Business of Major League Baseball's Urban Youth Academy *131*

Chapter 7: Three Reasons Black Kids Will Play Baseball *155*

Chapter 8: The Surefire Plan- Three Actions for Major League Baseball *166*

Chapter 9: The South is Rising! Georgia Leads a Black Baseball Revival *175*

Chapter 10: Glass Walls, Broken Hearts, and Final Thoughts *187*

Extra Innings: Baseball's Ultimate Fantasy Team- Ten Black Athletes Who Could Have Been Hall of Fame Baseball Players *189*

Appendix A: Results of 1975 MLB Census *201*

Appendix B: Census of 1981 MLB *203*

Appendix C: Census of 2011 MLB *207*

Appendix D: 2011-2012 NBA Census *210*

Appendix E: African-American 2011 NFL Players from Select Cities *220*

Appendix F: African-American Census of 1959 MLB *224*

Appendix G: Survey on Attitudes of African-American Athletes Towards Baseball *226*

Appendix H: African-American All-Stars *229*

Appendix I: Letter to Darrell Miller Regarding Miami Urban Youth Academy Site *231*

Appendix J: Cuban Major Leaguers at the 2013 All-Star Break *233*

Appendix K: 1st-Round Drafted African-American Players by High School State Since 2000 *234*

BIBLIOGRAPHY *235*

INDEX *238*

NOTE FROM THE AUTHOR

This is not about increasing diversity in baseball. This is about increasing talent.

Let me explain my perspective.

I was once the biggest baseball fan in the world. Not only do I lack my youthful passion for major league baseball, but I wonder if I'd have liked it at all had I grown up today.

For my tastes, the major league game has become too slow paced and unathletic. The first has little to do with the declining numbers of African-American players; the second has everything. By losing the Black population, baseball is losing the best athletes who would inevitably become their most exciting players. What you're watching today is watered down talent. Were it not for the influx of talented Latinos and Asians, the league's entertainment value would be nil.

Growing up in the Detroit suburbs as the third child of Indian immigrants, I fell in love with baseball at age eight in 1979. Some would call it obsession; I watched or listened to nearly every Tigers game in the 1980s. It continued to distract me from my studies through the 1990s until I finally gave in and became a major league scout in the 2000s.

I still follow major league baseball. But if I have to wait five minutes for a pitching change in the third inning, I'll switch channels in a heartbeat.

Why? I don't think I'm different from any other sports fan. I enjoy watching sports because I want to see great athletes play like their life depends on winning. I want to see intensity; I want to be shocked and awed; I want excitement and passion and athleticism.

Baseball has somehow defied evolution by becoming both slower paced and less athletic over time. Meanwhile football, basketball, and hockey have evolved towards high-speed action and superior athleticism.

The fans have spoken with their remote controls. Though major league baseball is more profitable and more attended than ever before, the television ratings have fallen off a cliff the last thirty years.

While the early 1980s World Series games would regularly attract 40-60 million viewers, MLB is lucky to get 15-20 million today despite a greatly increased (by 33%) U.S. population. By comparison, the overall viewership for the Super Bowl, NBA Finals, and Stanley Cup have each improved.

Baseball has its niche; there are millions who follow the game through numbers and statistics and fantasy baseball is as popular as ever. There are plenty of children playing little league. But the dwindling television ratings reveal that baseball is becoming increasingly irrelevant as a spectator sport.

For further perspective, the most important baseball event of the decade was the deciding Game 7 of the 2011 World Series between the St. Louis Cardinals and Texas Rangers. It was out-watched by at least 25 regular season NFL games from the very same season.

The subsequent 2012 World Series was by far the least watched of all time, getting destroyed in the ratings by the NBA Finals eight months later.

Commentaries on the length of ballgames have become trite as have the analogies to watching paint dry and grass grow. As a child, I never once found it boring or slow because baseball wasn't played nearly as boring or slow as it is today. The numbers show that the length of games have nearly doubled since the early days of major league baseball; they are nearly an hour longer today than they were when I discovered the game in 1979.

It's still a nine inning game. The extra hour is dead time; pitchers holding onto the ball; hitters adjusting their batting gloves; pitchers making half-hearted pick-off throws. There are times where even I agree that major league baseball is excruciatingly boring to watch.

What's baffling is that this has happened while the NBA instituted a 24-second shot violation, the NFL shortened its play clock, and the NHL created penalties for delaying the game. All the other major leagues have implemented stiff timeout restrictions while MLB umpires are expected to grant them like candy. Society got faster, baseball got slower.

But enough said on the pace of baseball. This book is not about slow pace but my second complaint: slow athletes.

Speed is a guilty pleasure in all its manifestations. People who find baseball boring must put those thoughts aside when watching highlights of Willie Mays or Hank Aaron. There's nothing boring about an over-the-head catch in center field or a laser shot in the gap followed by a blitz around the bags. It's eye candy just like a thunderous slam dunk or a 90-yard touchdown run.

Today's style of baseball is station-to-station on both offense and defense. Displays of athleticism are increasingly rare.

Simply said, the premium athletes in America play football and basketball while the best in Canada play hockey.

As a baseball scout, I can't tell you how often I watched a high school football or basketball game with great envy. *What if he would have played baseball?* I'd ask. The fastest, strongest, and most athletic kids were on the gridiron and on the court. They were breathtaking to watch.

Most of them were African-American.

There are those who believe that Blacks just aren't good at baseball. A former major league general manager, who's spent six decades in the game, told me, "Black tools don't play in baseball" when I informed him of this book.

I can't disagree more. If baseball history isn't convincing, with its legions of superior Black ballplayers, then just look at how many Blacks are coming out of the Dominican Republic and how a 65% White nation like Cuba puts out powerful national baseball teams that are 90% Black. Where Black kids play baseball, they dominate.

Though I was color-blind as such in my childhood, it was ultimately the African-American ballplayers who piqued my interest during the early 1980s. Watching Ozzie Smith pogo-stick his way to a high bouncer in the hole; seeing 6'5", 230-pound Dave Parker run down a ball hit over his head and throw a bullet to strike down Jim Rice at the plate in the All-Star Game; Rod Carew's impossibly fast hands smoking an inside fastball to left-center field; Andre Dawson patrolling center field like a "Hawk"; Dave Winfield shrinking the ballpark with vicious swings and giant strides; Rickey Henderson exploding into full-speed after just one step towards stealing second base.

Just as Boomer Babies fell in love with Hank Aaron and Willie Mays in the 1950s, I was enraptured by the great African-Americans of the 1980s. The Ozzie Smiths and Rickey Hendersons brought something vital to the league. Flash, pizzazz, athleticism, charisma; call it what you want. It is its conspicuous absence today that has diminished baseball's appeal as a spectator sport.

So my plea to win back the Black athlete has little to do with the civil rights movement.

I am not requesting the predominantly White overlords of Major League Baseball to address Black participation out of a sense of inclusion and fairness. Nor do I necessarily blame Black exclusion on racism.

What I'm saying is that MLB needs Black America. They absolutely must have the great athletes from this demographic if the league is to remain in the national conscience. The NFL and NBA were wise to grow their brand among Blacks. By losing African-Americans, Major League Baseball is on a course to lose everyone else. If humanitarianism isn't rewarding enough, MLB should think about its own long-term survival.

I would not be writing this book if I thought it a losing cause. On the contrary, it is my belief that Major League Baseball can reclaim Black athletes in record numbers. I believe the glory days are ahead but only if MLB acts quickly and decisively.

When they do, African-American communities will again embrace this great game and share in the civic rewards that only baseball can bring.

It is in that spirit, with my love for both baseball and community, that I present to you *Curse of the Black Bambino*.

Anupam Sinha

Jupiter, FL

August 13th, 2013

PROLOGUE: The Black Bambino

"Some people say Josh Gibson died of a brain hemorrhage. I say he died of a broken heart."

-Attributed to Ted Page, former Negro league teammate

To understand this book and the issue at large, one must begin with the big catcher from Pittsburgh.

How good was Josh Gibson?

He was known as the "Black Babe Ruth". A Negro league superstar in the 1930s and 1940s, Gibson was said to have crushed 800 home runs and hit balls further than 500 feet.

No major league catcher then or now could hit like Josh Gibson. Not even Bill Dickey or Mickey Cochrane, both of whom were household names well on their way to Hall of Fame careers. Dickey and Cochrane could hit .320 like Gibson, but neither possessed his Ruthian power. Gibson had a tremendous throwing arm, was a good receiver behind the plate, and yet he could run like a centerfielder. Josh Gibson was a physical specimen, a freak of nature, and a gift to baseball.

Gibson had a charisma akin to later athletic celebrities like Willie Mays and Magic Johnson. He was a fan favorite, his rugged athleticism complemented with an easygoing off-the-field persona.

But by the 1940s, Gibson was setting his sights on something he could never have. That's when he started holding out for raises, threatening to jump ship from team to team, year after year. He took to drinking and carousing. He had forgotten his twin children and he was arrested multiple times for lewd behavior.

Somehow, Gibson was still the best catcher in the world. He didn't hit for the same power in the 1940s, but he still hit for high averages and knew how to lead a pitching staff. Gibson could stumble out of bed to hit .350 and that's often what he did.

But between the hits came fits of depression and thoughts of suicide.

One day, according to biographer William Brashler (*Josh Gibson: A life in the Negro leagues*, Ivan R Dee, 2000), teammates found Gibson alone in his hotel room having an imaginary conversation with Joe DiMaggio. Gibson was frustrated that Joe didn't remember him, a fellow baseball legend.

Gibson was hardly an isolated case. Black America was bursting with tremendous baseball players in his day. Players like Satchel Paige, Cool Papa Bell, Oscar Charleston, and so many others could have dominated the big leagues if just given a chance. One by one, year by year, the hearts of gifted Black athletes were torn out of their chests as Commissioner Kennesaw Mountain Landis refused to permit a man of color to enter the league.

Josh Gibson wasn't the only one, but he might have been the best, the most tragic, and the most symbolic. For when Branch Rickey's Brooklyn Dodgers finally reached out to sign a Negro league player in the fall of 1945, he chose Jackie Robinson. It wasn't long before other Black players signed, but they were young bucks like Larry Doby and Don Newcombe; talented ballplayers with their best days ahead. Gibson, at age 35, surely came to realize that his gifts were wasted. The game was rejecting him for the last time.

The once-chiseled and rock-solid 210-pound catcher had ballooned to a pudgy 230 during the 1946 season.

Then his body just withered away. Gibson weighed a flimsy 180 pounds in his dying winter. He spent his remaining days in a drunken stupor, as if he knew that coming back for the 1947 season was never an option.

When Gibson died at age 35 just months later, the initial reaction from friends was that he died of a broken heart. On January 20th, 1947, Gibson would be laid to rest in Allegheny Cemetery without leaving enough money to mark his headstone.

The broken heart of Josh Gibson, the "Black Babe Ruth", still emanates from his grave in Pittsburgh and forever lingers over the legacy of baseball. For there would be penance for Gibson if today's Josh Gibsons were able to achieve his dream, to play and glorify the game he loved and the game that broke his heart.

Sadly, there is not.

Chapter One: The L.A. Story and RBI

Many have anointed San Pedro de Macoris to be the greatest baseball factory in the world. In spite of a population comparable to Grand Rapids, Michigan, the Dominican town has produced over seventy major league players. The list includes superstars like Robinson Cano, Sammy Sosa, George Bell, Pedro Guerrero, and Joaquin Andujar.

But San Pedro de Macoris has nothing on Los Angeles. In its time, Los Angeles was truly the mecca of the sport, baseball's city of angels. Nobody produced a more staggering list of great ballplayers from the 1950s to the 1970s.

Almost all of them were Black.

"In our day," says veteran White Sox scout Tommy Butler, "Los Angeles baseball was so strong that you didn't just have to scout the nine players on the field. The guys in the dugout you had to worry about, too!

"Like George Hendrick, he hardly played at all for Fremont High School. Sat on the bench for them and he played 18 years in the big leagues! A couple other guys who got kicked off those teams played pro ball, too."

To truly grasp the impact of Los Angeles, one should look at the 1981 major league season (see Appendix B). There were 20 African-American players from Los Angeles in the big leagues that year. The list is highlighted by two Hall of Famers: shortstop Ozzie Smith and first baseman Eddie Murray who, incidentally, played ball together at Locke High School.

The L.A.-bred Black ballplayers behind them were not too shabby themselves.

George Foster's career was highlighted with a spectacular 1977 season that earned him the National League MVP for hitting .320 with 52 home runs and 149 RBIs as the cleanup hitter for the Cincinnati Reds. The Leuzinger High School product went on to club 348 homers over his career.

Foster led a particularly impressive group of outfielders: Chet Lemon (Fremont HS), Lonnie Smith (Centennial), Dan Ford (Fremont), Ken Landreaux (Dominguez), Mitchell Page (Centennial), George Hendrick (Fremont), Al Cowens (Centennial), Ellis Valentine (Crenshaw), Gary Ward (Compton), and Bob Watson (Fremont) were also starting major league outfielders out of inner city L.A. schools. The ten of them combined with Foster for a total of 19 All-Star Game appearances.

The Black L.A. infielders in 1981 included veterans Hubie Brooks (Dominguez), Lenny Randle (Centennial), and Enos Cabell (Gardena) along with Murray and Ozzie Smith.

The extraordinary list of Los Angelenos makes it hard to imagine the major leagues without them. Fittingly, it was the Los Angeles Dodgers who won the 1981 World Series and they did it with three native Black sons on their roster: starting centerfielder Ken Landreaux, veteran backup Reggie Smith (Centennial), and super utility man Derrel Thomas (Dorsey).

The very next year, three inner city L.A. "kids" led the St. Louis Cardinals to winning the 1982 World Series: Ozzie Smith, Lonnie Smith, and George Hendrick formed a third of their starting lineup.

Though L.A. players were still thriving in the big leagues, it was clear to scouts by the late 1970s that the great factory was starting to sputter. The Black inner city kids were leaning much more to football and basketball, even in the baseball mecca of Los Angeles.

The last gems to come out of L.A. were Darryl Strawberry (Crenshaw) and Eric Davis (Fremont) in 1980. Strawberry was the first overall pick by the New York Mets in the June draft while Davis inexplicably lasted till the 8th round.

One could say that inner city L.A. went out with a blaze of glory because of all their great ballplayers, none were as gifted as Strawberry and Davis. The childhood friends were tremendous athletes with electrifying skills.

Strawberry was a sculpted 6'6", 230 pounds in his prime with giant forearms and a lefthanded whip that could lift you out of your living room chair. Despite his size, Strawberry ran like a gazelle and he also possessed a powerful throwing arm. Had he wanted to pitch, Strawberry could have surely been an ace lefty.

Eric Davis was a razor-sharp 6'3", 180-pounder with power and speed by the gallon; fast twitch muscles from head to toe. His bat was so quick, Davis had to create a hitch; he started his hands below his belt because they were literally too fast for major league fastballs.

Both were the types of athletes who could have gone pro in just about any sport they wanted. Strawberry was an exceptional basketball player who also dominated his one season of football for Crenshaw High. Davis was a basketball-first athlete for much of his life and few doubted his boast that he could play in the NBA. Well into his big league career, the Los Angeles Clippers made serious overtures for Davis to pull a Bo Jackson and play two professional sports.

Though they fell short of the Hall of Fame on account of off-the-field issues (Strawberry) and injuries (Davis), they were exhilarating baseball players in their prime.

Sadly, they were the end. As the 1980s rolled on, the caliber of baseball deteriorated to the point that most scouts didn't even bother to visit Los Angeles. Especially with Orange County, the L.A. Valley, and San Diego more than picking up the slack.

Endangered species

One scout decided to take action.

For John Young, it was personal for he was a product of the glory days.

Young grew up in south central Los Angeles, graduating from Mount Carmel High School in 1967. Though the area wasn't as crime-ridden and gang-infested as it would become 20 years later, Young lived through the Watts riots and survived daily temptations to steer himself wrong. His tremendous athletic ability along with a strong support system kept him on a more virtuous path.

Young ended up attending Chapman College where he became a 1st round pick of the Detroit Tigers two years later in 1969. He reached the major leagues in 1971 for four glorious at-bats. His two hits gave him a lifetime big league batting average of .500.

But Young would never get another shot at "the show", in fact he played the next six seasons in the minors. Young put up huge numbers, but his bat wasn't quite enough to stick in the big leagues since he didn't bring much to the table with the glove or on the bases. Though Young was a speedster in his youth, he'd become a slow-footed 6'3", 220-pound first baseman by his late-20s.

He would join the Chicago Cubs as a scout and remain in the profession for 24 years. Young was appointed the Detroit Tigers' scouting director in 1981, the first African-American ever to hold such position in major league history.

His objective was clear in 1981. The Tigers needed to do a better job scouting and signing Black players from the south.

"When Bill Lajoie handed me a stopwatch and radar gun, he reminded me of the different mindset of southern scouts," said Young. "He told me that many quality Black players are overlooked."

Lajoie was tired of getting beaten on southern Black ballplayers and he was hiring John Young to put an end to it.

The Detroit Tigers had all the right intentions, but they were too late to the game. Young would soon discover that the Deep South was no longer a treasure trove of Black ballplayers by the early 1980s.

"So I hit the southeastern roads all excited, looking for the next Hank Aaron, Willie Mays, and Billy Williams. That's when I see the deplorable condition of inner city baseball in Atlanta, Birmingham, Mobile, Jackson, and New Orleans.

"What bothered me the most was the attitude Caucasians had toward the cerebral 'necessities', or lack of, by Blacks to participate in baseball."

Then there was the chance conversation in 1982 that really boiled Young's blood.

"I remember calling a premium high school prospect just before the June draft. I wanted to get the rain make-up dates. He graciously talked me through the remaining schedule with his opinion on the games that would be most worth my time.

"I will never forget his advice on one opponent when he said, 'I wouldn't waste my time on this game, it's a Black team and we will mercy rule them.'

"To this day, I don't believe the kid meant that as a vicious racial statement. I think it was in his mind the best way to describe most inner city baseball programs.

"Although I was peeved by the statement, my anger was directed by the fact that, in all honesty, I agreed with him; and the truth does hurt. I remembered wishing for a magic lantern or Rod Serling to send Jesuit High School back in time via the Twilight Zone to play some of Phil Pote's Fremont High School teams from south central L.A.

"So I guess anger was the initial emotional inspiration to improve the situation."

The unwitting young prospect was Will Clark.

Will Clark went on to play for Mississippi State University before enjoying an outstanding 15-year major league career as a first baseman. One of the greatest San Francisco Giants of all-time, Clark was a 6-time All-Star, finishing his career with a .303 average and 248 home runs.

While Will Clark went on to major league stardom, John Young kept beating the bushes and beating his head over the declining state of Black baseball.

By the late 1980s, he was back in Los Angeles working for the Texas Rangers. Young was now a veteran scout, long past his playing days, entering his 40s. Upon his homecoming, Young was horrified to find that his precious Los Angeles was not immune to what had plagued the south. Even worse than the loss of baseball, the city had developed a dangerous gang problem.

"Despite playing on an NCAA championship team (Chapman College) and in the major leagues (Detroit)," says Young, "my fondest memory of baseball anywhere was playing in the Compton Connie Mack League from 1965 to 1967 at Cressy Park. This league was extremely competitive and organized by Pop Syler, an African American. I would guestimate 75% of the participants were Black.

"Because Cressy Park was a stadium with lights, players from all ethnic and economic backgrounds rushed to play there. Caucasian players were not intimidated by the neighborhood. White players like Mike Paul, Rene and Marcel Lachemann, Rick Burleson, and the Pride of Compton, Duke Snider, all honed their skills there. Long before the Crips and Bloods, Marcel's only concern was how he was going to pitch Reggie Smith and Roy White while Rene's main concern was batting against Don Wilson and Dock Ellis.

"Along with me, the 1967 Compton Connie Mack class included future major leaguers Enos Cabell, Wayne Simpson, Lenny Randle, Derrel Thomas, and George Hendrick."

Fast-forward to 1988.

"It was difficult watching the poor caliber of baseball played by the predominantly African-American high schools. These were schools with basketball teams that could run you out of the gym; schools that had quality basketball coaches and uniforms and a history of sending graduates to college. How could baseball be received with such apathy?"

John Young had enough. "The Black ballplayer is an endangered species," he became famous for saying. In 1988, the percentage of Black major leaguers was down to 18% from the 19.1% of 1981. But Young knew it was going to crash a whole lot further if something wasn't done quick.

In response, Young came together with local scouts the following summer. They wrote a proposal to the commissioner's office which led to the formation of Reviving Baseball in the Inner Cities (RBI) in Los Angeles. Since producing both Eric Davis and Darryl Strawberry in 1980, the once bountiful City of Angels had gone hollow. Young's hometown was the perfect starting point. His dream was to extend RBI to inner cities across America and reclaim the great Black athletes who would both gain from and give so much to Baseball.

Commissioner Peter Ueberroth blessed the operation and did everything in his power to help. Ueberroth knew his way around the local bureaucracy having run the hugely successful 1984 Summer Olympics in Los Angeles.

Still, it took incredible effort to get off the ground. Young battled to get financial support. Battled to get baseball fields. He went into the schools with ex-big leaguers like Hubie Brown, Eric Davis, Darryl Strawberry, and Chris Brown and recruited young Blacks, face-to-face, to join RBI.

"With the resources, support from MLB and the city of Los Angeles, kicking off RBI appeared to be a slam dunk, right? Not quite," said Young. "There was another challenge that was not factored in the equation; the Crips and Bloods. I was no stranger to gangs in L.A. During my youth there were the Slausons, Gladiators, Businessmen, and

Watts gangs. However, the violence differential between the Crips versus the Bloods and the Slausons versus the Gladiators is like David trying to defend Hiroshima with a sling shot."

Parents balked at permitting their children to play on fields in gang territory. It seemed an intractable issue until Andy Williams with the Los Angeles Department of Parks and Recreation stepped forward. Among other things, Williams set up a meeting with gang leaders and introduced Young to the Los Angeles Youth Gang Task Force. An understanding was reached and gangs were no longer an issue in the early years of Los Angeles RBI.

Reviving Baseball in the Inner Cities was on its way.

"A very expensive public relations thing."

Young believed he was turning the tide; that baseball would once again be fed with Black players from the inner cities and everywhere else. He bragged "give me a million dollars and I'll blow away all those little islands" referring to the Dominican Republic's pre-eminent status as a baseball factory. Young envisioned the next 10-20 years of a league bolstered with Black stars to dwarf MLB's 18% representation in 1988.

RBI proved a success only in that it expanded to 200 cities (according to Major League Baseball). But it didn't solve the problem, not in Los Angeles nor anywhere else. In fact, the percentage of Black ballplayers has been cut in half; 8.8% in 2011 compared to the 18% of 1988.

Inner city Los Angeles is represented by only two major league players in 2013: outfielders Coco Crisp and Trayvon Robinson. Crisp is putting together a fine career as a fleet, leadoff-hitting centerfielder for twelve seasons (and counting) in the bigs. Robinson is more a 4A player; shuttling between Triple-A and the major leagues.

Needless to say, it's a far cry in quantity and quality from the 20 Black big leaguers L.A. produced in 1981.

"Once we gave it away to Major League Baseball, it started going bad," says a former scout who assisted Young with RBI from its inception. "Early 1990s, mid-1990s, I'd say... They were not out to run a league.

"Anyway, that's why I'm upset at baseball and what they did with RBI. John Young had a good program in L.A. It's too bad MLB doesn't understand how they get players. They don't understand."

Still, with or without RBI, the decline is shocking. How could L.A. go from a mecca to an embarrassment? From twenty Black big leaguers to only two?

"I don't think it just pertains to L.A., I think it pertains everywhere that there's a Black population," says Phil Pote. Pote has scouted for both the Oakland A's and Seattle Mariners for more than 40 years in southern California. Prior to scouting, Pote was a hugely successful baseball coach at prep powerhouses Fremont and Locke High Schools between 1957 and 1968.

"Football and basketball weren't very big in the 1940s, 50s, and 60s. The NFL and NBA were in embryonic status. Since then, they've done a tremendous job growing those sports and promoting them.

"It's a societal change. Baseball is America's game, I'll still say that it is America's game. But it was born in a much slower paced society. Now we're in an electronic world where everything is 'bam, bam, boom, crash'! Basketball and football are action-packed sports with very little down time.

"It's not just L.A. and it's not just Black kids, brown kids, White kids, but all kids today grow up in a faster paced society and those with the most athletic tools are attracted to those sports. It was a slow-paced society in the 1950s. Football and basketball are more to today's pace and they are glamorized. This is one of many reasons why those sports are much more popular among Black athletes than baseball now."

Inner city-bred players as a whole have dropped 83%; from 60 to 10 over a thirty year span (Appendix B and C). So Los Angeles alone produced twice as many big leaguers in 1981 as all the inner cities combined in 2011.

L.A. has deservedly received the most attention, but take a look at the other productive cities of 1981; not only for their baseball decline but for their coinciding productivity in football and basketball.

Table 1

African-American Players Produced by City (ranked in order of 1981 MLB)

City	1981 MLB#	2011 MLB#	2011-2012 NBA#	2011 NFL*
1. Los Angeles	20	2	15	16
2. Oakland	7	0	0	3
3. New York	4	0	15	2
4t. San Francisco	3	0	0	2
4t. Miami	3	0	3	29
4t. Cincinnati	3	0	0	3
TOTAL	**40**	**2**	**33**	**55**

#See Appendix B, Appendix C, and Appendix D for MLB and NBA figures

*Figures determined through 2011 NFL Census by USA Football, see Appendix E for summary

Oakland held their own in 1981; considering its population is barely a tenth of L.A.'s, Oakland's seven Black major leaguers may be even more impressive than L.A.'s twenty. Also consider their quality; Oakland's list is headlined by Hall of Famers Joe Morgan (Castlemont HS) and Rickey Henderson (Oakland Tech). Then there's outfielder Lloyd Moseby (Oakland) and pitcher Dave Stewart (St. Elizabeth), both youngsters in 1981 who would soon become All-Star contributors.

Right across the bay, San Francisco was a Black baseball factory in its own right adding three players led by A's ace righty Mike Norris. That made 10 inner city ballplayers from the Bay Area alone.

New York contributed Hall of Famer Rod Carew along with All-Stars like second baseman Willie Randolph and slugging outfielder Ben Oglivie. Andre Dawson, Warren Cromartie, and Mickey Rivers were a fine triumvirate for Miami. Tony Scott, Leon Durham, and former N.L. MVP Dave Parker certainly did Cincinnati proud.

More revealing are the columns to the right of the table. The six cities produced 40 Black ballplayers in 1981, but just two in 2011 and both were from L.A.

Both New York and L.A. have significant RBI presence, in fact they are likely the two programs with the highest endowment. According to its tax filing, Harlem RBI received $10.7 Million in donations during 2010 alone. L.A., of course, was where RBI was born and has had numerous benefactors. Despite the enormous funding, there has been little production by New York and L.A. at the big league level.

Baseball's demise in the nation's two largest cities proved the NBA's gain; New York and Los Angeles are pro basketball's greatest factories. The 2011-2012 NBA season featured 15 Black hoopsters from each city.

Like the NBA, the NFL has also capitalized on Los Angeles (16 Black football players) but they really struck gold in Miami (29). By comparison, there is not a single African-American major league baseball player from Miami today.

Consider four more cities that are loaded with excellent young Black athletes: Chicago, Dallas, Indianapolis and Detroit. (Number of Black athletes for each league is in parentheses.)

NBA: Chicago (10), Dallas (8), Indianapolis (4), and Detroit (2). (Appendix D)

NFL: Chicago (8), Dallas (11), Indianapolis (6), and Detroit (11). (Appendix E)

MLB: Chicago (0), Dallas (0), Indianapolis (0), and Detroit (0). (Appendix C)

So that means 24 NBA, 36 NFL, and zero Black major leaguers from those four cities combined!

Some more numbers: The 2011-2012 NBA boasted a total of 95 Black players from the inner city compared to MLB's 10. While there are no exact figures on the NFL, it is surely over 250.

Any way you slice it, Major League Baseball is getting killed in the cities where so many of the nation's best athletes reside. This is despite the presence of an RBI chapter in each town.

There has been little effort by the league to re-examine RBI's failure to increase the number of Black major league players. On their official website, Major League Baseball boasts that RBI is in over 200 cities and has 200,000 participants every year. They also claim to have produced eight current big leaguers which is hardly a bounty for a nationwide program of 200 chapters. The list is still sketchy; it seems that RBI is taking credit for developing players they had little to do with. Justin Upton, for example, was raised near Virginia Beach and though he played for an RBI All-Star team in a single tournament, he's hardly a product of the program.

"It's a very expensive public relations thing and that's exactly what they're doing with it," said a veteran southern California scout who was once involved with RBI. "It's not about developing inner city players, it's about PR."

Considerable money has been poured into RBI; tens of millions of dollars from donors outside of Major League Baseball. Former righthanded pitcher Kevin Brown dropped $1 million into the L.A. program by himself after he signed with the Dodgers in 1998 and first baseman Mark Teixeira did the same for Harlem RBI after signing with the Yankees eleven years later.

So how did RBI fail?

Not every chapter is so well funded. A number of past RBI chapter presidents have come forward and complained of the lack of resources coming from Major League Baseball.

"MLB gives you a startup of $5,000 the first year, depending on how many teams you bring in," recalls Chris Nelms on running Cincinnati RBI. "After that, everything was on me. I was on my own."

Nelms was with the program for six summers.

"If you were part of the Boys and Girls Club, they would fund the program. But I wasn't, I was by myself, and I had to do it myself. We needed to raise $10-$15G a year to have a league and I did that. Ken Griffey Jr. helped a lot; he sponsored a bus for the kids to ride to Detroit. And I had some money the second year from various sponsors.

"MLB just gave you their name, that's all. No money. They might give some equipment, some literature, other than that not much. Some balls. After that, nothing much."

A prospective RBI proprietor in the south had an even worse story.

"Hell, they offered me $200. $200! They said, here's $200, now you start a league. I can't even pay for one team with $200.

"They say they care about bringing baseball to inner city kids, but it's all talk. If they really cared, they'd invest and not just talk."

The lack of MLB funding often kills the leagues before they even have a chance. It depends exclusively on outside donations. For programs like L.A. and New York City that do receive considerable benefaction, it is up to them to use the money effectively.

I myself was a coach and planning committee member for the RBI program in Pontiac, Michigan back in 1996. We did not have a single umpire show up to any of our games; I recall fathers taking up the chore. They had to cancel the end-of-year banquet for a lack of funds. We raised much of our money by working the concession stands for Detroit Pistons games at The Palace.

I wasn't privy to the budget, but if Major League Baseball was funding any part of our program, it wasn't tangible.

Houston: the inner city baseball factory that almost was

Martin Stringer was the assistant director for Houston's RBI program from 1997 to 2005. Stringer worked under Irvin Hall, who'd previously headed the Detroit/Pontiac program that I was involved with. Unlike two hundred other RBI cities, Houston worked.

As a matter of fact, Houston is the one inner city with increased Black representation in 2011 than it had in 1981. Four Black inner city Houston-bred players are in the 2011 big league census; Carl Crawford, Michael Bourn, Chris Young, and Jason Bourgeois all hailed from Hall's and Stringer's Houston RBI.

"The Houston program, and John Young would verify this, was one of the top RBI programs in the country," said Stringer. "Today the RBI program is much diminished. They only have two teams now, we had 16 to 18. What happened was the city funded it for years, then they privatized it. It had been funded by grants, city finances. You lose your sources, you lose your coaches. We have to pay coaches and we can't pay enough of them.

"All the programs came apart from a lack of funds in 2005."

Stringer had an impressive number of participants during the heyday of Houston RBI.

"In 1997, we had 1,716 total in our program. We had 956 African-American players, 480 Hispanics, 77 Asians, and 186 White players. That included 568 girls in the softball program.

"In 1998, we had 1,649 participants. Then it went to 3,636 in 1999. We increased because, one, we had a vibrant program where kids were playing. Two, kids were being coached well. Three, kids were being successful. And four, the program was no cost to parents. Kids were given uniforms, all the fields were redone."

Stringer fondly recalls his big league alumni.

"I coached Carl Crawford. I coached all four of them, one thing they all had was talent. But they came from schools that were not very good baseball schools. Carl came from Davis High School; he came to us with very raw baseball skills.

"Carl would have still played baseball otherwise (without RBI), but he wouldn't have been exposed and he wouldn't have been as polished.

"We opened a line of marketing for these kids. I worked 80 hours a week!"

Houston worked brilliantly when it had money and it remains a shining example of what RBI can be. Houston was becoming an inner city baseball factory in its own right, but the reduced funding of 2005 has severely derailed the effort. Since 2005, the inner city talent in Houston has taken a dive and the well may go dry again for a very long time.

"Indianapolis would bring a team that was all White!"

There has been minimal progress among the Midwestern programs.

The presence of an RBI program made no difference in Detroit despite their chapter winning the Junior RBI World Series three years in a row from 2006-2008. While the city boasts two Black NBA and 11 Black NFL players, it hasn't had a single major league baseball player since Northwestern High's John Mayberry Sr. finished his career with the New York Yankees in 1982.

"I'm not a fan of RBI," said local youth baseball and basketball coach Darryl Smith. Smith's son Myles is a pitching prospect in the Boston Red Sox chain. "As far as their intended mission to develop inner city kids, it's not even helping. There were only two inner city kids on those championship teams. They had two kids from Canada and the rest were from the suburbs."

Two hundred fifty miles south is Cincinnati, Ohio, a town that was nearly the Midwestern version of Los Angeles during the 1970s and 1980s. The cream of their African-American crop was Ken Griffey Jr., Barry Larkin, and Dave Parker.

Today Cincinnati has three Black NFL players and none in baseball.

Chris Nelms headed the Cincinnati RBI program from 1999-2004. A former minor league player in the 1970s, Nelms grew up baseball-mad in the Queen City, learning the game from his father and three uncles who all played in the Negro leagues. He grew disillusioned by the direction of RBI.

"Indianapolis would bring a team that was all white. Boston was all Hispanic. They were deviating from the philosophy of what RBI was all about," said Nelms. "RBI is really watered down. It's not focused on African American players for two reasons. One, it's hard-pressed. Two, to put together an all-star team to get out of the region for an all-expense paid trip, you had to go out of the inner city to get players.

"That became the goal (going to regionals), not developing African-American players. RBI became its own worst enemy. And everybody deviated from the philosophy of RBI."

Nelms argued his case to authorities but to no avail.

"Their goals are to get to the regional. I told them, 'I disagree'. Part of it is winning and going to the regional, but there should be player development. Because if you have good players and they get to the major leagues, they'll come back and give to the program. They'd serve as an example and a model to inspire other young men to MLB or to a college scholarship."

"Where's the inner city in Anaheim?"

This 'deviation from the philosophy of RBI' has become a running joke among major league baseball scouts.

"You were watching the Anaheim RBI team? Where's the inner city in Anaheim?" asked an incredulous Astros scout after a southern California tournament in 2006.

"Between the Goofy and Donald Duck parking lots in Disneyland," I responded with barely a straight face.

"Does RBI stand for 'reviving baseball in the inland empire'?" asked a Los Angeles Angels scout a few hours later. "Because none of the kids on the L.A. team are even from L.A."

It's not much better for scouts on the national scene.

"The RBI World Series has been real disappointing," a scout confided to me in Jupiter, Florida during the 2010 Regionals. "I go to scout it because my boss tells me I have to. But there aren't any players there and hardly any of them are Black, much less from the inner city."

Extinct

John Young himself looks back on his brainchild with both pride and regret. "I don't think Major League Baseball mismanaged it, necessarily. But I wish they had baseball people in the right position to make decisions. Jimmie Lee Solomon never played baseball. Neither did Thomas Brasuell. "

Young added another rather cryptic assessment.

"I used to say that the Black baseball player was an endangered species. Now he's extinct."

Chapter Two: The Saga of the All-Black Lineup

The last thing on Danny Murtaugh's mind was Black History. The ever-competitive Pirates manager just wanted to sweep the Phillies and put distance between he and the Cardinals.

The defending N.L. East Champions were well on their way to winning the 1971 World Series. But on September 1st, the 11,278 fans at Pittsburgh's Three Rivers Stadium were treated to a breakthrough of another kind.

Dock Ellis was due for his regular turn on the mound. Murtaugh made out his batting order with sluggers Roberto Clemente and Willie Stargell hitting third and fourth like they always did. Just the same, Rennie Stennett led off at second base and Dave Cash hit seventh and played third base.

Then the rest of the lineup was shaken and stirred until it all turned dark.

Hard-hitting first baseman Bob Robertson was out, so Al Oliver moved from center to first. Gene Clines took Oliver's place in center and Jackie Hernandez was at shortstop to sub for injured starter Gene Alley.

Soon after the nine Black Pittsburgh Pirates took the field, there was a rumbling both in the stands and from the dugout.

The NBA had its first all-Black lineup seven years earlier, on December 26th, 1964, under the guidance of legendary Boston Celtics coach Red Auerbach. No one has documented the first all-Black NFL lineup, but it was surely well after September 1st, 1971. The National Hockey League (NHL) has never come close.

The starting lineup was short-lived as Dock Ellis was knocked out after pitching just an inning and a third that Wednesday night.

Reliever Bob Moose was roughed up too, so Murtaugh called on his other Black pitcher, Bob Veale, to get the last out of the third inning. The All-Black lineup was in force once again.

Veale, a lanky 6'6" starter turned lefty specialist, struck out the Phillies' Ron Stone but didn't come back to pitch the fourth.

When Bob Veale headed for the showers, it was the end of the all-Black lineup. Not just for the ballgame, but for 42+ years and a running count of 95,000 major league contests.

In that respect, September 1st, 1971 was the pinnacle of Blacks in baseball. In just 25 years, MLB had gone from a league with no Blacks to a lineup with no Whites.

Black players drew fans and dominated the league

It was only fitting that a National League team like the Pirates would be the first to field an all-Black lineup. The senior circuit had been much quicker to integrate than the American League, starting with Jackie Robinson's debut in 1947. It wasn't until 1959 that all 16 teams had at least one Black player, with the American League's Boston Red Sox being the last.

According to research by *Sports Illustrated* writer Dave Perkin (see Appendix F), the National League consisted of 15.6% Black (American and Caribbean) players in 1959 while the American League registered much less (11.3%). Overall, Major League Baseball was 13.5% Black including Caribbeans and 8.6% with American Blacks alone.

Considering the racial intolerance of the time, it is remarkable they still had comparable African-American representation (8.6% versus 8.8%) in 1959 to what we had in 2011, 52 years later. Blacks couldn't even drink from the same water fountains or eat in the same restaurants as Whites in 1959.

But they played baseball and they played it well.

“Sabermetrics were not around in 1959,” Perkin said. “Attention was paid to traditional stats such as batting average, home runs, RBIs, runs, steals, and total bases. Black players are all over those lists.”

Perkin reported that four of the National League’s top-5 hitters were Black that season. So were all five of the top-5 home run leaders, three of the top-5 RBI men, four of the top-5 runs leaders, four of the top-5 total base leaders, and all five of the top stolen base kings. In other words 25 out of the 30, or 83.3%, of the leaders were Black in a league where only 15.6% were.

To delve into the decade of the 1960s, if you take the National League “triple crown” category leaders (batting average, home runs, runs batted in) for each season between 1960 and 1969, you’ll find that among the 31 leaders, 26 were Black (including Latinos). That’s an astounding 84%!

There were 12 All-Star Games in the 1950s; the National League went 8-4. There were twelve more in the 1960s (twice a year until 1962) and the American League couldn’t win a single one! They played to a 1-1 tie in the second All-Star Game of 1961 and lost all the others. That means the A.L. had a 4-19-1 All-Star record over the 1950s and 1960s!

It’s hardly a coincidence that the National League out-numbered the American League 119 to 45 in Black All-Stars over the same two decades (see Appendix H courtesy of the National Baseball Hall of Fame).

But more than win All-Star Games, the Black players gave the N.L. a boost at the gate.

According to Dave Perkin’s research, the more integrated National League out-drew the American League in attendance over 14 of the 16 seasons between 1953-1968. Despite the era’s inherent racism, White fans were more than willing to spend money to watch Black baseball players. The iconic New York Yankees were in the American League, a huge draw both at home and on the road; but the National League still edged out the junior circuit in attendance year after year.

Even the exceptions proved the rule. The American League had higher attendance in 1961 simply because they'd expanded to ten teams while the National League still had eight. The only other year they exceeded the N.L. was in 1955, when the American League had a down-to-the-wire pennant race eventually taken by the Yankees while the Brooklyn Dodgers clinched the N.L. crown early to make the senior circuit's regular season almost completely void of drama.

As much as the National League benefitted from having many more Black players than the American League, there was clear discrimination down the line of talent in both circuits.

Neither N.L. nor A.L teams hung onto Black fourth outfielders or utility infielders. Instead they picked White players for the lesser roles, often in disregard of talent. They were happy to have Black players who were stars, but a Black backup who could just as easily be replaced by a White player usually was.

When baseball was the model sport

That was changing in the 1970s; very much the unspoken promise of the 1971 Pittsburgh Pirates. Players like Jackie Hernandez (a Cuban Black) were useful on the bench, but hardly stars, and the future promised for a lot more Jackie Hernandezes to go with the Hank Aarons. Baseball was taking integration to another level.

This was not supposed to be the end, but a means to the end, something to grow upon as it was for the NBA. It was evident how many fine young Black athletes were waiting in the wings and surely baseball would have many more Black players and many more days of all-Black lineups.

The NBA routinely puts out all-Black quintets in 2012 and it's not unusual to see 11 Black football players lined up on one side of the ball in the NFL. So it's baffling that baseball has yet to have another after 95,000 games and more than 40 years.

There were more African-American role players in the 1970s than ever before and Black representation rose to nearly 20%. Nevertheless, the game's Black talent pool was gradually undermined. Both the NFL and NBA were integrating much faster and there were noticeably fewer Black superstars in baseball by the end of the decade. The very best Black athletes were just starting to go to football and basketball.

So even as Murtaugh's nine took the field on September 1st, 1971, baseball was losing its grip on the elite Black athlete in America.

O.J.'s busted thumb

The floodgates were open in the NBA with big men Bill Russell and Wilt Chamberlain passing the torch to Kareem Abdul-Jabbar of the Milwaukee Bucks. Buffalo Bills running back O.J. Simpson was about to burst the scene as the NFL's most marketable star.

Baseball didn't lose Abdul-Jabbar and Simpson because it was slow or boring or a White man's game. Just the opposite, both Abdul-Jabbar and Simpson grew up playing baseball and have stated in their respective biographies that baseball was their favorite sport.

It just happened that Kareem grew over 7'0" tall and could no longer throw strikes as a young pitcher in New York City. O.J. busted his thumb and was forced to run track, which caught the attention of the football staff at San Francisco's Galileo High School.

Clearly, their physical tools were more attuned to excellence in basketball and football than they were to baseball, yet baseball was the sport of their fancy.

Baseball was truly the national pastime when Abdul-Jabbar (then known as Lew Alcindor) and O.J. Simpson were raised. And they weren't the only great athletes to fall back on other sports after "failing" at baseball. The lure of basketball and football just wasn't as great for the Black athlete of that time.

As it was, baseball was far and away the most popular sport in America for both Caucasians and African-Americans throughout the first six decades of the 20th century. A review of old team photos will reveal more Black MLB faces during the 1950s than there were in the NBA or NFL.

According to renowned basketball expert Bill Simmons (page 96 in *The Book of Basketball*, ESPN Books, 2009), the NBA reached 26% Black representation during the 1961-1962 season. That meant there were only 25 Black NBA players that year compared to over 60 major leaguers.

Along with the higher MLB numbers, there was arguably more Black star power in baseball than there was for either football or basketball in the 1950s and 1960s.

Jim Brown, Bill Russell, and Wilt Chamberlain aside, Blacks didn't have quite the impact on football and basketball as Mays, Aaron, and Bob Gibson did on baseball. Baseball was still the national passion and they were primary contributors to its popularity.

An age where Shaquille O'Neal played baseball

Hank Aaron said it himself in his book, *I Had a Hammer* (with Lonnie Wheeler, Harper's, 1990), that he and his Black peers in Mobile, Alabama loved baseball and saw football as the White man's game. Such a characterization would seem preposterous today with roles greatly reversed between the two sports.

The various Negro leagues co-existed with MLB throughout the 1930s and 1940s; most people think they were better. They certainly held their own in exhibitions and historians typically agree the Blacks won much more than they lost.

"Every Black athlete played baseball back then," says former scout and baseball executive Muzzy Jackson. "Buck O'Neil was my mentor when I worked with the Kansas City Royals and he said it all the time. Imagine an age where Shaquille O'Neal is playing baseball. You've got Magic Johnson on the mound. Barry Sanders in center field. That's what it was like then. That was Negro league baseball!"

There are many experts who believe that Satchel Paige would have out-pitched anyone in MLB. Many say Josh Gibson would have been the best catcher and Oscar Charleston the best major league centerfielder had they been given the opportunity. Buck O'Neil, the Negro league first baseman-turned scout-turned icon, claimed that Charleston was the greatest player he ever saw over nine decades of watching baseball.

That is why so many Negro league players have since been inducted into the Baseball Hall of Fame in Cooperstown. They may not have played Major League Baseball, but no one doubts they should have.

During the first half of the 20th century, professional football was struggling to grab hold and professional basketball as we know it did not exist. That certainly played a role in the lesser Black participation in football and basketball at the time.

But there was also among African-Americans a genuine love for baseball that is nowhere to be found today. Even though they were banned as a group from competing in MLB, Blacks continued to play and excel. The White man couldn't get rid of them, they were too good and too motivated. That persistence played no small role in why the color barrier was finally broken in 1947.

The growing concern with MLB commissioners

There was a steady decline through the 1990s not only for Black athletes playing baseball but for Black fans paying to watch it.

Peter Ueberroth recognized the arising problem in the 1980s and was of great help to John Young in creating Reviving Baseball in the Inner Cities. Bart Giamatti lived merely five months into his five-year term as commissioner, but continued RBI and shared the same concerns as Ueberroth. Upon Giamatti's untimely death in 1989, Fay Vincent was named his replacement. Soon after, Vincent ordered a study of African-Americans and their attitudes towards the sport.

Vincent's survey had disturbing revelations. (NOTE: I've requested the report from Steve Arocho at Major League Baseball, but after much correspondence he was unable to find it. The National Baseball Hall of Fame Library does not have a copy, either.)

"We found, by and large, that African-Americans viewed baseball as the White man's game," Vincent told me 22 years later. "The lack of Black leadership in baseball (referring to managers, general managers, MLB executives, etc.) was definitely a root cause.

"The research showed that we weren't going to be able to fix the problem in a short period of time. It was going to take a long time and that we'd have to get to the Black churches, Black schools, Black leaders, and Black magazines. I remember, we went and talked to the man who ran Ebony Magazine out of Chicago. We met with him and the owner and I was the first commissioner to ever come to him. He was pleasantly surprised that I came, but we didn't get a whole lot done."

Vincent immediately set out to hire minorities to work in the commissioner's office and it was during his reign that Len Coleman became National League President. Vincent was also the commissioner who brought in Jimmie Lee Solomon as director of minor league operations, many years before Solomon would spearhead the Urban Youth Academy initiative (see Chapter 6).

"It was a problem and I wanted to correct it. We had a lot of good ideas and good people like Len Coleman. Unfortunately, other things got in the way. I got in trouble over the labor issue and the union had other concerns.

"I wasn't there long enough (served three years), but yeah, I would have liked to have done more. If I could have given it to good people, like Len and some others, and given them ten years, it would have worked. We might not have seen results at the big league level for 6-7 years, but they eventually would have made the difference."

Chapter 3: How Did Baseball Became So Slow and Unathletic?

Our prologue introduced the sad saga of Josh Gibson, the Hall of Fame Negro league catcher who passed away at age 35 only months before Jackie Robinson broke the color barrier.

Would Josh Gibson be able to play in the big leagues if he grew up today? I say "yes" but with only a sideways nod.

That's because the question is almost moot, 66 years later. Today's Josh Gibson can play baseball if he wants to. He just doesn't want to.

Legality is no longer the issue, it's culture and desire.

There was a time when Black men wanted to play baseball and White men ran them off. Today White men are begging Black men to play and it's the Black men who are responding with "no thanks".

Let's reconsider Josh Gibson himself.

Gibson was a powerfully built 6'1", 210-pound man, who could easily weigh 230-240 pounds of solid muscle if he were raised today in the age of weightlifting and enhanced nutrition. He was very aggressive and ran extremely well, ranking among the fastest Negro league players during his prime. Gibson was mighty tough and nobody wanted to go toe-to-toe with him in a bench-clearing brawl.

That description makes him sound like Lawrence Taylor, an iconic outside linebacker from the 1980s. Or Adrian Peterson, a superstar 6'2" running back in today's National Football League. Considering his powerful throwing arm, perhaps Gibson could have also been a Donovan McNabb-type quarterback.

The one thing he doesn't sound like is a baseball player, much less a catcher. Russell Martin (who happens to be biracial) is the only "Black" catcher playing major league baseball today. It's not just his color, there's no backstop in 2013 blessed with anything approaching Gibson's level of power, speed, and athleticism. Just look at the pictures of Josh Gibson; it's like Bo Jackson decided to put on the tools of ignorance. Could you imagine Bo Jackson behind the plate?

Furthermore, Gibson spent his teenage years growing up on the outskirts of Pittsburgh. Western Pennsylvania has since become a famous breeding ground for football players; not only do the Pittsburgh Steelers enjoy a tremendous following, but the region boasts a number of prestigious youth and high school programs that have produced NFL players by the barrel.

How could a young man of Josh Gibson's athletic talents escape the football craze of western Pennsylvania today? The city of Pittsburgh alone was represented by 10 NFL players in 2011 (according to NFL Media), six of whom were Black. By comparison, there is not a single Black man from the entire state of Pennsylvania who played major league baseball in 2011.

Remarkably, I find no written accounts of Josh Gibson ever playing football while growing up in the 1920s. William Brashler's biography (*Josh Gibson: A life in the Negro leagues*, Ivan R Dee, 2000) claims that Gibson played baseball, swam, and ran a little track but did nothing else athletically in his youth. When the "Black Bambino" was growing up, baseball was king, especially among working class Blacks. It was also a way to make a living while football and basketball were not. In the 1920s, those sports were not even an afterthought to baseball.

Also of note during the Black Bambino's time, there wasn't the talent disparity between warm and cold weather-bred baseball players as there is today. Back then, plenty of big league ballplayers came out of the North and it wasn't nearly as regionalized a sport. Gibson's teams, the Pittsburgh Crawfords and Homestead Grays, recruited heavily from the Steel City as did the Pittsburgh Pirates in the years before the MLB draft.

But the culture of western Pennsylvania would change and change quickly from Gibson's time. The region would soon embrace football and baseball would in turn suffer.

There's a striking parallel between Josh Gibson and another powerfully built catcher born 45 years later. Lance Parrish started his life in Clairton, just 17 miles south of Gibson's hometown of Allegheny.

Parrish, an 8-time All-Star who went on to a 19-year career with primarily the Detroit Tigers and California Angels, is not far from a 1980s Caucasian version of Josh Gibson. He didn't have Gibson's speed by any stretch, but hit 324 home runs and his outstanding throwing arm helped earn him three gold glove awards. He was a tremendous athlete with a football body (6'3", 240 lbs.) and football tools.

But Parrish wasn't raised in Pennsylvania. His family moved to southern California in 1962, on Lance's 6th birthday.

"Had we stayed in Pittsburgh, I very likely would have focused on football," Parrish told me. "I mean, it was a football hotbed. If I was lucky enough, I would have played in the NFL."

Parrish grew up to become an All-American in football and basketball for Walnut High School in southern California. He was recruited as a quarterback by a number of prestigious football schools. Parrish eventually accepted a scholarship to play both baseball and football at UCLA only to spurn it by signing a pro contract with the Tigers upon high school graduation in 1974.

"I played all three sports growing up in California, that's all we did. But I didn't play tackle football until I was a freshman in high school and my mom was real hesitant to let me even then! I played with my friends or played flag football.

"I didn't even know tackle football existed for the younger age; I imagine I would have played it earlier in Pennsylvania and gotten caught up in it. Not that I couldn't play football out of California because I did and I had an opportunity to keep playing. But I could play baseball year-round there and that really allowed me to develop. By the time I was drafted, it was what I loved the most."

Had Parrish's father not moved the family to southern California, baseball would have likely been robbed of one of its best catchers during the 1980s.

The Parrishes moved from western Pennsylvania more than fifty years ago. The region's love affair with football has since expanded to even greater heights while baseball has taken a precipitous decline among both Blacks and Whites in the area.

So going back to Josh Gibson, what are the chances that an incredibly strong and aggressive young Black male, who could run like the wind, grows up in cold-weather Pittsburgh today and decides to play baseball instead of football?

Zero. He'd be lucky to still be playing baseball in high school and forget it after that. If you don't believe it, just count how many Black Pennsylvanian NFL players there are compared to the big zilch in MLB. The state of Pennsylvania produced 57 NFL players for 2011 (according to NFL Media). Given that 67% of the league's players are African-American, it's reasonable to estimate that 37-40 of the Pennsylvanian NFL players are also Black.

So how bad would the Pittsburgh Crawfords and Homestead Grays have been if they were around today? Where on earth would they get their Black baseball players?

Josh Gibson wouldn't have had a chance. Or rather, baseball would have never had a chance at Josh Gibson.

Therein lies the very core of the problem; the very reason why Major League Baseball must find a way to attract Black athletes.

A dozen Black Ty Cobbs

It's hardly a stretch to say that Blacks saved baseball in mid-century; in fact, one would have to bend the truth to state otherwise. The altruism of Branch Rickey's "Noble Experiment" aside, baseball was becoming bland and boring prior to Jackie Robinson's 1947 debut.

Early in the century, home runs were the exception. In fact, not a single player slugged 20 home runs during the first 10 years (1901-1910) of what would later be known as the "Dead Ball Era". Frank Schulte hit 21 in 1911 and only one more player would surpass 20 before Babe Ruth's 29-bomb explosion changed the game in 1919. Home runs are literally ten times more prevalent today than they were in the Dead Ball Era.

Ballparks were much larger and baseball players much smaller during the Dead Ball Era. According to research published in the December, 2008 issue of *Economics and Human Biology* (pages 482-488, Onge, Krueger, and Rogers), the average height of a major league player during the 1901-1918 Dead Ball Era started at 5'8" and never quite reached 5'10".

(There isn't reliable data today because players and clubs lie about heights; my fair guess as a scout would be to project an average 6'2" among position players and pitchers combined.)

Another overlooked aspect is the bats, which were much heavier with thicker handles in the early days of MLB. The old bats were conducive to slap-hitting, not for power.

"Gorilla Ball" was not an option in 1910 so teams were forced to manufacture runs. A premium was placed on the ability to get on base, but also to run the bases and play good defense. With the spacious outfields at stadiums like The Polo Grounds and Forbes Field, you better have a centerfielder who can "go get 'em" or you'll be giving up doubles and triples like there's no tomorrow.

As badly as today's game needs more Black players, it was truly a black hole in the completely segregated Dead Ball Era.

Speed and athleticism were the trademarks of superstar outfielders like Ty Cobb, who regularly hit .370, stole 60-100 bases, and caught everything hit in his zip code. For all we know, there might have been a dozen Black Ty Cobbs playing town ball across the country.

Shortstop Honus Wagner never hit more than 10 home runs in a season. Nevertheless the "Flying Dutchman" is considered by many as the greatest shortstop to ever play the game based on his outstanding glove work, .328 career average, and 728 stolen bases. Legendary baseball scout and executive Branch Rickey still rated Wagner the greatest player of all-time in his 1965 book (*The American Diamond* with Robert Riger, Simon and Schuster); Rickey saw everyone to that point, including Ty Cobb and Babe Ruth.

There was no such thing as a hit-and-miss slugger when Cobb and Wagner played. Babe Ruth, who hit his prime in the 1920s, never struck out a hundred times. So while Ryan Howard can strike out 200 times a year as long as he hits 35 HR and drives in 120 runs in 2010, anyone who struck out even 70 times in the Dead Ball Era was generally considered a reckless 'batsman'.

There were a lot more fielding errors committed in the Dead Ball Era; while the cumulative fielding percentage in 2011 was .983, it was only .942 in 1901. By 1918, it had risen to .964. Even then, errors were twice as frequent as they are now but it's not so much to do with lesser athleticism as it was for much inferior gloves and rougher playing surfaces. Anyone who has seen the floppy mittens of years past can surely understand how difficult it must have been to catch a fly ball or to cleanly field a grounder.

Nevertheless, Babe Ruth broke the mold in the 1920s. The game became more stationary as stolen base numbers fell off a cliff. In 1916, there was an average of 1.1

stolen bases a game, but the 1933 rate was less than a third (0.35) of that (according to www.Baseball-Reference.com). The game had become less athletic overall with teams relying more on the long ball, allowing slack defenders to play the field as long as they drove in runs at the plate. The best athletes were in the Negro leagues.

Baseball was still the national pastime going into 1947, but had Jackie Robinson not joined and been followed by Larry Doby, Roy Campanella, Don Newcombe, and the host of other Black ballplayers, it's likely that baseball's demise in popularity would have come about sooner. Not only did these outstanding players attract attendance from a growing African-American population, but they boosted the talent of the league and made it considerably more exciting to watch. Fans of all colors were flocking to the park when Black superstars like Mays, Aaron, Frank Robinson, and Bob Gibson made their debuts in the 1950s. They saved Baseball long before the phrase became fashionable.

From 1947 through the entire decade of the 1950s, there was a great pipeline of Black players to the big leagues. It has since been clogged to where we stand at a mere 8.8% in 2011; our numbers dwarfed by the NFL's 67% and the NBA's 78% Black representation.

Willie Mays is in the NFL and Bob Gibson is sticking to basketball

Baseball could have died again in the 1990s and early 2000s if it hadn't been for a Latino pipeline. I have no reservations in stating the Latinos saved baseball, this time. Especially considering how much talent fell through the cracks when Blacks fled the sport for football and basketball.

There have been Latino major leaguers as long as there've been Blacks, but the real explosion came in the 1990s. According to studies performed by Dr. Richard Lapchick's group (Institute for Diversity and Ethics in Sports, University of Central Florida), the Latino percentage in MLB was a mere 13% in 1990. It doubled to 26% by 1999, peaked at 29.4% in 2006, and stands at 27% in 2011.

That 27% includes superstars like Jose Reyes, Miguel Cabrera, and Mariano Rivera. It does not include stars like Albert Pujols, Adrian Gonzalez, and Alex Rodriguez, who are of Latino descent but raised in the United States. One can only imagine how dull major league baseball would be had they not graced us with their skills.

It would have been like reliving 1960 without African-Americans.

If you consider that Black players have decreased from 18% to 8.8% over the same period (1990-2011), the extra Latino participation is nothing short of a life raft. The impact of Asia has also been palpable (2.1% in 2011, according to study). Japanese outfielder Ichiro Suzuki was one of the game's biggest stars in the 2000s and South Korean outfielder Shin-Soo Choo was, for a few years, the marquee player for the Cleveland Indians. There are a number of other Asians who are considered impact players for their organizations.

It is wonderful that baseball found other avenues for talent, but the sad fact is that the league should be a lot better and much more exciting than it is. We've gained Ichiro Suzuki and Shin-Soo Choo, but we've lost Willie Mays and Bob Gibson.

That's because today, Willie Mays is in the NFL and Bob Gibson is sticking to basketball.

Willie Mays was an "all-world" high school quarterback near Birmingham, Alabama and also quite exceptional in basketball. He could have reached the top in either of those sports and his high school (Fairfield Industrial) didn't even have a baseball team!

Bob Gibson grew up in inner city Omaha. He was a broad jumper and basketball player for Omaha Technical High School; they had a baseball team but inexplicably excluded him on the color of his skin. Gibson went to nearby Creighton University on a basketball scholarship and proved exceptional in both sports. Prior to becoming the most dominant World Series pitcher of all-time, Gibson was a Harlem Globetrotter. He easily could have been an NBA superstar had he continued that route.

What are the chances that any athlete, Black or White, would end up playing baseball today from those environs? Mays and Gibson simply loved baseball and they were determined to play. Such passion is nowhere to be found in Black America today.

When you look around the Black communities, you're hard-pressed to find thriving little league programs, particularly in the inner cities. Unfortunately, that is when baseball has to get a hold on the best athletes; when they are eight years-old.

I got my start as a bird-dog scout for the Detroit Tigers in 1993; I spent the following spring trolling Detroit for inner city baseball talent. I was stunned to find Detroit Public School League teams playing only nine games a year and on fields at Belle Isle with craters and broken glass. There was typically no JV or freshman team, and most of the varsity kids had only little league experience. Many had quit for 3-4 years as middle schoolers before coming back. The real athletes never came back to baseball, if they'd ever played to begin with. At that time, basketball was clearly the king sport in the Motor City with football second and track third.

Baseball is undoubtedly the most technical sport of the "big three". It's become cliché that even the best must play 3-6 years of minor league ball before even thinking of the majors; meanwhile top collegians step right in and dominate both the NFL and NBA. Over the last 20 years, there have been a handful of high school hoopsters like Kobe Bryant, LeBron James, and Dwight Howard, who've made immediate impact on the NBA as teenagers. That will never happen in baseball today; even the exceptionally precocious Bryce Harper needed to go through the minors for a year and change.

Sheer athleticism is a wonderful thing, but hitting a baseball, pitching a baseball, fielding it in the hole, and throwing off-balance are skills that take a million repetitions each. Rarely will you find a major leaguer who didn't play baseball since his early childhood.

"That's the key," says Los Angeles Dodgers scouting director Logan White. "To make it in baseball, you had to play the game from when you were little. If you're seven-foot, you could pick basketball up in college almost. Like Manute Bol and Hakeem Olajuwan. In football, Christian Okoye never played football until college!"

White brought up another interesting football late-bloomer; the father of one his Dodger draftees who now pitches for the Pittsburgh Pirates.

"James McDonald's dad played four years in the NFL and he never played football in his life," said an incredulous White. "Not high school or college. He was a basketball player at Southern Cal and he wasn't NBA caliber. Then the football coach at USC (John Robinson) went to the Rams and asked James Sr., 'why don't you try out for the team?' And so that's how he ended up playing football. They put some weight on him and he ended up playing tight end.

"You don't do that in baseball!"

Over the last twenty years, the closest baseball story that comes to mind is that about an African-American athlete named Al Martin. The 6'2", 220-pound Martin debuted with the Pittsburgh Pirates in 1992 and spent most of that decade as a starting leftfielder.

As a youngster growing up in southern California, Martin played football and hardly ever touched a baseball. As legend has it, Martin attended a tryout camp after his sophomore year not to play, but solely to support a friend as a spectator.

One of the scouts running the tryout saw the athletic-looking Martin in the stands and motioned for him to come to the field. Martin was crude, but he showed he could both run and crush a baseball, standing 6'2" to boot. The feedback from scouts inspired Martin to start playing baseball his last two years in high school. His baseball skills would develop at a breakneck pace.

Martin was an 8th round pick by the Atlanta Braves out of Rowland High School in 1987 and would take just five more years to make the majors with the Pirates. Over 11 big league seasons, Martin would hit .276, slug 132 HR, and steal 173 bases. It was quite a career for someone who picked up baseball so late in life.

Even more miraculous is the life story of Ron LeFlore, who played baseball in jail for the first time in his 20s. LeFlore was paroled in 1973 and signed with his hometown Detroit Tigers immediately after at age 25. He was in the big leagues to stay by the end of 1974 and enjoyed a 9-year career in which he hit .288, stole 455 bases, played in one All-Star Game, and received MVP votes in four separate seasons (according to www.Baseball-Reference.com).

"We signed him for his tools. We didn't expect him to hit like that so quick," the late Bill Lajoie told me back in 2009. Lajoie signed LeFlore as an area scout for the Tigers a few months before he became the club's scouting director. "He could hit the ball quite well, but he couldn't center it. Fred Decker down in Lakeland was our farm director and he moved him up quickly. He had (general manager) Jim Campbell's ear and he pushed LeFlore to him."

Lajoie also remarked on LeFlore's tremendous athletic ability, so rarely found on a baseball field.

"I was afraid the Detroit Wheels (an upstart pro football team) would find him. If they ever got a hold of him, he was 215 pounds of muscle and could run like hell. Ron ran a 6.4 60 yard-dash on grass at the stadium, beating both Hampton brothers (local speedsters Rodney and Robert) in two different runs.

"Ron LeFlore was the fastest righthanded hitter to first base I'd ever seen," said Lajoie, who had seen many as a professional player from 1955-1964 and a scout from 1965-2010. "I watched some of those great football players in the NFL, with their agility and all that stuff, and they didn't have anything on him. So we were lucky to get him."

Incidentally, both Al Martin and Ron LeFlore are African-American. One can only imagine what kind of players they would have become had they played baseball from an early age and received expert instruction. One could argue LeFlore in particular as one of the greatest pure athletes ever to play major league baseball, given not only the great strength and speed but his remarkable hand-eye coordination to hit big league pitching just a year out of jail.

What kind of player would LeFlore have been had he played baseball growing up?

"Along with that speed, he would have hit for more power," said Lajoie. "He would have been a better defensive centerfielder. He used to run past balls, he would have been better."

If LeFlore could have added a power and defense dimension to his already impressive game and kept it together for longer than nine seasons, he'd have been a Hall of Famer.

As difficult as it is to play baseball at the highest level, these are two fairly recent examples of exceptional athletes who still brought excitement to the sport despite a late introduction. Two Black athletes who'd surely be relegated to football in this day and time. One can only wonder how many Al Martins and Ron LeFlores there are in the 21st century who simply don't go to that tryout.

Not my father's Cardinals

Because baseball is the most technical of the big three sports, it should be duly noted that even the greatest athletes need to be developed after high school. Martin and LeFlore would have never made it had they not received expert coaching in the minor leagues; or to use baseball lingo, good "player development".

Many veteran baseball people don't see today's minor league systems as equipped to develop raw athletes as they were in the 1970s. This effect skews towards Blacks because so many Black ballplayers fall into the "raw" category.

Benny Latino was notorious for signing high-end Black athletes as an area scout for the Tampa Bay Devil Rays in the 2000s. Latino believes minor league player development, or lack thereof, has a leading role in the decline of Black major leaguers.

"I'm going to give you an example. I saw a high school kid this year named Jervenski Johnson who'd committed to Arkansas to play football. He didn't have the test scores. Wide receiver, he was a 70 runner (well above-average on the 20-80 scale) with a 65-70 arm. A lot of raw power. The best natural athlete I've seen in a long time. He plays right across the street from my house. I talked to a couple of area scouts and they said, 'our club told us we need to get more polished players, we don't have time for him.'

"But this guy, ten years ago, somebody would have taken this guy decent and given him five years (to develop in the minors). When it came down to it, when he didn't get the test scores and no one drafted him, he went to a smaller school (Southeastern Louisiana University) to play football and they said he could play baseball, but I won't be surprised if he never plays baseball again.

"Jervenski really loved the game but he had a ways to go. Major league clubs, a lot of major league clubs, aren't set up for this. They aren't set up to develop that guy. My philosophy (as a scout) was to take five crude guys with a lot of tools and athletic ability for $100,000 and if one out of five make it, you're over the bar. If two make it, you're really ahead of the ballgame!"

Latino doesn't believe that every great Black athlete can make it in baseball, but is nonetheless disturbed by how many slip through cracks.

"If it's a good kid and he's got some kind of discipline, he's got a shot. It's going to take a while and the organization has to be patient. A lot has to do with the organization and a lot of them think it's cost efficient not to get these guys. But like I said before, if it works out for you then you'd be saving money."

Longtime MLB executive Pat Gillick has also seen changes in the mindset of player development over his Hall of Fame career. Gillick entered the administrative side of baseball in 1964 with the Houston Astros. As a general manager, Gillick went on to win two World Series crowns with the Toronto Blue Jays (1992, 1993) and one with the Philadelphia Phillies (2008). His teams in Toronto were particularly successful at developing Black ballplayers.

"They (major league teams) aren't as patient as they were then. One of the reasons is that when we got our franchise in Toronto about 35 years ago, we paid $7 million. Now they go for $700-800 million, and one (the Los Angeles Dodgers) just went for $2 billion. Consequently, I don't think these owners are patient anymore. They pressure the people in scouting and player development to develop players more quickly."

It's affected drafting strategy just the same.

"So there's a lean to college players more than high school now because high school players take longer to develop. General managers are feeling the heat to get players up here as fast as they can because by the time the high school players come up, they say, 'Well, we might not be here'."

The lean towards drafting collegians adversely affects African-Americans because so few of them are playing college baseball.

I myself worked for an organization that drastically shifted their philosophy from the 1980s to the 2000s in terms of the players they signed and how they were developed.

The St. Louis Cardinals I grew up watching in the 1980s were all about speed and defense. Incidentally, their rosters were loaded with Black players. Willie McGee and Vince Coleman were in the same outfield; two of the very fastest players and best base-stealers in the game. Ozzie Smith was a phenomenal shortstop, perhaps the greatest to ever field the position; he was a superior athlete who could also make things happen on the bases.

It seemed like every year, the Cardinals called up another speedster who knew how to play "Whiteyball"; an ode to manager Whitey Herzog who perfected the style so well that the Cardinals made three World Series appearances (1982, 1985, and 1987) during the decade.

Fred McAlister was the Cardinals scouting director for much of that run. Until his death at age 80 in 2008, McAlister was still working part-time and through him I learned much about the old Cardinals.

"We were all on the same page," McAlister told me back in 2005. "I drafted the kind of players Whitey Herzog wanted. I drafted speed, athletes. The farm director, Ted Simmons or whoever, they knew how to develop that kind of player. They could take a really fast kid like Vince Coleman and teach him how to play baseball. How to use his speed on the bases, in the outfield. They knew how to get them ready for Whitey. That's why we won."

By the mid-2000s, the Cardinals were still quite competitive but more of a station-to-station ballclub. I worked for the organization from 2005-2008 and we had plenty of bats and some good arms, but there was very little speed or pure athleticism to be found at any level. Our farm directors were Bruce Manno and Jeff Luhnow and both showed a clear preference for the polished ballplayer over the crude athlete with big upside. This usually meant college kids over high school and excluded many Blacks, like the Vince Colemans and Alex Coles of yesteryear.

In my first year as the Cardinals' southern California area scout in 2005, I signed a Black outfielder named Malcolm Owens out of San Bernardino Community College. For me, Owens was the epitome of an "old school Cardinal". Despite standing a sturdy 6'3", 210 lbs., Owens possessed blazing speed. I'd timed him under 4.0 seconds going home-to-first from the right side (4.3 being major league average) and fell in love with his overall athleticism.

Now don't get me wrong, Owens had big holes in his game, especially with the bat. He was a tremendous athlete; I couldn't believe it when he told me had no interest in football because he would have made a heck of a wide receiver or safety. But Owens hadn't played much baseball, either. He was oft-injured at Canyon Springs High School in nearby Moreno Valley and then he'd taken two years off before enrolling at SBCC. At age 20, he was SBCC's #9 hitter for most of the year. Owens had a lot of work to do; he was undoubtedly a longshot from day one, but I believed we had nothing to lose and potentially much to gain.

I discovered quickly after signing Owens that these were not my father's Cardinals. The minor league coaches were mystified by his crudeness, unable to share my appreciation for his upside. Owens was unfortunately released after two years for a lack of progress in their eyes. I learned a hard lesson about catering to your club's player development; to this day I feel I didn't look out for Malcolm Owens and that I shouldn't have signed him that year. Perhaps with another year of junior college ball under his belt, Owens would have been better prepared to play in the minors for somebody else.

Nevertheless, I still believe that had the Cardinals signed him 25 years prior, Owens would have had a chance to become a major league outfielder and a good chance at that. The physical ability was definitely there and if he was willing to put in the work, they would have done everything they could to mold him into another running Redbird. He just didn't fit the mold of what the Cardinals had become in the 2000s.

While football was speeding past Tony Dorsett, baseball got lapped by Ron LeFlore

Today's NFL players are much faster at every position than they were in the 1970s. Tony Dorsett and John Stallworth would have a hard time hanging with even an average running back or wide receiver today.

One might expect the same to be true of baseball. One might think that Ron LeFlore must have been left in the dust by today's base-stealers.

Think again.

"You know, he's still the fastest guy I've ever timed on a full swing from the right side to first base," says Joe McIlvaine. "I timed him in instructional league, my first year as a scout. He ran down the line on a full swing from the right side in 3.8. I've never to this day gotten that again. I've gotten 3.9, but never 3.8 on a full swing. A bunt yes, but I've never gotten a guy in 3.8 on a full swing."

Bill Lajoie told me much the same when we were writing *Character is Not a Statistic* in 2008.

So while football was speeding past Tony Dorsett, baseball got lapped by Ron LeFlore.

It explains why the universal scouting scale for speed remains unchanged over forty years. An "average" runner is still one who goes from home-to-first in 4.3 seconds from the right side and 4.2 seconds from the left. (Scouts start the stopwatch upon bat-to-ball contact and they stop it when the player touches first base.)

Not only have times not improved, but most scouts swear they've gotten slower. It's inspired many to exclaim the ultimate oxymoron: "Hardly anyone is an average runner in the big leagues anymore!"

Or: "The average major leaguer is a well below-average runner."

Some teams have actually lowered their scale. When I worked for the San Diego Padres back in 2004, they considered 4.4/4.3 to be average running times home-to-first; a tenth of a second slower than the industry.

The old-time scouts scoffed at the Padres but they were simply responding to the times. It's a sad commentary on the league's lack of athleticism and one that is rooted directly in the declining number of African-American major leaguers.

At the same time, NFL Sundays have turned into track meets. The number-oriented sabermetric baseball fan can talk all day about the importance or lack thereof for speed in baseball. But I can't imagine there's a single living soul who finds it more exciting to watch a slow runner than a fast one. When you exclude speed, you exclude spectators.

Lloyd Moseby wasn't even talked about then...

In a recent discussion with Bill Caudill, the former major league closer who now works as a scout for agent Scott Boras, I asked about the differences between today's centerfielders and those of thirty years ago.

"I pitched with Lloyd Moseby behind me in Toronto. Lloyd Moseby was as good defensively as just about any centerfielder today, and he wasn't even talked about then. It's not even close. We had Dwayne Murphy, Chet Lemon, Andre Dawson, Dale Murphy, Gary Maddox, so many other guys in the league who could run them down."

Any scout old enough to remember would agree that centerfielders were much more far-ranging in the early 1980s than they are today. I wrote an article myself on the topic (*Are There Any Pure Centerfielders in the High School Class of 2011?*) for ProspectWire.com back on February 18th of that year.

In that article, I stated that, as a scout, I would have graded 14 of the 26 starting MLB centerfielders in 1981 as having "plus-plus" range, grading a 65 or higher on the 20-80 scouting scale in which a grade of 50 is considered major league average. By comparison, I graded 11 of the 30 in 2011 as having plus-plus range.

Blacks represented 19.1% of all MLB players in 1981 and just 8.8% in 2011. The change in Black centerfielders is not quite as drastic (15 out of 26 starters, 57.7% in 1981 versus 15 of 30, 50% in 2011) and the increase in Latino starters have helped (from 2 to 6). But it's enough to make a difference and the loss of Black athletes is in direct correlation to the trend. The Black centerfielders of 2011 are also less athletic and slower runners in general than their 1981 counterparts.

There was so much more athleticism in 1981 that the game's three best speedsters were relegated to left field instead of center.

Rickey Henderson, Tim Raines, and Willie Wilson are three of the best basestealers of all-time, in fact ranking 1st, 5th, and 12th in baseball history.

Raines led all of MLB with 71 as a rookie in 1981 while Henderson was second, leading the A.L. with 56. The tall, wiry, long-striding Willie Wilson ranked 6th overall with 34 in the strike-shortened season.

Needless to say, Henderson, Raines, and Wilson were burners; there may not be a single player today who goes from first to second as quickly as they did. If they were in their prime in 2013, they would all be shoe-ins to play center field.

But the A's had Dwayne Murphy and he covered even more ground than Henderson. Raines was a converted infielder and he had no chance to move the fleet Andre Dawson away from center. Young Willie Wilson was still a little ways from inheriting center from veteran fly chaser Amos Otis. That's how athletic the game was in 1981!

Center field is the "Blackest" position and the one that requires the most running speed. So it should be no surprise the position isn't played nearly as well today as it was thirty years ago.

Devalued or misrepresented

It doesn't stop in center.

If you look around the diamond and compare 1981 to today, which era had the better fielders?

I have posed this question to numerous scouts and former players alike who've watched baseball extensively in both eras. No one has vocally disagreed with my assessment that at least eight of the nine positions on the field are less athletic and less defensive than they were 30 years ago.

Every position except shortstop.

"There's no question they were better athletes thirty years ago," said Dale Sutherland, who scouted southern California for 28 years. "Faster runners, better athletes, no doubt. As far as fielding, it also has to do with teams promoting players on their bats. They're rushing players through before they can develop their fielding because there's no emphasis on that anymore. Their bats are ready quicker, but not their gloves."

Today's players are undoubtedly better hitters with more power at most every position. But back then, you had catchers like Rick Dempsey and Steve Yeager who were there for their gloves and their arms.

You had shortstops like Mario Mendoza and Mark Belanger who hit .200 but played every day because of great defense. Frank White and Lou Whitaker were second basemen with superior quickness, softer hands, and much stronger arms than their counterparts today.

There were any number of acrobatic third basemen like Buddy Bell, Graig Nettles, and Mike Schmidt. There were first basemen like Eddie Murray, Keith Hernandez, and Cecil Cooper who were agile, sure-handed, and strong-armed enough to play anywhere. By contrast, today's first basemen are often put there because it's the position where they are least of a defensive liability.

The only reason I think today's shortstops are better fielders is the influx of Dominican and Venezuelans. There were some very good shortstops in 1981. Ozzie Smith may have been the greatest ever and you can still make an argument for Robin Yount, Alan Trammell, Rick Burleson, Alfredo Griffin, and Gary Templeton that they could flash the leather with the best today. But overall, I believe today's shortstop is more athletic and farther ranging.

A lot of fans don't care or even notice the loss of athleticism, especially fans who share Bill James's perspective on the game. Bill James is a noteworthy author of numbers-based baseball books who has worked in the Boston Red Sox front office since 2002.

Mr. James has repeatedly referred to baseball as a game not to be watched but to be analyzed. Whether we agree or not, it's clear that there are millions of baseball "fans" who take the very same approach. I'm often shocked and sometimes horrified how fans want to talk more about stats like WAR and VORP and WHIP rather than the play Troy Tulowitzki made in the hole. I believe there are still fans who enjoy watching the game and taking in its visual beauty, but there are growing numbers of those who hardly watch it at all and only enjoy it through the numbers.

Billy Beane, the Oakland A's GM who championed Bill James's theories and essentially began the "Moneyball" craze in the early 2000s, is notorious for his disinterest in watching baseball. As detailed in *Moneyball: The Art of Winning an Unfair Game* (by Michael Lewis, WW Norton, 2003), Beane didn't even watch the team he was running! He had to be coerced to watch the A's during their fantastic 20-game winning streak in 2002.

Until recently, fielding, speed, and athleticism had been largely ignored by the sabermetric community (a term derived from the well-respected Society for American Baseball Research, SABR) simply because they had no way of measuring it the way they did for hitting statistics. In recent years, statistical analysis has become fashionable for defense, but "range factor" (RF) and "ultimate zone rating" (UZR) are highly flawed metrics that, in my opinion, do not come close to accurately quantifying the value of a fielder.

Nevertheless, front offices were quickly Bill Jamesed and Moneyballed. You have a number of general managers today with little scouting acumen, who've put all their eggs into the sabermetric basket. They won't recognize the ground Garry "Secretary of Defense" Maddox just covered to save a triple with two runners on if it doesn't affect his RF or UZR. And if you study the mechanics of how those statistics are determined, you discover plenty of holes in the process. As a scout, I can say I've seen numbers that are nearly opposite of what I would have attributed defensively to a player.

How this relates to Black players is simply that many of the skills with which they have blessed our game have since been devalued or misrepresented.

"Overall, I don't think we have as many athletic teams as 15-20 years ago," says Pat Gillick. "We have guys with more strength, they are bigger and stronger, but I don't know that they are more athletic."

So in effect, what we've ended up with after thirty years is a league that is slower, less athletic, and slower-paced. There's no question there isn't as much speed in the game today. Athleticism and fielding are definitely worse. And games have gone from just a little over two hours to three-plus with much more dead time between pitches than ever before.

Meanwhile, the NHL, NBA, and NFL have all gotten much faster, much more athletic, and much faster paced over the same time. Whenever their respective commissioners make changes to the league, it's always to improve the pace and demand on athleticism to satisfy an increasingly action-hungry population. Baseball has done the opposite; the game's pace has slowed particularly since Bud Selig became commissioner at the end of 1992.

As I alluded to in my author's note, I would not have been a baseball fan had I been born 25 years later. My parents did not introduce me to baseball; I'm the son of Indian immigrants who happened to stumble upon it on my own.

I discovered the sport watching television as an 8 year-old on May 31st, 1979. The game that made me fall in love with baseball was a 1-0 pitcher's duel. The Tigers' Pat Underwood made his big league debut by defeating his brother Tom in Toronto. It was certainly not a slugfest, but it was tension from the first pitch to the last. (And it took only an hour and 52 minutes to play, an unfamiliar pace to fans in 2013.)

I loved athleticism. I loved speed. I loved defense. The home run ball was exciting, but the other things are what kept my attention in between. Even in a slugfest with five homers; that means there are 65 other at-bats where something else has to happen.

With slower players (and a slower pace), I have a hard time believing a random first generation American boy will turn on a television and fall in love with baseball today as I did in 1979. I can say with good certainty that I wouldn't because the things I loved about the game then are much diminished now. The next generation of fans will overwhelmingly be those who were introduced to the game by their fathers. That's a good base, but it can't be the only source of support because it's destined to dwindle.

This absolutely correlates with the decrease in Black players. Though I never would have given it a second thought in 1979, it was the Black players who made the game so exciting. I took them for granted simply because I knew no other way and never imagined that the Cecil Coopers and Jim Rices and Dave Winfields were going to disappear.

"And if you turn that faucet off..."

Baseball is more profitable now than ever as Mr. Selig has reminded us many times over. Nevertheless, it is clearly less popular than it was in the early 1980s and perhaps at any time in its history. The television ratings are in the toilet; regular season NFL games regularly exceed World Series ratings which was unheard of through the 1980s. Attendance is higher so more people are going to games, but it's a drop in the bucket when you consider how many fewer people are watching baseball on TV than ever before.

The previous commissioner, Fay Vincent (1989-1992), thinks the profitability of Major League Baseball has thrown a band-aid on a bleed that's turning into a gusher. "Basketball and football have gone right by baseball in the Black community. A lot of that is economic but some of it is leadership and attention from Baseball.

"One of the reasons is that baseball is doing so well, they're making a lot of money, attendance is good. All the clubs are rolling in cash. I think, to some extent, that people are saying, 'we may not be doing well in the Black community, but what's the big deal?'

"I think it's terrible because what you're missing.... you're missing generations of fans. And if you turn that faucet off, it takes a while for the effects to be felt."

As the former commissioner points out, it's not just Black players we're losing, but Black fans. Fewer Black fans means fewer Black parents to raise future Black baseball players.

Is it a surprise the percentage of Black baseball players has been cut in half in the twenty years since Fay Vincent left the office?

"I'm not surprised," says Vincent, "because I think that the factors were all there and we could see it going the wrong way. I'm surprised it happened so quickly. I knew it would happen, but not that quickly. It was marketing and there was not enough attention put on the Black audience.

"Part of the problem, again, is that the game is doing well. When it's doing well, it's hard to get people terribly agitated. They say the Blacks are gone, but the Dominican players have come here and taken over and they say 'no big deal'.

"I don't think baseball is spending a lot of time on this issue."

Nerds and number freaks

The sabermetric fans are the loudest, but it's my belief the vast majority of sports fans are a much different sort. When you listen to football fans, they don't throw out numbers to compare John Elway to Dan Marino; they talk about quick releases and leadership. I've never heard a basketball fan break out stats comparing Magic Johnson to Larry Bird, or the great Chicago Bulls teams of the 1990s to the Celtics of the 1960s. Sidney Crosby to Wayne Gretzky? You hear about spin moves and puck-handling, but I couldn't tell you any of their statistics much less break them down into VORPs and WARs.

Baseball today is appealing more to the intellectual numbers-oriented fan, but less to those who actually watch the game. People who dislike baseball often think of our fans as nerds and number freaks and there's more than a little truth to that. Those who enjoy watching other sports have walked away from baseball because it is not as fun to watch as it used to. It's more friendly with numbers, but it's not nearly as aesthetic to the eye.

It seems more journalists and media types have jumped on the numbers bandwagon. The MLB beat writer for *Sports Illustrated* is a young man named Joe Sheehan who makes no bones about his angle on the game; there's very little discussion of humanity or technicality in his weekly columns. The magazine has groomed Albert Chen as his understudy. Peter Gammons and Tom Verducci throw nothing but numbers (like WAR and OPS) out to the public on MLB Network, rarely mentioning tools or anything aesthetic even when speaking of a player's Hall of Fame consideration.

For example, Gammons' argument for former Detroit Tigers shortstop Alan Trammell to be in the Hall of Fame is not that he was an all-around star with a clutch bat and great hands, but that his "adjusted OPS" was almost identical to Derek Jeter's and Barry Larkin's in their prime. All three enjoyed outstanding careers at the same position, but anyone who's watched them play would hardly call them identical players. Gammons made no attempt to subjectively compare their bats or gloves or their importance to their team as leaders. Again, would anyone call Magic Johnson and Larry Bird "identical" players because their stats are alike?

Gammons and Verducci are not alone among the media, which is evident in the voting for the major awards. Despite a mere 13-12 record for a lowly Seattle Mariners team in 2010, Felix Hernandez was given the A.L. Cy Young Award in a landslide over playoff aces David Price and C.C. Sabathia (both coincidentally African-Americans) for "other" statistics that the new-wave sabermetricians sell as more important than winning. Whether you believe Hernandez should have won it or not, it's clear he would not have taken the award if the vote was done ten years prior.

It was even more evident with the 2011 N.L. MVP vote, when Milwaukee Brewer leftfielder Ryan Braun edged out Los Angeles Dodgers centerfielder Matt Kemp by the Baseball Writers Association of America. Braun had an outstanding season, very much comparable to Matt Kemp as an offensive and baserunning force, and it showed statistically. Now Braun is no slug, he's a fast runner with a strong arm but he's not the athletic freak of nature that 6'3", 235-pound Matt Kemp is. Braun is just a little bit above-average fielder at a less important position while Matt Kemp became a very good defensive centerfielder in 2011. Braun led his team to the N.L. East title and there's something to be said for that, but I still expected the other non-measurables to weigh in Matt Kemp's favor.

As an African-American, Matt Kemp has even more opportunity to be an ambassador for the cause. Had he won the MVP, the positive press would have had a ripple effect among prospective Black fans.

"When I saw Matt Kemp for the first time in 2004," says Dale Sutherland, "I told John Young that we need to get on him to help RBI. I said, 'John, this guy has Willie Mays tools and he's going to make a lot of money!'"

High praise for Matt Kemp; perhaps the now-29 year-old African-American has provided a glimpse of what could be. Despite his Mays-type season, Kemp couldn't bring home the MVP, but will hopefully be a candidate for years to come.

Matt Kemp is the rare, precious exceptional Black athlete playing baseball. Because right now Willie Mays is in the NFL, Bob Gibson plays in the NBA, and Josh Gibson is ignoring baseball altogether as he grows up in Pittsburgh.

Their absence is not reflected in Value Over Replacement Player or Range Factor, but if you actually watch the game in person or on TV, their absence leaves a deathly void with not enough Matt Kemps to take their place. This game is not nearly as exciting and entertaining as the one I and older generations grew accustomed to watching.

Chapter 4: Come On, Scouts! There's More to Dwight Gooden than Being Black and Righthanded

If you study the history of the MLB draft, you'll discover a recurring pattern of under-drafted Black players throughout the 1960s and 1970s. It's shocking to see how late some of baseball's best were drafted during that time.

Never was it more evident than in 1975.

For reasons soon to be explained, the first round of the 1975 June draft was the weakest first round of all-time. The 1st round produced no better player than Rick Cerone, the 7th overall pick who was more or less a part-time platoon catcher for the bulk of his 18 big league seasons. There was not a single All-Star Game appearance among the 24 first-rounders. The #1 overall pick Danny Goodwin hit a mere .236 in 636 at-bats while the next four choices failed to play even a day of major league baseball.

Danny Goodwin is Black. He was a catcher from Southern University in Louisiana and he had also been the first overall pick four years prior. Goodwin was drafted out of an Illinois high school in 1971 before shocking the baseball world by not signing with his home-state Chicago White Sox.

Needless to say, Goodwin was a well-known quantity going into the 1975 Draft; once again the consensus #1 prospect in the country. There was no hiding of Danny Goodwin's talents, but the story was much different for three other very talented southern Blacks who proved the real treasures of the draft.

Young Lee Arthur Smith was a fire-balling righthanded pitcher out of Castor High School in rural Louisiana. The Chicago Cubs took him with the fourth pick in the 2nd round and Smith went on to enjoy an outstanding 18-year career that could very well land him in the Hall of Fame.

Smith's 478 career saves were the major league record until Trevor Hoffman topped him on the final day of the 2006 season. He grew to 6'6" and over 250 lbs. Lee Smith's dominance was legendary, the stories never-ending. His right arm was like a giant, muscular whip. Hitters who faced him could hardly see the ball; with his size, velocity, and super-long limbs, it was as if he were handing it to the catcher right underneath their nose.

If a young Lee Smith were to step on an amateur field today, scouts would trip over themselves even with his control issues and hoop dreams. A tremendously large and athletic Black kid with a 95+ MPH fastball and devastating breaking pitch would be unlikely to last more than a few picks in 2013, but Lee Smith was still available at #28 for the Cubs in 1975.

"I just stumbled onto Lee Smith," says Joe McIlvaine. McIlvaine scouted the area for the Baltimore Orioles back in the mid-1970s before becoming a scouting director and general manager later in his career. "It was my second year as a scout. I mean he had a great delivery, just perfect mechanics and this was a guy who'd never been taught. He'd hardly played baseball. Lee was chiseled, like 6'5", 205 lbs. He threw really hard and had a good curveball."

McIlvaine was the man who drafted Dwight Gooden in the 1st round just seven years later as the New York Mets scouting director. "Until I saw Gooden, I always said Lee Smith was the best high school pitcher I'd ever scouted.

"I really thought we would take him, he was the sleeper in the draft. We picked 23rd overall (in the first round, five picks before the Cubs choice) but we took Dave Ford instead. He was pretty good at the time, but obviously wasn't Lee Smith.

"A lot of people didn't think he would sign, but Buck O'Neil (then a scout), my God. He was something. He spent two weeks with the kid and got it done."

While working on my first book, *Character Is Not a Statistic*, I asked another former scouting director, Bill Lajoie, what he thought of Lee Smith as a high school kid.

"I didn't see him. I don't even know if we had him on our list!"

How could someone with such unworldly talent not even be on the Detroit Tigers' scouting list? Sure Smith was new to pitching and in love with basketball, but was he not good enough to be on the list? Lajoie responded that racism was par for the course among southern area scouts, who were overwhelmingly Caucasian and raised in the Deep South.

"Sometimes you have an old-time scout down in that area and you didn't get a true picture."

"I should have sent someone down (to scout Lee Smith) from the North," he added with regret.

In the 5th round of the same draft, Lajoie did strike it rich on another southern Black. The Tigers selected Lou Whitaker, an infielder from Martinsville, Virginia. Whitaker reached the big leagues to stay just two years and three months later at age 20. Over an 18-year MLB career, Whitaker was a 5-time All-Star and one of the premier second basemen of the 1980s. He was an all-around performer with a great glove (three gold glove awards) and a strong left bat for the top of the order.

Whitaker was the American League Rookie of The Year in 1978, just three years out from being a mere 5th-round pick out of high school. Was Lajoie really that much smarter than everybody else?

"No, I didn't even see him in high school," Lajoie refuted back in 2009. "Wayne Blackburn (the area scout) saw Lou as a junior and wrote a nice report on him. He tried to go back to Martinsville and his car broke down. I relied heavily on Billy Jurges (who worked for the Major League Scouting Bureau) and on what Blackie wrote before. I don't recall hearing anything about him from other scouts."

So the Tigers took Whitaker in the fifth round without even seeing him play as a senior. That tells you how little interest the other teams must have had to let him last that long.

As inexplicable as I find the stories of Lee Smith and Lou Whitaker, there's another southern Black who was the best of them all and unselected through the first ten rounds of the same draft. Outfielder Andre Dawson lasted all the way to the 250th pick (11th round) before the Montreal Expos pulled him off the Tallahassee campus of Florida A&M University.

Anyone who's scouted knows it's an inexact science and that players change quickly once they get into pro ball. There are 1st-rounders who bomb just as there are 31st round picks who end up with major league careers. It's not to say that mistakes aren't made, even by the best.

But Andre Dawson is and was a physical specimen, a man and an athlete impossible to ignore. Even if he didn't hit, his exceptional arm, speed, and tapered 6'3" physique should have been worth an early round selection on their own. Just walking off the bus should have earned him a higher slot than the 11th round! That's not even mentioning Dawson's outstanding character and fierce determination to become a major leaguer. Beyond his talent, it was Dawson's incredible threshold for pain that paved his path to Cooperstown. I recall a trainer who'd worked for both the NFL Chicago Bears and Chicago Cubs exclaim to WGN Cubs announcers in the 1980s that Dawson played through more pain than anybody on either of those teams.

How on earth did Andre Dawson last until the 11th round of the 1975 Draft?

Lajoie knew about Dawson, but like Lee Smith and Lou Whitaker, he never saw him.

"I've got a scout. He complains, 'Bill, I've been tied up on the road. I've been on the road a long time.' I say, 'Can you stop in and see this guy Dawson at A&M?'

"His response to me: 'Well I already saw him and I didn't think too much of him.' I said, oh, okay. Honest to God truth. That happened."

I asked Mr. Lajoie how and why that scout could say something so ludicrous.

"A Black player in the south, basically a Black player anywhere, did not get the same attention. I had a guy who told me a Black player had to be twice as good. That was still going on! Jesus Christ!

"Tremendous (how the black players overcame prejudice). With Dawson, it was prejudice, you're damn right!"

Andre Dawson went straight from Tallahassee to Lethbridge, the Expos' rookie-level Pioneer League affiliate, and hit .330 with 13 HR and seven triples in just 300 at-bats. So his bat couldn't have been *that* bad in college considering he hit for a .695 slugging percentage as a sophomore (according to *1975 Official Collegiate Baseball Guide*) and was able to dominate pro ball out of the chute. The pitching in the Pioneer League is much greater than anything Florida A&M University faced. If Dawson's bat was really that weak at FAMU, there's not a minor league hitting coach on earth who could have made so quick a correction.

Dawson made his major league debut the very next year. So it wasn't long before every other team in baseball realized they'd blundered on the former FAMU Rattler and that the Expos were onto something special.

"The Hawk" proceeded to become a Hall of Famer and one of the best players of his era. Among other accomplishments, Dawson played in 8 All-Star Games, won the 1987 N.L. MVP, hit 438 HR, collected 2,774 hits, and earned 8 gold gloves awards for his fielding excellence.

The draft looks pretty good if you put Smith, Whitaker, and Dawson in the 1st round where they truly belonged. The Cubs, Tigers, and Expos reaped the rewards of everyone else's racism.

Lajoie later hired John Young to become the Detroit Tigers' scouting director in 1981 with the idea that Young would help prevent the misevaluations of Dawsons and Smiths in the future. Naturally, as a Black man, John Young would be the last one to ignore a prospect on the color of his skin.

It's not to say that every southern Black was hidden away in that era, because there's Danny Goodwin and a handful of other MLB stars who went in the first round; quite notably Vida Blue (1971 out of a Louisiana HS), J.R. Richard (1969, Louisiana HS), and Jim Rice (1974, South Carolina HS). But it seems that those talents were well-known and unmistakable from the beginning. The Dawsons and Whitakers proved to be great talents, but their identification required more hustle and open-mindedness on the part of the scouts.

It was worse in the 1950s and 1960s; the early days of integrated baseball. The National League caught on well before the American League and teams like the San Francisco Giants and Pittsburgh Pirates were particularly willing to sign Black players. But most teams weren't and the racism was even less veiled among scouts than it would be in the 1970s. The American League clubs were particularly awful, passing on Black players in their own backyard.

The Detroit Tigers had two very fine ones stolen underneath their nose right about the time Bill Lajoie was a phenom prospect himself coming out of Denby High School in 1952.

"There were a few Black guys the Giants signed that the other scouts stayed away from," said Lajoie, recalling the early 1950s in Detroit. "Willie Kirkland and Leon Wagner hit a lot of homeruns in the big leagues and I'd never heard of them until they signed. That scout did a great job."

Indeed, Kirkland and Wagner, from Northwestern and Inkster High Schools, went on to hit a combined 359 major league home runs. Scout Ray Lucas became a hero for the Giants largely because the Tigers were negligent, overlooking the great Black talent in their own city. It was the pre-draft era and had the Tigers wanted Kirkland or Wagner, they would have just had to say “hello” to sign them.

(Wagner had actually played baseball and football at Tuskegee University in Alabama after Inkster HS, but none of the southern area scouts thought to sign him, either.)

At least the Tigers would wise up to sign Willie Horton out of Detroit Northwestern High School in 1961. It wasn’t long before Horton became a hometown hero and one of the franchise’s most feared sluggers.

Racial profiling

Scouting has changed as have scouts themselves. Today’s scouts are more educated but younger, less experienced, and more willing to cave in their opinions and convictions for a promotion. One of the positive side effects is that racism has subsided though I’ve still received less than subtle reminders that it hasn’t disappeared entirely from the scouting trail.

I worked with one White scout in particular who did little to hide his feelings against Blacks and other minorities. While he never directed a racist remark to me in person, it was obvious that I was spoken to in a much different tone. The disrespect was petty to the point where he once offered gum to the scouts around him, but refused me, his own teammate.

One afternoon at Auburn University, I became very upset with an elderly White male usher who didn’t believe I was a scout and literally yelled at me for asking to leave the stadium to retrieve a coat. I was already battling with my spring allergies and the dropping temperatures were making it worse.

I mentioned it to the scout and his wife. His wife ignored it and he thought it was funny, making no effort to confirm to the usher that I was a scout. Later on, this scout made a point of walking right past the usher to go to his car. He came back, lifted his coat, and said, "See, I had no problem! It's just you!"

From the more conscientious White scouts, I'd heard stories of this man defending his use of the "N-word" and claiming that in his town it was perfectly all right. In a drunken rage, he once yelled out a series of racial slurs at Asians who entered a restaurant, leading at least one of the White scouts in his group to go home early.

It most certainly affected his work as a scout. He typically under-graded Black players and threw down one stereotype after another, preventing his club from even considering players who wound up doing quite well. Once he even argued against a Black prep outfielder from Mississippi because he was dating a White girl.

This individual is still in the game and has in fact been promoted by people who've seen at least as much as I have. He has many friends in baseball who, if they don't share his beliefs, have no problems defending someone who does. So I won't deceive anybody in saying that the practices of 1952 or 1975 are out the window. It still lingers, it's just not as pervasive. Instead of nearly every southern scout having this attitude, we have only a handful.

And for every one or two scouts like this one, there are ten more who are just trying to do their job.

"As a scout, we see a Black athlete on the field, we immediately focus on him to see what kind of athlete he is," says Jake Wilson, who covers southern California for the Tampa Bay Rays. "We try to get a running time to see what kind of runner he is. And you watch in the field, see what position he plays. There are so few Black players, your inclination is to scout the guy and give him as much opportunity as you can."

Scouts like Jake Wilson are more than eager to find that future big league star. No one wants to miss out on the next Andre Dawson, no matter what color his skin is.

So I don't suspect that Black athletes are losing opportunities to play baseball on account of racism today. Black players aren't overlooked, in fact there are so few that they tend to stand out. Scouts who see one all-White team after another can't help but notice when there's a Black player on the club. Whether or not he's a prospect, he's going to be etched in their memory bank.

I won't accuse the whole scouting industry of racism, but I do accuse many of being "default scouts". I accuse them of "racial profiling" to borrow an infamous descriptor attributed to law enforcement. I do believe this scouting mentality has adversely affected the Black pipeline, even if unintentional.

Scouts are all about comparing amateurs to big leaguers, but the way they do it is not always intelligent or accurate when it comes to Black ballplayers.

Every tall Black outfielder who throws and hits lefthanded is just like Darryl Strawberry.

Every Black catcher is Charles Johnson.

Every Black righthanded pitcher gets compared to Dwight Gooden. If he's under 6'0", he's Tom Gordon. If he's lefthanded he's Vida Blue unless he's very big; then he's C.C. Sabathia.

A Black bad-bodied righthanded power hitter is Cecil Fielder. A Black bad-bodied lefthanded power hitter is Prince Fielder. Doesn't matter if they are strong or athletic or as determined to succeed as the Fielders, just that they are fat and Black.

Dexter Fowler was a thin-as-a-rail 6'4" high school outfielder who could swallow up ground with long strides around the bases. But he hit for very little pop and had a below-average arm when the Colorado Rockies drafted him out of high school in 2004. *Baseball America* quoted a scout who referred to him as "Andre Dawson".

Aside from the plus speed and color of skin, there was absolutely nothing else in common.

Fowler is playing in the big leagues today; he's a high-strikeout, slap-hitting centerfielder with good outfield range and only occasional power from both sides of the plate. No one in their right mind would compare him to Andre Dawson now and it was completely unfair in 2004.

Baseball America, PerfectGame.org, ESPN, and other media outlets are just as guilty as the scouts for a different reason. They feel it's necessary to compare Black players to Barry Bonds or C.C. Sabathia because it's alluring to their readership.

Every now and then a comparison is insightful; but my overwhelming impression is that scouts see skin color first and the person second. Too often Black players are described as raw, athletic, toolsy, and crude, whether they are or not. Too often they are compared to other Black players with whom they have little in common aside from subcutaneous melanin. There are often better player comparisons among Whites or Latinos but such comps are institutionally taboo.

I have a million stories, but one that stands out is about a 5'10" Black righthanded pitcher I was scouting at San Diego State University in the mid-2000s. He threw hard, but it was straight and he had little command. This young man was just an average athlete, not particularly loose or easy, and he threw a flat slider.

"Turn him in! He reminds me of Tom Gordon," said a supervisor.

I just about lost it. In fact, I said it straight out. "The only thing he has in common with Tom Gordon is that he's Black!"

Tom Gordon, of course, was 5'9" and he did throw hard. But he also had one of the greatest 12-to-6 curveballs ever seen. It was his signature pitch, the one that allowed him to pitch so long in the big leagues as both a starter and reliever. Comparing someone to him who doesn't even throw a curveball is insane and misleading. It's like comparing the voice of Marvin Gaye to the voice of Jimi Hendrix; it's skin deep if that.

I remember another scout in the early 2000s (still employed and since promoted) who told me about a Black pitcher playing college ball in south Florida. He was "Gooden this" and "Gooden that".

When I saw the pitcher, he was a big blocky kid with, again, no curveball and a straight fastball with average velocity. He only had one thing in common with Dwight Gooden and that one thing wasn't going to help him strike out 260 National League hitters at age 19 or win a Cy Young Award at 20.

(A few years later at the Santaluces Baseball Complex in Lantana, Florida, this same scout peeved an over-hearing African-American mother by loudly describing the 2003 Florida Marlins World Series ring as so gaudy that "even Lenny Harris thought it was too big and he's Black!")

I offer three explanations for why baseball scouts are so prone to racially profiling Black prospects.

One, today's scouts simply aren't as shrewd about the game as the scouts in the past. They are younger and more educated, but they learned how to evaluate players in scout school or by studying statistics; they learned how to make their bosses happy. They didn't learn by experience, they didn't learn by watching players over decades and finding out which ones make it and which ones don't. The old scouts usually did and there's something to be said for that experience.

There are definite exceptions, but the vast majority of today's scouts don't see past a body type, a profile, or the color of a player's skin. It's an easy way out that requires zero experience. You don't have to watch a player that closely nor do you have to watch the big leaguer you're comparing him to. You say someone is "just like Sabathia" and it gets everybody's attention.

I recall a second-year scout I worked with as a St. Louis Cardinal who wrote a report in the spring of 2006 describing an obese and grossly unathletic college player as being just like Prince Fielder. This scout watched him in a single game and never once saw Fielder as a prep. The scout was, in fact, a college student in Rhode Island while Fielder was finishing high school ball in Melbourne, Florida.

I can't even call his beloved player a first baseman. He took a pre-game there and after tripping over his own cleat, it was understandable why the coach put him in the lineup as the designated hitter.

Yet this scout tried hard to sell me, claiming this was the most impressive hitter he'd seen thus far, and if I don't like him then I'm going to miss another Prince Fielder.

The young player was soon kicked off the team and never heard from again.

(The scout is now a scouting director.)

A second reason that Black players are often misevaluated: most scouts are Caucasians who grew up in predominantly Caucasian areas. Blinded by a lack of exposure, scouts often make blanket assumptions both on talent and attitude. They assume every Black kid prefers football and basketball to baseball.

Now I've met Black scouts who are just as bad with the racial profiling, so it's more about ignorance than latent racism. I remember a Montreal Expos scout telling me back in 2004, "Most White guys just can't scout Black players and some Black guys can't, either."

It partially explains how Domonic Brown lasted to the 20th round in 2006 coming out Redan High School near Atlanta.

Brown is one of baseball's up-and-coming stars, a chiseled 6'5", 220-pound leftfielder for the Philadelphia Phillies. Brown possesses an exciting blend of power and speed, with a strong throwing arm to boot.

After struggling to catch up to big league fastballs his first three years in the majors, Brown figured it out and hit his stride in 2013. He's loosened up his hands and learned to handle the inside heater that used to tie him up.

Chip Lawrence signed Brown for a bargain $200,000 in 2006 while he was a Georgia and northern Florida area scout for the Phillies.

"He'd signed a football scholarship to Miami. A lot of people thought he was just using baseball as a hobby. But when you talked to the kid, you found out he really wanted to be a baseball player," said Lawrence seven years later. "I think a lot of people walked away from him because of the football obligation. But it wasn't the case and it worked out for him.

"You saw the body, you saw the power/speed combination, the athleticism. Those guys are hard to find to play baseball, it's getting fewer and fewer."

Did Domonic need a sales job to play baseball over football?

"It wasn't hard to convince him at all, not at all. When I met him and his family, he made it clear that he wanted to be a baseball player. Baseball was #1 and football was #2."

Why couldn't the other scouts see that? Did his being African-American have anything to do with their preconceived notions?

"Yeah, I think that may have something to do with it. The fact he was in a Black school had something to do with why there weren't many scouts in the stands. Unfortunately, I think that played a role in it too. Black scouts shied away as well, it wasn't just the White scouts.

"There was some crudeness to him, some rawness, and sometimes you wondered how that would play at the next level. But when you got to meet him, you got excited about the rawness and lack of playing because he wasn't playing all year round yet and so rawness can be good. More upside."

He didn't say it straight out, but it's fair to assume that Lawrence being African-American was an asset in scouting and signing Domonic Brown. Lawrence could see through a lot of the distractions his competitors could not.

A third reason for default scouting: there are so few Black major leaguers these days that scouts have limited comparisons.

By the same token, the NBA and NFL are loaded with Black players. If an NFL scout says a running back reminds him of Eric Dickerson, he's not just saying he's Black because there are about 975 examples of Black NFL running backs of all shapes and sizes in the last decade alone. That scout probably means he runs high, has a tall and rangy build, long strides, and the ability to cut like nobody's business. He might even be referring to the arrogance and propensity to fumble. But if the NFL scout is comparing someone to Eric Dickerson, it's surely a legitimate talent and not just some tall Black kid who plays running back!

Same thing with an NBA scout; do you think they call every 7'0" Black kid Patrick Ewing? No, because they could just as easily call him Hakeem Olajuwan, Kareem Abdul-Jabbar, Dikembe Matumbo, Shaquille O'Neal, David Robinson, Moses Malone, or Dwight Howard if all they mean to say is that the kid is 7'0" tall and Black. If an NBA scout drops Patrick Ewing's name, it represents a talent much different from the other players mentioned regardless of their common color. He's probably a great rebounder and inside player who can also hit some jumpers. Not just some 7'0" Black kid in a tank top.

When you hear a baseball scout or magazine compare a player to Bob Gibson or Carl Crawford, there's only one safe assumption: he's Black! It's a sad reality.

The "raw" or "crude" label gets to me as well. I've known several White scouts who've used those words to describe every single Black player they ever saw. It may be true with some, particularly with players from the inner city, but there are plenty of other Black players who are just as polished as their White counterparts.

The "athletic" label is also trite even when it's meant as a compliment. They'll throw that label on a Black player without actually watching his actions. If he happens to also be a prospect in football or basketball, forget it! He's labeled as a great athlete and 5-tool player, no matter what he brings to the table.

I remember the 2003 MLB draft, which was loaded with high school outfielders. Ryan Harvey was a White kid from Dunedin High School in Florida, a 6'5", 210-pound physical specimen; Harvey had fluid actions, a plus-plus throwing arm, power at the plate, and good speed.

Delmon Young was a pure hitter from southern California with a thicker body, average speed, good arm, and less than fluid actions. There was no question who the better athlete was, but you heard the label "athlete who can hit" put on Young while Harvey was a "polished Dale Murphy-type". (Young, of course, made it to the big leagues and is in the midst of a successful career.)

The racial profiling extends to positions. Rarely will scouts consider putting a Black player on the mound or behind the plate; they are almost always moved to the outfield, a phenomena Dr. David Ogden at the University of Nebraska-Omaha refers to as "stacking".

"Don't worry about Matt Kemp, he's gonna play basketball."

The Moneyball movement has also unintentionally served to exclude Blacks.

"You can say Moneyball is racist," joked a veteran area scout from the Northeast. "Because you're looking for college players and there aren't any Black college players. You don't care about athleticism and you want guys who take walks. Well, that sounds like you want a lot of stiff White guys!"

There are some Black players who fit the "unathletic patient college slugger" mold so desired by Billy Beane and other statistically-minded scouts and executives, but there are many more Blacks who don't. Most are coming out of high school or junior college, and the Moneyball teams were not interested in that pipeline.

Such thinking was particularly prevalent in the early 2000s. The Los Angeles Dodgers made a killing with high school players and many of them were Black. In fact since 2002, scouting director Logan White has signed more than twice as many Black big leaguers as the next highest team (11 to 5). Among them are big league starting first baseman James Loney, catcher Russell Martin, shortstop Dee Gordon (Tom's son), and pitcher James McDonald. But the crème de la crème was unquestionably Matt Kemp.

The outfielder was a mere 6th round pick in 2003 out of Midwest City High School in Oklahoma. How on earth were the Dodgers able to get one of the game's most exciting all-around players in the sixth round?

"What helped me was the time," says White in retrospect. "If you can recall back then, a team like Toronto wouldn't even go to see a high school player. Oakland, Boston, St. Louis, the Padres, there was that time where five teams or maybe as much as ten were automatically out of the running for a player like that because they didn't draft out of high school."

White believes the Moneyball "college first" movement gave him the edge on other Black players as well. "That's how we ended up with Xavier Paul, Trayvon Robinson, and James Loney."

But Matt Kemp slipped through the cracks for even the teams who believed in scouting high school. White saw him by accident.

"What happened was, Mike Leuzinger was the area scout and he took me in to Oklahoma City to watch a pitching matchup between these two pitchers. They both got drafted (Michael Rogers from Del City HS and Brent Weaver from Midwest City HS). That's the reason I went to the game, the pitchers. There were twelve scouts there besides us.

"While I'm there, there's a rightfielder with a pretty good body. And I'm like, 'my God!' There's a little baby fat in his rear, a little thicker than now, but he was big, physical, in right field. So he comes to the on-deck circle and I ask a scout who he is and he says not to worry about him because he's a basketball player.'"

White watched him go 1-3. It was a tournament and Midwest City HS was going to play another game right after so White and Leuzinger stuck around.

The twelve other scouts who watched the pitcher's duel were long gone. Only the two Dodger scouts stayed back for Matt Kemp's second game.

Though the Dodgers had him graded out as a 3rd round talent, White ultimately drafted Kemp in the 6th round because there was such little interest from other teams.

Kemp had all the physical ability in the world, he was just crude. Baseball had been a distant second to basketball in his mind, but after a nice talk from White and follow-up by Leuzinger, Kemp came to realize he could have a big future in baseball. White had no trouble signing the future All-Star for $130,000.

"Matt Kemp is a pure athlete," adds Dale Sutherland, who was working for the cross-town Angels when he scouted Kemp in the minor leagues. "He's a basketball player who really came on when he got to play baseball full-time. I think his natural ability is better than Willie Mays, he's bigger and stronger. He's that kind of talent."

White admits the talent was there, but not easy to see on that day in Oklahoma City. Between the two games, Kemp went 1-6. He played right field, not center where a coach usually puts his fastest runner. His home-to-first times were 4.4, slightly below-average. But from looking at his body, watching his swing, and watching him glide on the bases from first-to-third, White was convinced that Kemp had big league potential.

What would Matt Kemp have done had nobody drafted him? He may have fallen through the cracks like so many great Black athletes before.

"If nobody drafted him, I believe Matt would have gone out and played basketball," says Logan White. "I would have to ask Matt but I don't even know if he had baseball scholarships. He might have had some people talk to him for baseball, but he had more people talk to him for college basketball. Matt would have probably gone and played Division I basketball somewhere rather than college baseball."

So easily, baseball would have lost one of its most exciting and marketable talents.

There are three reasons why teams will miss a multi-dimensional, high-ceiling talent like Matt Kemp in the draft. Black or White.

First, today's scouts don't recognize what can't be seen with the naked eye in the way of their predecessors. This is, again, because of their comparative lack of real-world experience on the scouting trail. If it doesn't show on a radar gun, a stopwatch, or on a stat sheet, the new age scout is not nearly as keen.

Second, most of their scouting directors and general managers want more polished players who'll move quickly and make them look good.

"I got chastised for it," says Logan White, the Los Angeles Dodgers scouting director since 2002. "We took an inner city guy from Kansas City named Justin Chigbogu (in 2012) and he's got big power and everything and I got crushed in his first season. They're like, 'this guy is far away, why not get that college guy who is closer?' 'By the time this kid becomes a player, I'll be gone,' and all that."

High school kids who take 5-6 years to develop are high risk and long term and not many SDs or GMs keep their jobs for that long. You can just wind up the disciplined college slugger and let him go because he will get to the big leagues quickly if he hits. Meanwhile the high school kid is going to take time and effort.

"My thing is, I never drafted a player because he was Black," says Logan White. "Not one time. I tried to draft the best ballplayer and it turned out that's how it worked."

White used to work for Paul DePodesta, the Dodgers general manager from 2004-2005. DePodesta was Billy Beane's right-hand man in Oakland and one of the faces of Moneyball. But because of White's success with high school players, DePodesta did not impose his will to change their strategy in the draft. But White still had to face the farm system.

Which brings us to #3; there isn't nearly the investment in player development as there used to be. Teams were strongly committed to turning 18 year-old raw talents into major leaguers in the old days, but there's been a noticeable increase in college drafting over the 2000s.

The Detroit Tigers of the 1980s were built by great drafting and player development in the 1970s. Notable was the quick ascent of high school players like Alan Trammell (less than two years to MLB), Lou Whitaker (less than three), and Lance Parrish (3+).

The Tigers weren't pioneers. They were just modeling the powerhouse teams who preceded their success in the 1970s. Teams like the Boston Red Sox, Pittsburgh Pirates, Oakland A's, Cincinnati Reds, and Los Angeles Dodgers were quite successful in developing their high school draft picks into major league players

Was player development that much better in the 1970s?

"Yeah! I think so," Lance Parrish told me back in 2010, comparing his days as a minor leaguer to those as a minor league coach thirty years later. "I say that with no equivocation whatsoever. My experience with those guys and the Tigers organization at that time, it just seemed that they knew what they were doing. They had a better sense of things than what I see going on today.

"To me, the guys who are more successful are the guys who have put the time in and learned from the failures and successes of all the people who came before them; and then go on from it.

"Absolutely, most farm directors today don't have that experience. I think it's a concern."

Baltimore Orioles scout Jim Thrift grew up following his father Syd to minor league parks in the 1970s and he sees much the same as Parrish.

"Financial restrictions have changed development; not as much time put into them as there used to be. Back then, you signed a player and you had two months of instructional league, even in 1995 and 1996. Be there from September 10th to November 10th."

Instructional league is not a league per se, but a fall camp that teams have held for as long as anyone can remember. The point of the "league" is just what its title implies; to bring the best lower-level prospects to one setting to be instructed by the minor league coaches. It's difficult to make major mechanical adjustments during the season; the work accomplished through instructional league has hastened many a prospect's rise to the majors.

Nevertheless, the two-month instructional league is a thing of the past.

"Today, some have 'instrux' for two weeks, some don't have it at all," says Thrift. "Financial restrictions cut it off. If we keep paying guys $25 million a year (at the big league level), they push these things farther and farther away; forcing people to draft college players, walking away from ceiling players who need to develop. Teams need to ask themselves, 'aren't you cutting off your nose to spite your face?'"

Amateur players drafted in June used to sign very late until MLB instituted a mid-July signing deadline in 2012. This affected high school players and "athlete" types more than anyone else. Even with a mid-July signing deadline, players often miss their entire first summer of pro baseball and then have just an abbreviated instructional league. It's a double-whammy for the less developed player, right from the get-go.

All of this has a clear effect on the development of Black ballplayers. Most of the Blacks who've made the majors in recent years were not the "raw" types when they signed.

Matt Kemp is a notable exception; the 2011 N.L. MVP runner-up is an outstanding example of what player development can do with a pure talent. Kemp was a great athlete but quite crude when he signed out of high school in 2003. Dodgers scouting director Logan White remembers more than a little pessimism during Kemp's first year in pro ball.

"He hit like .240 with 1 HR to start and I remember our coach saying, 'I don't know about this Kemp kid. He went 0-3 again today with three strikeouts'. He'd say this on the game reports on his voicemail. They'd complain his swing was too long and all that."

White believes that Kemp's intelligence made the difference.

"But I credit Matt because Matt is a smart kid. Comes from a good family, from a good background of good people. And what Matt did quicker than anybody I've ever seen, any player that I've ever drafted, he made adjustments. That next year I saw him in the South Atlantic League, Anup, and I really got to take a look at him and I realized we have a star on our hands here. He hit .288 with 17 home runs.

"And a lot of it was in the second half. The first round picks in the league that year, he out-played them. It was something to watch and it was amazing to me how much better he was in a year's time, one year away from high school. Crazy, scary how good he got in one year."

It took "The Bison" only three years to get to the big leagues, four full years of to stick, and five pro seasons to become All-Star caliber for the Los Angeles Dodgers.

To the point that executives prefer quick fixes while they still have a job, the Dodgers had three different general managers from the day Kemp was drafted in 2003 to when he made his big league debut in 2006. It wasn't quick or easy and former GM Dan Evans was long gone before reaping the benefits, but did Matt Kemp ever turn out?

Most of today's other prep-drafted Black big leaguers are along the lines of Justin Upton, B.J. Upton, Adam Jones, C.C. Sabathia, and Prince Fielder; players who grew up playing lots of baseball with active parents in warm weather climates. They were not crude or raw (even if so racially profiled by the default scouts who saw them). Prince Fielder hit his way up and both Uptons fell into the category of freaky athletes with advanced baseball skills and smarts. Fielder, of course, is the son of Cecil, a former major league superstar, while Manny Upton was around sports his entire life.

It's no coincidence that 10 of the 75 Blacks on 2011 rosters are second-generation big leaguers while only Bump Wills (son of Maury) was second-generation among the 134 Black players in 1981. It's no coincidence that the game's two greatest Black players the last twenty years, Barry Bonds and Ken Griffey Jr., are also sons of major leaguers.

Those aren't the only great Black athletes in America; they were just fortunate to be born into situations where they wouldn't fall through the cracks. The problem for baseball is that for every Ken Griffey Jr., there are a hundred Chris Pauls and Adrian Petersons with transcendent athletic ability who don't have MLB fathers to steer them to baseball.

A tale of two "beasts": Megatron and Cobra

It's no longer uncommon for an exceptional athlete like Adrian Peterson to grow up in American without ever gripping a baseball. But even if he does, he could still get weeded out by economics or the inability of scouts to recognize his talent.

Jim Thrift once scouted an outfielder in the Atlanta suburbs who was committed to play football for Georgia Tech. Calvin Johnson was a straight-A student and a top wide receiver recruit out of Sandy Creek High School in 2004.

There were no plans to play both sports for Georgia Tech because of Johnson's commitment to his academics. High school would be his last baseball hurrah unless somebody pulled a huge upset and signed him to play pro.

"I was crosschecking in Georgia with Steve Kring, who was our Southeast supervisor," says Thrift. "He says 'let's go see him and then we'll eat', and I say 'What if I like the guy?' He says, 'You'll see him'.

"So I go and watch the guy, 6'4", 225 lbs., Black guy playing center field. He's hitting balls under the trees. He's playing center field and the left and rightfielders are about 20 feet from the foul lines!

"I say to Steve, 'where is the father?' He says he's going to Georgia Tech to go play football, but I say I want to talk to the father.

"I talk to the father, and I haven't seen anything like this in a long time. He says, 'Calvin loves baseball but he hasn't played a lot of it and if he doesn't get drafted where we think he should get paid, we'll send him to Georgia Tech and he'll play football. He wants to play in the NFL.'

"Calvin Johnson. Now there's opportunity for baseball to add a great Black athlete. He was special. He got better as a football player in college because I know NFL scouts who had some concerns. If you saw him play baseball, you would have said, 'I have to have this guy right now'. You would have spent money on him!"

"I said, 'Mr. Johnson, thank you very much. I'd love to sign him, but it's going to be a hard sell for me in the first round.'"

Thrift regrets he didn't push the Cincinnati Reds scouting director to pursue Johnson.

"I mentioned Calvin Johnson to Terry Reynolds and so forth. I said, 'We have a special case here, but let him play football and go to the NFL'.

"But I look back at that and say, God! I went against my bloodlines. My dad would have gone after him! But I had to make a business decision."

How much would it have cost to sign Calvin Johnson?

"I think Mr. Johnson told me $3 million. I'm not sure what we were budgeted for."

Other scouts are unsure that even $3 million would have done it. Some recall the Johnsons setting their figure at $6 or $7 million.

Los Angeles Angels scout Chris McAlpin called him the best athlete he'd ever seen. Despite the loaded coiffeurs of his organization, McAlpin was unable to entice Johnson.

Chip Lawrence was also enamored with Calvin Johnson's baseball skills. Johnson came out of high school two years before Domonic Brown.

"He was #1 on my list, no question. I had him higher than Domonic. He would have been a sure 1st-rounder if he would focus on baseball.

"Calvin was a lot stronger, faster, had an even better arm. More power. They both had plus arms, but Calvin's was even stronger. It was impressive, he would just walk out for baseball and show all that.

"Amateur-wise, he's up there in a special class of players I've seen. He falls in the group of the Uptons and David Wright. They played a lot more baseball but he grades up with them on the tools. Along with Andrew McCutchen, they were the special ones."

So why didn't the Phillies take a shot at Calvin Johnson?

"I talked to him, he just had no interest in going out for pro baseball. We didn't even get to talk dollars. He said, 'I'm pretty good at football, too.' Guess he was right!"

Nevertheless, it's still surprising that for the kind of talent and athleticism brought to the table, Calvin Johnson went completely undrafted in 2004. Why wouldn't anyone take a 50th round stab in the event Johnson gets hurt playing football or simply changes his mind?

"I'm shocked too," says Muzzy Jackson, comparing Calvin Johnson to a two-sport athlete he was involved with back in 1998. "When I was with the Reds, Adam Dunn told us he wanted to play quarterback for the University of Texas and go to the NFL. But our scouts really liked him as a baseball player and gave him a lot of money just to play pro baseball part-time on the chance something would happen."

Something did happen. The University of Texas settled on Chris Simms as their starting quarterback and asked the 6'6" Dunn to move to tight end. Dunn decided he'd rather crush baseballs than linebackers and after just a year in Austin, he became sole property of the Cincinnati Reds. Dunn rose quickly to the big leagues, receiving the call barely three years into his pro career. He's since grown to a defensive end-like 285 pounds and has become one of the game's most prolific lefthanded sluggers.

Adam Dunn paid off handsomely on the Reds' $772,000 gamble. But for every Adam Dunn, draft history is littered with many more frivolous selections of "athletes" like Michael Vick, the Virginia Tech quarterback who went in the 30th round to the Colorado Rockies in 2000 despite quitting baseball in 7th grade.

Instead of wasting a pick on Michael Vick as a public relations ploy, why not take someone like Calvin Johnson who, though a longshot, could change the entire fate of an organization?

It brings us back again to the realities of the modern day scout. Trained more on statistics, radar guns, and stopwatch readings, they are susceptible to miss what can only be seen by the naked eye.

I've come across the 2004 preference list of one Georgia scout who had Calvin Johnson ranked 45th. His area consisted of three states: Georgia and the two Carolinas and he saw 44 players he considered better prospects than Calvin Johnson! The same Calvin Johnson whom veteran scouts like Thrift, McAlpin, and Lawrence evaluated to be a once-in-a-generation talent.

True to form, this scout also had Matt Wieters ranked 36th. Wieters was then a Charleston-area high school senior; he would go on to star at Georgia Tech before becoming the powerful centerpiece catcher of the rebuilt Baltimore Orioles. Neither he nor Calvin Johnson were particularly recognized in 2004 by publications such as *Baseball America*. So in that respect, it's not surprising that "yes-men" scouts would overlook them. Fear of going against the grain is endemic to the extent that scouts will misjudge even the greatest of talents if they fail to draw a crowd.

It's immaterial in this case because today Calvin Johnson is "Megatron", one of the NFL's great drawing cards and the franchise player for the Detroit Lions. He's changing the sport with every sensational down-field grab.

We'll never know what kind of major league player Calvin Johnson would have been but as longtime MLB scout Phil Pote points out, his case hardly constitutes an American tragedy.

"I can't throw anyone under the bus for not playing baseball if they are doing well in those other sports. As long as they're doing well for themselves, well, then that's great for them and I have to be happy for them. As long as they get an opportunity."

The point is not that Calvin Johnson made a mistake, but simply that baseball is losing athletes both early and late in the game.

The Dave Parker story from 34 years prior has common threads with Calvin Johnson. There were bumps and bruises along the way, but in the end this story benefitted MLB and not the NFL.

"The Cobra" was one of the National League's premier players during the late-1970s and seemed destined for the Hall of Fame. He was derailed by an early-1980s drug problem, but came back strong to end his 19-year career (1973-1991) with a gaudy .290 batting average, 339 HR, and 1,493 RBIs.

Anyone who saw Dave Parker in his prime can appreciate the kind of athlete and physical specimen he was. At 6'5", 230 lbs., Parker would be considered a big man in any era but was especially so amongst outfielders in the 1970s. Still, he was a plus runner, a plus thrower, a 25 HR threat, and despite his size Parker was able to win consecutive batting titles by hitting .338 and .334 in 1977 and 1978.

Jim Martz was then a scout for the Baltimore Orioles and he first heard Dave Parker's name in the summer of 1969, just before his senior year at Courter Technological High School in Cincinnati

But there was to be no senior baseball season for David Gene Parker.

"Parker was not eligible to play high school baseball, he had been suspended for assaulting a teacher at Courter Tech," Martz remembered.

"Courter also had another prospect, Burnell Flowers, who was drafted by Cleveland as the first pick in the 2nd round. The first time I laid eyes on Parker was in street clothes while scouting Flowers at CTHS.

"Wow, what a body! He was 6'5", 195 lbs., well-proportioned, lean, and muscular. I knew I had to see this guy. Only way was to work him out (since he was ineligible to play for the high school team)."

Martz did get Parker to a workout in front of the Orioles' scouting director, Walter Shannon.

"Parker ran a 6.6 60 yard-dash (MLB average is 7.0), showed a plus arm, and plus power. He hit in a Pete Rose-type crouch, would swing and miss some balls and then drive one 400+ feet. Overall raw, but no denying the tools and potential."

Martz wanted Parker badly and he did his due diligence talking with teachers and classmates to investigate Parker's character. The teacher assault incident was difficult to overcome, but in the end Martz believed his upside more than worth the risk.

On draft day, Shannon decided not to select him and Parker fell all the way to the 14th round for the Pittsburgh Pirates. Incidentally, Parker would help the Pirates beat the Baltimore Orioles in the 1979 World Series just nine years later.

"For years, each time I saw Shannon he would apologize for not drafting Parker but allowing hearsay from outsiders instead of utilizing my report, extra digging, and recommendation.

"Credit the Pirates' Jim Maxwell for doing his own work and fighting to get Parker. What a steal! Very few scouts had Parker on their list, if so low just to C.Y.A."

Even in the 1970s, a toolsy but raw (and northern) Black player like Dave Parker was overlooked, but at least somebody was on him and someone ultimately pulled the trigger. And Parker came with real and serious character issues unlike Calvin Johnson, a model student-athlete if there ever was one.

When Martz asked a young Dave Parker what position he played in football, Parker's response was an emphatic "Whatever position I want!" He claimed on numerous occasions in the 1970s that the world never would have heard of O.J. Simpson had Parker himself played football instead of baseball.

Like Calvin Johnson, Dave Parker was an incredible football talent coming out of high school. But Dave Parker was willing to sign out of the 14th round while Calvin Johnson wanted $7 million and a 1st round slot. Johnson had other options, Parker didn't. That's the biggest difference between 1970 and 2004.

Parker would have had serious options in 2004. His football exploits would have drawn much more acclaim than anything he'd done on a baseball field. There's a good chance Parker wouldn't even be playing high school baseball today, but even so, it's hard to imagine he'd fit through the final filter of choosing pro baseball for 14th-round money over a big-time college football scholarship.

We have Jim Thrift chasing Calvin Johnson in 2004 and Jim Martz going after Dave Parker in 1970. They represent a dichotomy of similar Black athletes from different eras who went in different directions due in part to the circumstances of their times.

The kid who was going to me make me famous liked McDonald's better than Mountain Jack's

As Phil Pote said, Calvin Johnson is hardly a tragedy. He's doing quite well in the NFL; he's simply baseball's loss.

But I have a personal scouting story that does qualify as tragedy for both society and the sports world; one that can be prevented in the future.

It all began when I was a bird-dog scout for the Detroit Tigers in the mid-1990s. I was an idealistic 25 year-old graduate student looking for athletes on my spare time.

Sometimes the search for athletes took me to the gridiron and I'll never forget a September Friday afternoon in Pontiac, Michigan. Pontiac Central High School was hosting West Bloomfield High and Central had the consensus #1-ranked football player in the state.

His name was Donte Robertson and Donte did it all that day. I could only stay for a half, but I saw him play quarterback, running back, safety, and kickoff returner. He never left the field. Robertson had a gun for an arm, the body control to make plays on the run, and the toughness to run over players who were much bigger. Nobody could tackle the 5'11", 185-pound Donte Robertson one-on-one.

And my God was he fast! The rest of the field was standing still. I was convinced at the time that he was the best high school athlete I'd ever seen.

The last thing I watched Donte do that day was make a diving, over-the-head interception that brought visions of Willie Mays at the Polo Grounds and Chet Lemon at Tiger Stadium.

I walked out of the stadium shaking my head, wondering what kind of baseball player Donte Robertson could be if football was out of the picture.

I should have heeded the old cliché and been more careful what I asked for!

Several months later, I read the *Detroit News* and *Detroit Free Press* on football signing day to learn that Robertson wasn't academically eligible for NCAA athletics. There was a story about how his mother had left him to move to Tennessee and that he had no idea he was off track academically; the bottom line was that Donte couldn't get a football scholarship.

I hit the phones and eventually got a hold of Robertson's football coach at Pontiac Central, a man named Irv Speaks.

"He did play baseball till 8th grade, but," he laughed, "I encouraged him to run track instead. Maybe I shouldn't have done that."

Coach Speaks told me he wanted to help Donte and would tell him to call me, but weeks went by and I heard nothing.

I finally got a hold of Donte through his track coach, Bobby Kaiser. Kaiser was an energetic 50-something Black man who ran a community recreation center where Donte frequently played pick-up basketball. Kaiser happened to be the son of Cecil Kaiser, a 5'6" pitcher affectionately known as "Asprin Tablet" during his Negro league days.

I met with Donte at the rec center and played catch with him in front of the other kids. Then I took him to a fancy restaurant in Bloomfield Hills called Mountain Jack's. Donte was as polite as he knew how to be, quite relaxed, and interested in what I had to say.

"I was really good at baseball. I'm just an athlete, I wanna play something. I'd even play hockey if I had a chance, it doesn't have to be football."

After dinner, I asked him if he liked his meal.

"I like McDonald's better."

I'd called Mark Monahan, the Tigers scout I worked for, all excited about my discovery. After all, in my overly ambitious mind, I was onto the biggest find in baseball history. The best athlete I'd ever seen; nobody else knew about him and I was going to make him a star. (That's the way my mind worked at age 25!)

"He hasn't played any high school baseball?"

"No, but he's a phenomenal athlete, Mark, it's like watching Allen Iverson. Fast twitches like you wouldn't believe."

"You want to bring him all the way out here to Ypsilanti for a workout?"

"With an athlete like this, I'll drive him anywhere!"

Monahan also worked as the facilities coordinator for Eastern Michigan University, which was more than an hour's drive from Pontiac.

It was a very cold February day. The roads were bleached with snow and salt. I picked Donte up early in the morning as a well-dressed man waved him off.

The man was not Donte's father.

"My father could walk in here right now and I'd have no idea," Donte told me over dinner the day before. With his father a relic and his mother having moved to Tennessee without him, Donte was living with another family who'd kindly taken him in.

I gave Donte the choice of any radio station and he picked WJLB which played all rap music, all the time. I was not into rap, but I thought it a small price to pay for his comfort.

Shortly after we turned onto I-696, Donte pointed to the light on my dashboard and said, "You're on empty."

I, of course, knew my Honda Civic better than anyone. "Nah, there's enough for us to go to Ypsilanti and back, don't worry."

When we got to the facility, Mark played catch with him. Donte had a little bit of a football hook in his arm-action, but there was clearly some arm-strength. Then Mark threw him pop-ups in different directions; going over his head, coming in, running to his left and right.

"He's got a lot of hand-eye coordination and body control," Mark whispered.

He called Donte into the batting cage. "We all know you can run, so we don't need to time you. Let's see you swing the bat, Donte."

Mark was an excellent batting practice thrower, but for some reason he asked me to pitch that day. I never had much of an arm to begin with and I was afraid my 50 MPH fastball wouldn't be a challenge to Donte.

So Donte stood in the box, but I couldn't get myself to throw after I saw how Donte was holding his bat.

"No!" Mark yelled and rushed into the cage. Donte was trying to hit righthanded with his left hand on top of his right; cross-handed, so to speak. I couldn't help but look down in embarrassment.

When he dug back in, I threw one a little high and over the plate. Donte swung like a caveman, missing the pitch by a mile.

I kept throwing and he kept missing. He popped up a few, hit a few grounders, but no ropes. My dream was dying with every swing.

He asked if he could get water and while he was gone, Mark put on a stern face.

"He has a long way to go, Anup."

"Yeah, but he's a great athlete. Once he starts playing, he'll figure it out."

"He told me he doesn't plan to play high school baseball."

"No! He told me he'd try out tomorrow. He's gonna play."

"Okay, but this has to be on you. Do what you want, if you believe in him."

The whole workout couldn't have taken more than half an hour. So we got back in my car, turned on the rap music, and headed east.

About 30 minutes into the drive, my car ran out of fuel.

"I told you!"

AAA came by and gave me enough gas to get to a station in Farmington Hills off of Orchard Lake Road. This was back in the days before "pay at the pump" so I filled up, parked the car, and went inside with my credit card.

Now this next scene is right out of a sitcom. This has never happened to me, before or after.

While waiting in line, I simultaneously smell perfume and feel a soft tap on my back.

"Excuse me," says a pretty young blonde who must have been 20 years-old. "Are you from around here?"

"Yes," I gulped, guessing she was from California.

"Well, me and my friend..." She pointed to her car where another blonde waved back. "We are looking for bathing suits. Do you know a place where we can find some?"

I think for a minute. It's winter, there's four inches of snow on the ground, and she's looking for swimsuits.

"There's a place called Dunham's a couple miles up. And then a sporting goods place up in Keego Harbor." I give her directions, but she doesn't seem attentive.

"Well, will they have bikinis that we can try on?"

"Um, yeah, I think they will. It's winter, but yeah."

"It's just that, well, we don't know our way around and I wanted to know if you could come with us."

The idea of helping two pretty girls try on bikinis was more than a little tempting. But my little fantasy ended when my gaze caught a sleeping Donte Robertson in the passenger seat of my car.

"You know, I'd love to. But I gotta take this kid home."

When I dropped him off in Pontiac, I reminded Donte about baseball practice the next day.

"Yes Mr. Sinha, I'll be there."

The Pontiac Central High School baseball team was a joke, there's no other way to put it. The school was almost entirely Black, as were the football and basketball teams; somehow the baseball team was 95% White and those were hardly the school's best athletes.

I'll never forget their coach, a 50-something ruddy-featured man named Melvin Nuss. He was a teacher with no appreciable baseball knowledge, but he'd been the varsity baseball coach since the 1960s.

I'd spoken to him before to find out if Donte had ever played ball. At the time, Mr. Nuss was congenial and intrigued by my idea. I remember him saying, "Most of those really great football and basketball players don't look good on a baseball field, but if you get them early and work on them, wow!" To his recollection, Donte had never tried out for his team.

I thought Mr. Nuss would be thrilled with the idea of the best athlete in the state coming out for baseball, but when I called him again, he unloaded on me.

"You think you're a scout and you're going to tell me how to do things, sir? This might be the right thing for you or the right thing for him, but it's not the right thing for my program and the other kids who have worked so hard."

I was stunned, but he wasn't done.

"We've already started practicing and Donte is going to be too far behind. Absolutely not!"

"Well, how long have you been going for?"

"What does that have to do with it? Why does that matter? Whether I've been going a day or a month, why do I have to tell you that?"

"Well, you said he would be too far behind and I just wanted an idea how much Donte would have to make up."

"I have a lot of work to do, sir. Goodbye!"

Just like that, Mr. Nuss hung up on me.

I called Donte to tell him not to bother going to practice, but he had something else in store.

"I can't go out for baseball because I have my son this week."

"Your what?"

"My son."

"Okay, well when does your girlfriend take him back?"

"I don't have a girlfriend."

"Who is the mother of your child?"

"I hardly know her, it's just some girl I met at a party."

So that was the end of the Donte Robertson baseball experiment. I did make a phone call to the Detroit Lions and spoke to one of their scouts, Rick Spielman, on Donte's behalf. Spielman told me there was nothing they could do; no matter how good he was in high school, he needed to at least get into a junior college if he wanted a chance to play professional football.

I was going to work that angle with him. I ran into Donte at Bobby Kaiser's rec center.

"Hi Anup."

"Hi Donte. I talked to a Lions scout, he says you should get into a junior college. You don't need the same grades; you play football there and transfer to a D1 school after two years."

"Thanks Anup, but that's okay. I don't need football, I need to get a job and get an education."

I stared at him, but he didn't budge. He wasn't joking one bit.

"Okay Donte, that's your call, but if you change your mind, let me know and we'll all try to help."

I never saw Donte again. That summer I helped coach an RBI team of 11-12 year-olds based in Pontiac and one of the other coaches thought he saw Donte on a corner selling drugs. I didn't believe it and he couldn't confirm.

About nine years later, I'm living in southern California and scouting for the St. Louis Cardinals. I get to thinking about Donte Robertson one night, realizing I'd never heard his name in the NFL. What happened to him?

He was murdered in a drive-by shooting. I found stories on the internet that described his descent from celebrated local athlete to gang member/drug dealer. He'd supposedly ordered a hit on this gang and then was shot in retaliation. The other young man in Donte's car survived the barrage but came out a paraplegic. (He also passed away a few years later.)

I thought about the calm, quiet kid who sat in my car for more than two hours and told me he liked McDonalds better than Mountain Jack's. Donte never showed me even a tinge of violence. He spoke in disgust of his fullback for getting into fights and carrying a knife. Never did I foresee him with this demise.

In the article they had pictures of Donte's dad. The dad Donte had never met was a church pastor and he looked exactly like him. Pastor Robertson was quoted on how the school and society had failed his son.

I cringed at his hypocrisy as I did recalling Mr. Nuss. I wondered if Mr. Nuss shared any of my guilt. Donte Robertson should have been playing in the NFL in his mid-20s, not dead. He might have even had a fighting chance at baseball had Nuss been pro-active, who knows for sure?

I'd coached in RBI with a man named Frank Russell who graduated from Pontiac Central HS in 1968. His younger brothers Campy and Walker were also Pontiac Central grads and all three ended up playing in the NBA.

But Frank Russell told me in 1996 that he loved baseball and so did Campy.

"It was our best sport, I'm telling you. Campy was a great pitcher. He threw 90 MPH. But none of us made Mr. Nuss's team and we were better at baseball than we were at basketball!"

At the time I wondered how many great Black baseball players have been lost to negligence. After Donte Robertson's murder, I wondered how many lives.

Indeed, teachers and coaches can influence the young like no one else aside from their parents. I find it hard to believe that every inner city school has someone destroying their baseball program, but there are probably more default high school baseball coaches than football or basketball because it's simply not a priority nor a money-maker at that level. Baseball in lower socioeconomic areas will always be compromised.

Robertson had other barriers, of course. Like any young man, he needed money. With no education and no parental guidance to speak of, his choices were to work at McDonalds for $5 an hour or sell drugs and make thousands of dollars a day. It's not hard to see how that's going to end up.

What I learned first-hand is that it's a great struggle for a scout to "create" a player, so to speak. I couldn't make Donte Robertson, I couldn't help him more than he was willing to help himself. Scouts can encourage and go the extra mile, but it's awful hard to fight the battles Donte had to fight.

More than just twirling a stopwatch

While I was working for the San Diego Padres back in 2004, one of my colleagues was Jake Wilson. Wilson scouted the four corner states of Arizona, New Mexico, Utah, and Colorado. It was the summer before that Wilson had caught onto a jumbo-sized biracial kid from rural New Mexico.

That man-child was Kyle Blanks, who has now played in the big leagues for five years and running. He's a swing-and-miss power hitter who's found a niche as a platoon player. Regardless of where he goes from here, Blanks is a great story for how scouts can help bring Black athletes to baseball.

"Greg Trammell told me about him," says Wilson, now a scout in southern California for the Tampa Bay Rays. "I watched his Albuquerque Connie Mack team in Arizona and he had some good players. James Parr and Jordan Pacheco both ended up playing in the big leagues. But he told me he had another good one who couldn't make the trip, but would be at their University of New Mexico Tournament on the 4th of July.

"So I went there and there were four other scouts watching. I couldn't believe how big he was! A little soft in his shape, but 6'6", 260 lbs., and very, very strong. He had this big swing, like he does now, and there was obvious power.

"I ended up pitching to him in the home run derby and he finished second to John Potterson, an Arizona kid who would be a 1st-round sandwich pick for the Yankees."

While Blanks had great size and strength, most of the other scouts considered him much too crude to be a prospect. The raw power was impressive, but Blanks had a long swing that seemed hopeless to ever catch up to a big league fastball. He also needed a defensive makeover, having no defined position at the next level.

On his Moriarty High School team was a freshman lefthanded pitcher named Matt Moore. Moore would be an 8th-round draft pick in 2007 before becoming a big league ace for the Tampa Bay Rays. But this was 2004 and Moriarty was still a strange town to baseball scouts. With a population less than 2,000, and an average household income in the $20,000s (according to 2000 and 2010 U.S. Census), it was also a town where few residents moved up.

But Jake Wilson wanted to help. He wasn't entirely sure that Blanks would be a prospect, but he had enough talent to be of interest.

Blanks somehow avoided football, but he was a premium high school basketball player who was bigger and often quicker than his competitors. Blanks played shortstop for the baseball team as well as pitcher.

On the diamond, Blanks not only had raw power in spades but he showed unheard-of speed for someone his size; solid-average on the major league scale. For arm-strength, Wilson clocked him at 86-88 MPH throwing off the mound.

Even if Blanks didn't turn out draft-worthy, Wilson figured the least he could do was help put him in position to get an education through baseball so he could one day take care of himself and his family.

To say that Wilson took him under his wing is an understatement. Other scouts have told me that Wilson essentially "made Kyle Blanks" by working tirelessly to throw him batting practice and hit him fungos. A former Angels farmhand himself, Wilson worked with Blanks on fielding mechanics and was pleased to find the big New Mexican a willing pupil.

"He probably could have played college basketball somewhere, but he never really looked into it. Baseball was his first love; he made two commitments, to the University of New Mexico and to Yavapai College."

Wilson was persistent on the final draft day, calling the Padres from the Denver airport, pleading his case for his supervisors to make the pick. No one else on the Padres had seen Blanks to that point, so Wilson knew he'd have to force the issue. Finally, in the 42nd round of the 2004 draft, the Padres selected Blanks and Wilson slept easy.

"I wasn't the only scout on him, I think four others liked him. But it was the 42nd round, I can't be sure he would have been taken after that."

Blanks went on to attend Yavapai Junior College in rural Arizona. Most believed it would take him at least two years to become pro-ready but lo and behold, Blanks made leaps and bounds his freshman year. Thanks to Wilson's workouts and to his coaches at Yavapai, Blanks was pro-ready after just a season of college ball. The Padres held his rights under the old draft-and-follow rules and they signed Blanks at the end of spring. He reached the big leagues four years later and hit .250 with 10 HR in just 148 at-bats as a rookie in 2009.

Even if his career ends tomorrow, Kyle Blanks is a success story. Beyond living the dream as a big league player, he's also made enough money to take care of himself and his family. So many opportunities have come for Blanks whether or not he becomes a star.

And whether or not he takes credit, Jake Wilson's proactivity is why Blanks wears a San Diego Padres uniform. If more scouts would go so far, not just to scout a player, but to guide him and make him better, we'd have a lot of Kyle Blankses; great athletes, Black and White, who don't end up in other sports, on the street, or in my case of Donte Robertson, in a grave.

Scouts can do good, there's no question about it. They have to really care, as Jake Wilson did, and go the extra mile to help someone they literally have just a 1 in 30 chance of ever drafting. They have to be unselfish; do some community work, get involved with inner city programs, and not just stand around the suburbs and twirl their stopwatch.

The problem runs much deeper than scouts, but here's hoping that more of them follow the lead of Jake Wilson because to an individual, scouts can make a whole world of difference.

Jake Wilson proved it.

Chapter 5: How Desire, Access, and Opportunity Made Football the African-American Dream

Desire, access, and opportunity: three parts of a filter that have ultimately excluded African-American athletes from baseball.

Desire comes first because great desire can move mountains.

No desire to play baseball? It's already done, game over.

Baseball's biggest obstacle is simply that African-Americans prefer the other sports in overwhelming numbers.

Harris Interactive Polls asked 2,331 adults about their favorite sport back in December of 2010. Among African-Americans, 45% chose professional football to only 6% picking baseball. By comparison, the overall rate (among all races) was 31% choosing football to 17% baseball.

In 1999, Simmons Market Research Bureau did a survey that revealed only 7.5% of major league attendance comprised of Black fans. By comparison, the NFL boasted 9.2% and the NBA 14.7%. Keep in mind that football and basketball tickets are considerably more expensive.

Anyone who's attended a game more recently can see it's only gotten worse. The Kansas City Royals have expressed frustration with what they have determined to be a 3% Black attendance rate at Kauffman Stadium. Aside from perhaps the Atlanta Braves and Washington Nationals, it is doubtful that any big league team still averages 7.5% Blacks in the 2010s. The NFL and NBA have only added to what was already a sizable advantage in 1999.

This wasn't always the case. Baseball was truly the national pastime for the bulk of the 20th century; it was the preferred sport among Blacks even more so than Whites.

But most of the Black faces in today's major league venues speak with Caribbean accents.

Why do Caribbean Blacks love baseball so much more than Blacks in America?

"It's the only way out!" says Pittsburgh Pirates international scouting director Rene Gayo.

"In the Dominican Republic, the only way out of poverty is to hit, throw, and steal bases."

Gayo describes a racial dynamic almost polar opposite to that found in the states.

"I heard a White kid from a pretty good family here (in the Dominican Republic) say to his parents, 'I want to be a baseball player'. His parents say, 'what are you talking about, that's for Black people!

"Not just the D.R. Danys Baez (from Cuba) told me that's what his mother told him, that when he grew up saying he wanted to be a baseball player, his mother said, 'what are you talking about, that's for Black people!' He said, 'well I know it's for Black people, but I still want to be a baseball player.'"

Needless to say, Baez would have faced no such stigma had he grown up in America.

The irony of specialization in America

A big part of the Caribbean success is that their players specialize in baseball by playing all year-round.

But in America, specialization does more to filter than enhance.

"The #1 reason for the lack of Black baseball players?" asked Logan White. "They don't play football, basketball, and baseball, they are forced to specialize. And you know the kids are going to want to play football and basketball when they are little, but especially football. Because you get a lot of attention in football, you get a lot of fans, and the cheerleaders at the games. In baseball you don't have that. So I think you lose kids right away because of specialization."

You lose kids right away and then you lose kids down the road.

"When you have kids who are getting (baseball) lessons from age three, these other kids who are playing multiple sports, mostly Blacks, they could be playing football, basketball, track, whatever, they can't keep up with the kid who's been getting the lessons. Guess what? They're going to go to football and basketball!"

The irony is that specialization filters out kids who are ultimately best-suited for baseball. It favors those with means who are not necessarily the most gifted. Every sport suffers for it to an extent, but none more than baseball. More often than not, when a Black kid has to quit a sport going into junior high it's baseball that goes.

Not only is it harder for a multi-sport player to keep up in baseball, but they are more likely to be dominant in the others. Baseball doesn't need to be #1 necessarily at that age, but it needs to stay in the picture. For most of the athletes, it doesn't.

"I believe strongly in playing a lot of sports," says Virginia Beach-area youth coach Manny Upton. "Football teaches you both mental and physical toughness. Basketball teaches you quick feet, agility. Baseball teaches you hand-eye coordination, mental toughness. They make you better. I don't believe how many kids are only playing one sport, I think the coaches who force that on kids are not looking out for them."

Does this happen even at the younger ages?

"I run into that all the time. Lots of good Black athletes get tied down by basketball early. Even kids who end up only 5'9". That kid might be good at baseball, but to play in the NBA? LeBron can do all the things that 5'9" kid can and he's 6'8". Specialization is hurting baseball, especially."

Upton's sons, B.J. and Justin, played every sport growing up and Upton believes that only enhanced their development into major league baseball players.

"I'm all for multiple sports because it's great to develop the kids," agrees former major league general manager and scouting director Joe McIlvaine. "Every sport has something special to offer. Any time you can get into pressure situations, whether it's basketball, baseball, football, whatever, you know, it's a situation in which you are developing and learning how to handle pressure."

"It's fun to play baseball but watching it is different."

Why do little kids play sports?

The same reason they do anything, because it's fun. An 8 year-old isn't thinking about scholarships or a signing bonus, he's playing baseball because he just loves swinging the bat.

If Black kids think baseball is fun, they will play it. If they don't think it's fun, they don't play. It can't get any simpler than that.

The late Kirby Puckett, baseball's last inner city Hall of Famer, described in great detail how he overcame barriers (*I Love This Game*, Harper Collins, 1994) while growing up on the south side of Chicago. Ultimately, it was Puckett's abiding love for baseball that led him to Cooperstown immortality in spite of having only street ball experience prior to 9th grade.

Baseball simply can't depend on Kirby Pucketts to fall out of the sky; there aren't many gifted Black athletes willing to take the path of most resistance to choose the sport that provides the least short-term adulation. It's quite possible that the 5'8" Puckett, a roundish but muscular 220 pounds in his prime, would have ended up an NFL running back had his mother agreed to sign a youth football waiver. The exception proves the rule; the one inner city baseball player to make it to Cooperstown the last thirty years did so out of great desire and because his mom wouldn't let him play football.

I sent a survey (see Appendix G) to local non-baseball athletes gauging their attitudes towards baseball. I hand-picked my subjects to be top-level athletes; those I considered (as a scout) to possess the raw ability to become baseball prospects. Most of the non-baseball athletes I surveyed were African-American, but I also contacted Caucasians to see if their reasons differed for avoiding the sport.

The answers were hardly surprising. The far-and-away #1 complaint was that baseball was too slow. That showed up on just about every survey but more often on those coming from African-Americans.

The distant #2 complaint was baseball's lack of identity with the Black population; specified was the sport's racist past and the lack of African-American players.

None of the Black kids in the survey played baseball past junior high. Some quit long before and some never played at all. Hardly any watch it regularly on television.

Interestingly, 60% of the Black athletes surveyed believe they possess the talent to play Major League Baseball had they received proper instruction and repetitions growing up.

Travis Rudolph, a four-star wide receiver/defensive back recruit from Cardinal Newman High School in West Palm Beach, is a telling example. (I am a teacher at CNHS.) In addition to his football exploits, the sculpted 6'1", 190-pound Rudolph is also a star point guard in basketball and a sprinter in track. Rudolph does not play baseball for Cardinal Newman.

Some football coaches insist their skill players run track in the spring, but Rudolph's isn't one of them. Steve Walsh himself was a three-sport letterman for Cretin-Derham High School in St. Paul, Minnesota prior to his All-American football career at the University of Miami.

"I don't care what sport they play in the spring," said Walsh.

"I loved to play baseball. If I didn't get a football scholarship, I would have probably gone to a smaller school and tried to walk on to the baseball team. But I didn't enjoy watching baseball.

"I was just talking to Travis. He said the same; that he played baseball growing up and he liked it. He just couldn't stand watching it and it veered him off. It's fun to play baseball but watching is different."

Erwin Pierre is also a sprinter at Cardinal Newman; he was encouraged by Walsh to try football for the first time as a senior. Pierre is about the same size as Rudolph and has already garnered attention from college football recruiters.

"I've never played baseball," Pierre told me. "Never had a baseball mitt. I feel that Black men like aggressive sports and baseball is pretty slow."

I surveyed only a small sample, but it's safe to assume these responses are how most young African-Americans view the game. They simply don't like it and don't consider it fun. One can only imagine how many great athletes are excluded just on the basis of dispassion.

Passion and desire can get you inside the filter and that's a start. But the holes of a filter become more narrow when the issue of access comes into play.

From the late 1800s through much of the 20th century, America was inundated by amateur baseball. This is not dissimilar to what is found in Cuba and the Dominican Republic today. All thirty teams have built academies allowing Dominican youth easy access to the game.

The irony is that the Dominican Republic, a third world country, provides its citizens with more access to baseball than does the United States of America.

But one is hesitant to call baseball the Dominican Republic's national pastime. It's less pastime and more necessity.

Sammy Sosa and Pedro Martinez grew up dirt-poor and they would have died dirt-poor were it not for baseball. In the Dominican Republic, there is no access for such children to go to law school, study medicine, or earn an MBA. They can't even get a high school education. You either make it on the baseball field or you spend the rest of your life working the fields; a dire reality that favors Major League Baseball at the expense of Dominican society. Baseball is there, higher education is not.

Major League Baseball exploits this advantage to the point of encouraging talented Dominican teenagers to devote all of their attention to baseball. They drop out of school and lose access to other endeavors.

I've been to Venezuela and Puerto Rico; two other Latin American countries that have produced a large number of major league players. There are barrios in Venezuela where homes are literally made of cardboard boxes; forget about running water or electricity, they don't even have walls or roofs. The worst ghettos in America are havens in comparison. Puerto Rico is much better but it still has its ghettos. Baseball provides a way out of poverty for both Venezuelans and Puerto Ricans.

Opportunity needs a knocker

The final filter is opportunity. A Black kid can have the desire and access to play baseball, but he isn't getting to the major leagues without an opportunity. The smallest part of the filter is where opportunity resides.

As thoroughly as major league teams have mined the Caribbean through academies and tryout camps, a Latin American teenager (outside of Cuba) has even more opportunity to sign a pro contract than his state-side peer. Players from the D.R., Venezuela, Colombia, Panama, and Nicaragua can sign at age 16 without even going through the draft. (Puerto Ricans are subject to the draft and every MLB team has a scout assigned to the island.)

What they don't have in these countries is football and basketball. If they want to play a sport, it has to be baseball.

"It's their best alternative," says Joe McIlvaine of the Dominicans. "The Black players in America have a lot of choices."

Good luck finding a football league in the Dominican Republic, first of all, and then even better luck finding and academically qualifying for a college football scholarship. You can't play in the NFL as a 16-18 year-old. Only the most precocious basketball players can jump a la Kobe Bryant to the NBA at age 18 but even if Latin America had such an athlete, he'd be hard-pressed to get the repetitions required to develop such skills.

Haiti, a cohabitant with the D.R. on the island of Hispaniola, has attracted attention for the influx of Haitians into the NFL. Washington Redskins wide receiver Pierre Garcon highlights an impressive group.

But Garcon and his fellow NFL Haitians grew up in the states. Within Haiti itself, there is no football access or opportunity; the only Haitians who make it to the NFL are those who move out young.

Baseball became America's national pastime for the same three reasons it dominates the Dominican Republic: people loved it (desire), people had access to it, and the game offered opportunity. The filter was at one time flexible enough to allow their most outstanding athletes to play the sport.

Aside from the attributes of the sport itself, widespread access was a great stimulus to the growth of basketball. At one time, however, baseball was more accessible in America than basketball.

Until the 1970s, it was easy to find a game; everybody had a team. Fields were everywhere, sea to shining sea, and kids played pickup games even more often than they played in leagues. Baseball was practically inescapable for Blacks in the late 19th and early 20th centuries, which is why it had a near monopoly on the country's best athletes.

Of course, such a scenario is unrecognizable today. For every baseball field, there must be a thousand hoops and backboards inside every community.

Basketball costs a single ball; two kids can play against each other all day. Baseball costs a whole lot more and the only thing two kids can do is play catch. Inner city basketball courts have sprouted while baseball fields have sprouted with weeds.

Detroit is one of many that transformed from a baseball town to basketball.

"The Northwestern High School complex was outstanding," says Frank Orlando, who coaches both baseball and girls basketball at suburban Detroit Country Day School. "The city was where all the best baseball was and you could see everything from the littlest little leaguer on one field all the way up to Bill Freehan, Willie Horton, and Dave DeBuscherre on another."

Inner city Detroit was not on a par with Los Angeles, but it produced its share of Black sluggers like Horton, John Mayberry, and Alex Johnson. The Detroit Public School League played its games in Belle Isle as well as at the Northwestern High baseball complex on the west side of town. Manz Field and Butzel Field were two other busy locales. In the 1950s and 1960s, they were considered excellent facilities. Today they have fallen into disrepair and Butzel Field is not even playable.

The Detroit PSL teams play only nine intra-league contests compared to the 20+ game schedules of their suburban counterparts. Many PSL squads don't even practice and very few have junior varsity teams. The summer leagues so prevalent in Frank Orlando's youth are no longer.

All things considered, it is little wonder why only two Detroit PSL players have been selected in the major league baseball draft over the last 15 years.

What's happened in Motown has happened to inner cities everywhere. Legendary programs like McClymonds High School in Oakland (alumni includes Frank Robinson, Curt Flood, and Vada Pinson) and Manual Arts in Los Angeles (Paul Blair, Lyman Bostock) have disbanded their baseball programs altogether. Their gifted Black athletes are playing the other sports.

The "separate but equal" stigma from the Jim Crow era still applies to portions of the South, according to Louisiana-based New York Mets scout Benny Latino.

"Let me give you an example, the high school that Jervenski Johnson went to, Amite High School in Louisiana. The two summer leagues there are still segregated. Just giving you an example. One league has money and one doesn't and I'll let you guess which one is more financially stable. By age 14 there's nowhere for Black kids to play, the numbers just drop."

Foam rubber salesmen

For at least half of the 20th century, there was minimal opportunity in professional football. While college football started gaining popularity at the turn of the century, it would be well into the 1950s before professional football could be described as anything more than fledgling.

Apathy to pro football in comparison to baseball was evident in its first draft. The very first NFL draft pick was Jay Berwanger out of the University of Chicago in 1936. He was so ambivalent to play pro football that (according to the University of Chicago News Office) he turned it down to become a foam rubber salesman. Berwanger, the first Heisman Trophy recipient, never played a down in the pros.

Even 15 years later, 1951 Heisman Trophy winner Dick Kazmaier turned down the Chicago Bears offer to earn his MBA at Harvard.

Though such a decision seems inconceivable today, it was not at all unusual for outstanding college football players to spurn the NFL to become salesmen, sportswriters, or businessmen. The league didn't pay much, careers had a short shelf-life, and nobody was sure how long the whole thing would last.

Professional basketball emerged even later. In 1891, James Naismith invented the game at a YMCA in Springfield, Massachusetts. It spread quickly and the popularity of college basketball increased steadily into the next century, but the jump in Black participation didn't begin until after World War II. In 1946, youth leagues around the country started opening up to Blacks. The National Basketball Association (NBA) was born that same year (initially called the Basketball Association of America); it became an option for talented athletes, but hardly as stable or attractive as major league baseball. The NBA was fledgling itself until the 1980s, actually having to compete with the American Basketball Association (ABA) for athletes and survival from 1967-1976.

A number of talented basketball players chose baseball on the basis of opportunity rather than preference. Caucasian Hall of Famers Hank Greenberg, Johnny Bench, and Sandy Koufax have all at some point expressed the opinion that they would have considered pursuing professional basketball if the NBA economics were like they were today. One has to imagine Black baseball Hall of Famers like Bob Gibson and Willie McCovey, prep basketball stars in their own right, could have also gone the hardwood route.

In 1968 and 1971, Major League Baseball won over two exceptionally talented White basketball players who did quite well on the diamond. Ron Blomberg was the first overall pick in 1968 and turned down a basketball scholarship to play for John Wooden's UCLA; who were in the midst of the greatest collegiate sports dynasty of all time. Blomberg was a potential NBA player as was Frank Tanana, who turned down a scholarship to Duke to sign with the California Angels as a 1st-round pick in 1971. Blomberg's career with the Yankees and White Sox was plagued with injuries, but he was a powerful lefthanded hitter who gained notoriety as the first-ever designated hitter. Tanana went on to a brilliant 21-year career as a lefthanded pitcher.

The competition for players was directly with the NCAA as opposed to the NFL or NBA. The NFL and NBA did not have nearly the allure so if MLB could keep the kids from playing those sports in college, they were going to get them. Furthermore, the NCAA wasn't nearly as formidable as today.

Colleges did bend the rules to lure athletes, but it wasn't until 1952 that the NCAA actually legalized the athletic scholarship. Until that point, football and basketball scholarships were not readily available and they were particularly sparse for Black athletes. There were a scattering of Black collegians on the west coast (like Jackie Robinson at UCLA), but their representation was nothing like today and there were absolutely none in the southern conferences outside of the Historically Black Colleges and Universities (HBCU).

By 1973, the NCAA realized the need for scholarship regulation; they split member schools into Division I, Division II, and Division III, with the latter being disallowed from offering athletic freebies.

College baseball coexisted with football and basketball, but it was never as lucrative or as vital to the professional game because the best baseball players could sign professionally right out of high school.

So professional baseball was the entity that provided the most opportunity; it was the "ticket out" for most of America and especially Black America; at least through to the 1970s.

Until that time, very few schools were offering athletic scholarships to African-Americans. The Southeastern Conference (SEC), Atlantic Coast Conference (ACC), and the schools that made up the future Big-12 remained lily white throughout the 1960s; unimaginable in this day and time when African-Americans dominate their football and basketball rosters.

A look at the outstanding African-American NFL players of that era reveals an inordinate amount who graduated from Historically Black Colleges and Universities. Jackson State University in Mississippi produced a long list of NFL stars highlighted by Hall of Famers Walter Payton (running back) and Lem Barney (defensive back).

Southern University is another HBCU that was incredibly productive, counting legendary defensive back Mel Blount and game-breaking 6'8" wide receiver Harold Carmichael among its top alumni.

Then there was Eddie Robinson's Grambling State program, with an NFL alumnus to rival the very best football schools in the country. Quarterback Doug Williams, defensive back Willie Brown, defensive tackle Buck Buchanan, defensive end Willie Davis, and wide receiver Charlie Joiner are just a few of the NFL stars who came through Grambling during the segregated era of college football.

Those Black athletes hailed mostly from the Deep South. The ACC and SEC wouldn't take them, so the HBCUs reaped the benefits.

The Midwestern-based Big-10 jumped into the action in the 1960s.

"Little Beaumont, Texas was a particularly good breeding ground," says *Sports Illustrated* writer Dave Perkin, who himself played both football and baseball for Long Beach State in the late 1970s.

"They had great Black players and neither Texas, Texas A&M, nor Oklahoma would recruit them. That's how Gene Washington and Bubba Smith ended up at Michigan State."

It was bad in Texas but even worse in the Deep South. If Mel Blount was coming out of Georgia or Walter Payton out of Mississippi today, one can only imagine the recruiting war bestowed upon them. The NCAA would have their hands full making sure neither young man drove home with new Porsches in 2013. But in the 1960s, Blount and Payton had limited options.

So while baseball may have provided the best opportunity for young African-Americans in 1950, it's far from the case today.

"The opportunity for football is greater than the other sports for the sheer number of scholarships that are available to go to college," says Steve Walsh.

"There are 85 scholarships available (for each program) for D1 football. Those are full scholarships, they pay for everything. Baseball, I'm just going to throw out a number, has 15 or 18 scholarships (actually 11.7). Some will be on full, but not many. Basketball probably has 15 (actually 13), kids will split them."

Seattle Mariners assistant general manager Joe McIlvaine agrees.

"It's hard to tell a kid who's a good athlete to give up basketball and give up football and say you're not going to get a college scholarship, but in the end you'll be a better baseball player."

According to the NCAA, there are 247 Division I football programs. These are split amongst FBS (formerly Division I-A) and FCS (formerly Division I-AA). The 120 FBS schools are permitted 85 full scholarships. The 127 FCS schools are permitted 63 scholarships which can be spread amongst 85 players. If every school used their full allotment, it would mean that there are 18,823 full Division I football scholarships available.

There are 345 Division I NCAA basketball programs. They are each permitted 13 full scholarships which means 4,485 basketball players can get their college educations completely paid for if every program is fully funded.

NCAA Division I baseball has 296 member schools. They are permitted 11.7 scholarships which can be split amongst 27 players. Though the vast majority of college baseball programs are under-funded and full scholarships rare, there are a maximum of 3,463 available.

Combined, the number of Division I scholarships available for football and basketball adds up to 23,308. Granted that not every program is fully funded, but it is still likely that there are over 20,000 athletes on full scholarships between those two sports. It dwarfs not only the maximum 3,463 on baseball scholarships but also the 150 or so spots available in rookie ball for baseball players who sign professionally out of high school.

In other words, a high school athlete can be one among 150 who get paid $1,100 a month for half a year to play baseball in the sweltering heat of Arizona or Florida in front of five fans; or he can be one of 20,000 who gets to be the big man on campus playing football or basketball in front of huge crowds with his entire education paid for.

No comparison.

And it really skews to the Black athletes.

According to Dr. Richard Lapchick's research for TIDES at the University of Central Florida, 45.8% of NCAA Division I football and 60.9% of basketball players were African-American during the 2011-2012 school year. If we apply those percentages to the number of scholarships available, it comes out to 14,194. Even given the presence of Ivy League and other programs that lack 100% funding, we can safely assume that at least 12,000 African-American athletes are on Division I football or basketball scholarships.

That's 12,000 outstanding Black athletes, nationwide, that baseball loses from the get-go. Major League Baseball has no way to compete with that. The 12,000 number is not even counting the other collegiate sports (i.e. Track and Field) or other levels (Division II, NAIA) that also offer a significant number of scholarships to Black athletes.

How many Blacks are playing college baseball?

"If you notice a Black player in college, it's unusual," says Joe McIlvaine. "I told a guy once, I want to count how many Black players on all the college teams this year. It was less than ten!"

"Excluding the Black colleges, I'll bet the Black players are one-half of one percent," says an incredulous Logan White. "It's a joke."

It isn't quite that low, but it often seems that way.

According to TIDES, there was 5.8% representation of African-Americans among all NCAA Division I baseball teams in 2011. Applying that to the maximum allowed 3,463 baseball scholarships would mean that there are 200 Black baseball players on scholarship.

Most baseball scholarships are half or less, anyway. But let's take a leap and pretend the 200 number is legitimate; it does almost nothing to close the 12,000 gap against football and basketball.

Of that 12,000, perhaps eight or nine thousand of those Black athletes would have been excluded from playing college sports altogether in 1950. Baseball could exploit that tremendous pool of athletes in 1950 but today it can't!

"You can get a full basketball scholarship, you get a full football scholarship, but almost all baseball scholarships now are 75% or less," says Joe McIlvaine. "It's the rare one that goes to 100%. So if you're a two-sport athlete and you get a full-ride in one sport, you're going to do that especially if you come from a poor family."

Baseball's peculiar role in collegiate integration

Bruce Larkins believes there's another factor that decreases Black representation in college baseball.

"I do believe that an average Black player will be passed by for an average White player in college. Predominantly White coaches and a lot of them take the easy way out; go with what they're comfortable with. Maybe a Black kid did something stupid (in the past) and they decided 'not to deal with that' anymore. Unconscious decision, too. Not comfortable dealing with different races."

Larkins also cited the lack of Black college baseball coaches in 2012.

"There are about 50 colleges and 150 college coaches in Florida. Me and the FAMU head coach (in 2012) are only Blacks I know of, out of 150!

"I can only think of two Black D1 coaches (in 2012), Tony Gwynn at San Diego State and Jay Alexander at Eastern Michigan. I don't know of any Black assistants."

Out of nearly 270 integrated D1 schools, there are only two Black coaches? It gets even worse.

"Some Historically Black Colleges and Universities (HBCU) don't even have Black coaches anymore. Grambling and Southern do. Delaware State is all White. North Carolina Central is all White, North Carolina AT&T has one Black assistant. Bethune Cookman and Alabama State have no Black coaches."

And the HBCU baseball teams have fewer Black players than ever. Bethune-Cookman is typically less than a third Black. Florida A&M was 100% Black for years, but even they have had to supplement with White and Latino players over the last decade.

"I have to get other players of other races now, if I want to field a team," says longtime Southern University coach Roger Cador. "When I first worked here it was all Black for a long time. More difficult to recruit now!"

It seems that the only White students at HBCUs are the baseball players!

"To force these kids to choose between baseball and education is crazy."

Former MLB commissioner Fay Vincent looks at the scholarship gap from the perspective of an academician. "I think the bigger problem is the financial aid for baseball programs. There are more educational opportunities for a minority kid in basketball and football. There are very few in baseball."

"I remember talking to Larry Doby (former All-Star, first Black A.L. player) about it and he said it's just about dollars. If you're a kid who excels at all three sports today, like Larry did, you're not surprised if he takes a basketball or football scholarship and gives up baseball. Baseball forces kids at age 17 to sign with a minor league team.

"They lose eligibility and lose their chance at an education and it makes no sense."

Vincent proposes a radical rule change at the collegiate level.

"The first thing they have to do is get the NCAA to give the players who sign at 17 or 18 a couple years of eligibility to where they can play again in college. Where they can play minor league ball and not lose their chance to play for the college game. Why would you ever want to choose at 17 to give up your educational future with a 1 in 50 chance of being a MLB player? But that's what baseball… they give these kids $100,000 signing bonus which, you know after taxes, goes by in about a year. And they come out, they blow out their arm, or they can't hit, and what do they do? They can't go back to college, they lose their eligibility.

"Bart Giamatti and I went to the NCAA in 1988 just as RBI was starting and the NCAA said 'okay, we'll think about it', but nobody did anything. They didn't do anything and that's just wrong. To force these kids to choose between education and baseball is crazy."

The closest thing Major League Baseball provides is the College Scholarship Plan (CSP) that many players have included as an addendum to their first pro contract. Those who sign out of high school can receive the CSP which will pay eight semesters of college tuition to whichever school they'd planned on attending. It is not entirely fool-proof. The CSP doesn't account for inflation and players who go part-time are punished because it will only make eight disbursements. There are also significant time constrictions on when the plan must begin and finish in order to avoid forfeiture.

Rather a difficult father than no father at all

College opportunity is certainly a barrier, but the truth is that baseball's problems with Black athletes begin at a much earlier age; this goes back to the filters of desire and access. Any effort to change fortunes must begin there. It is no longer a matter of picking which sport to play in college; most Black athletes have given up baseball way before, if they ever played to begin with.

The trend of baseball losing its Black athletes as small children is a direct consequence of missing father figures.

"African-Americans played a role in creating this problem, too, it's not just White people," says Roger Cador. "We lost that person who could be trusted, the father figure. The person who could pick the kid up. There's so much failure in baseball, you need a teacher. That person to be trusted and he's not there."

Football coach Steve Walsh believes it only snowballs from there.

"It's a generation of fathers who played different sports," he says. "This generation has played basketball. Their kids play basketball because their dads played basketball, they didn't play baseball. An entire generation of Black men didn't play baseball. They didn't like it so now they're playing basketball and football."

"No other sport is more father-son based than baseball," adds Muzzy Jackson, a former minor league player who went on to become a farm director, assistant general manager, and professional scout. Jackson currently advises athletes on behalf of Merrill Lynch out of Key Biscayne, Florida.

"I work with 18 African-American minor league ballplayers and 17 of them have strong father figures. That's not a coincidence."

What about the 18th?

"His father passed away when he was 14, but prior to that he was very involved as well."

Dr. David Ogden, an associate professor at the University of Nebraska-Omaha, has spent the last 13 years researching the relationship between baseball and the African-American population. In a soon-to-be-published survey of 488 college baseball athletes who played select ball growing up, only 12% were from single parent households compared to a national average of 30% (according to the 2010 United States Census).

Scouts and college coaches know the "strong father figure" phenomena all too well. Many fathers live their dreams through their baseball-playing offspring and make it difficult for those who coach them.

But the uncomfortable truth for scouts is that over-involved fathers are a necessity. It's rare that a player good enough to be drafted does not have a strong father figure behind him.

"Baseball is a hard game and you need a male role model and someone who instills discipline," Jackson said. "And you simply need someone to play catch with. When I grew up, I had a former Negro league pitcher next door who took me under his wing and taught me a curveball in 4th grade. You don't need that in football and basketball but it's essential in baseball."

There's been an alarming decline of at-home fathers among African-Americans since the heyday of Black baseball.

Studies by Steven Ruggles from the University of Minnesota have shown that the single parent household rate held steady at 30% for Black children through 1960. But according to Kids Count, a project of the Baltimore-based Annie E. Casey Foundation, 67% of African-American children were in single parent households in 2011. By comparison the rate was only 25% for Whites.

Way too many young Black men grow up without fathers in the United States. Is it any better in the Dominican Republic?

"It used to be a lot better, it's come down of late," says Rene Gayo, who grew up in Chicago many years before becoming a Latin American scout. "A lot has to do with the sugar mills. (Former president) Lionel Fernandez closed them down; it didn't just kill the economy but it affected the culture. The dad worked in the sugar mill, he provided for his family. And the mills all had baseball teams, dad played baseball for them. The kids would later play on these teams.

"Juan Marichal, Cesar Cedeno, they grew up playing on these sugar mill teams. Cesar Cedeno came back to play in the sugar mill league after he won the batting title."

"When Lionel Fernandez (D.R. President) closed down the sugar mills, he killed it. It was part of our culture for 300 years.

"It broke up families. Dads couldn't provide and they started leaving. But it didn't kill baseball. Baseball is so embedded in society that even that can't kill it in the Dominican Republic. It (losing fathers) killed it in America, but not in the D.R.

"In Latin America, baseball is not even a game so much as a way of life. It's part of our lexicon, our language. People will say, 'we're going to the bottom of the ninth', or 'it's a 3-2 count'. People talk like that. They'll say 'they bunted down the third base line' on us and it will have nothing to do with baseball. Just the way people talk. It could be a woman or a kid or a little girl, that's how people talk.

"That's how embedded the sport is with us," says Gayo, who was raised in Chicago but has grown to love and feel at home in the Dominican Republic.

Isn't football even more expensive?

Expenses are yet another element of the access barrier.

"I mean, a good glove is $200. Bat is $300-$500," says Orlando Reds travel ball coach Joe Logan. Growing up in St. Augustine, Florida, Logan was usually the only African-American on his youth baseball teams during the 1970s and 1980s. He went on to be drafted by the Montreal Expos and pitch four injury-shortened years at the minor league level.

"Uniform is at least $100. Pay at least $2,000 and you haven't even started to account for tournament fees. That's a lot of money and a lot of kids can't afford that. So I think that excludes a lot of Black kids."

"I feel that's the #1 reason for the problem," agrees Santa Fe College assistant coach Bruce Larkins.

"You have to pay $300 for a bat, a lot for glove and spikes. Basketball? Just need a ball. Football? You pay $50 and they give you the equipment for the season. Baseball is the most expensive."

Dr. Ogden from UNO determined that most parents spend upwards of $1,000 just for their kids to play select baseball in the summer. (The powerhouse programs I've spoken to charge much more.) According to his 2011 study of 6,500 select ball players (over 28 states), barely 3% are African-American. Clearly the expenses are discouraging to the Black participation.

It's easy to see how baseball could be more cost-prohibitive than basketball. But football?

"Football will never replace baseball as our national pastime," Branch Rickey boasted some fifty years ago (*Branch Rickey's Little Blue Book,* Macmillan Publishing, 1995). Rickey is considered one of major league baseball's greatest executives though he is most famous for signing Jackie Robinson in late 1945.

"It is too rough a contact sport for young limbs- and if you appraise the modern safety equipment, who can afford it?"

Branch Rickey made a great point but he's been proven dead wrong.

Football is flourishing in the inner cities; the very population Rickey thought it would exclude.

Isn't it too expensive to play football?

"Sure it's expensive," says Steve Walsh. "A majority of families aren't going to have the money to buy a $120 helmet, $65 to $70 shoulder pads, plus all the other pads you need. But they don't have to pay for all that. With the funding, these leagues are able to provide the equipment for $135 to $150 a year and that helps."

How?

"USA Football [an NFL partner] gives grant money to youth programs that struggle to purchase quality equipment. I wouldn't say they've funded the leagues, but it certainly helps out a little bit. A lot of these leagues have benefactors too, like (former rapper) Luther Campbell. He helps fund that league in Miami."

Pop Warner is to football what Little League is to baseball, but Pop has found a way to keep their entry fees at $150-$200 nationwide. The NFL's Football USA initiative has helped along with exceptional efforts from the ground. Together they've done the impossible; they've made football cheaper than baseball.

The National Hockey League is famous for being even Whiter than Major League Baseball; cost is often assumed as the culprit. But cost in America (running in the many thousands of dollars) is much different than cost in Canada where hockey is quite clearly the national sport.

Everybody plays hockey in Canada; much like baseball in its early days, hockey is played not only in leagues but also in pick-up games. A drive through Ontario in mid-winter will reveal many frozen-over ponds cleared out for a couple of hockey nets.

Hockey involves pads, sticks, jerseys, and skates. Not to mention ice rinks and their upkeep. On the surface, hockey is much more expensive than baseball, football, or basketball, yet it's the most popular and most accessible sport in the great north.

How?

"Because it's funded through the government," says Riley Batista. Batista is an African-American who grew up in Montreal before accepting a football scholarship to Georgia Tech in the late 1990s. Batista also played soccer for Georgia Tech and is currently on the planning committee for youth football and soccer leagues in Jupiter, Florida.

"It's not expensive at all to play hockey in Canada. Just like I try to make football and soccer accessible to kids of lesser means here, they have community funds to make hockey accessible to everyone in Montreal. It might cost them $100 to rent their equipment. Not even that."

The NHL is notorious for its paucity of Black players. If the sport is so accessible in Canada, to rich and poor, why aren't there more Black players?

"That's a misconception," says Batista. "If you go to Canada today, you'll see a lot of Black kids playing hockey. There haven't been many in the NHL because there weren't that many Blacks living in Canada in the 1950s and 1960s. Now there are. I played some hockey and the Black kids behind me are playing more.

"You can already see some really good Black players in the NHL. Like Wayne Simmonds, Jarome Iginla, Joel Ward. There's a lot more now because these are kids who grew up in the 1980s and 1990s. You watch," he grins, "because you're going to see a lot of Black Canadian hockey players in the future."

According to the 2011 Canadian census, the nation's Black population comprises only 2.8%. But forty years prior in 1971, the Black population was a miniscule 0.02%.

It's foolish to say Black men can't play hockey if the country that used to produce 95% of the league was 99.98% Caucasian at the time.

During the 2011-2012 season, the NHL claimed its Black representation to be 2.7%; the highest ever despite a league that is now 'only' 60% Canadian. While the finances of hockey may exclude the sport from most of Black America, the NHL has seemingly teamed with local communities to make sure that Black Canada is not excluded. Considering that MLB's Black representation was only 8.8% during the same season, is it possible for the NHL to surpass them one day?

"Maybe," says Batista. "Depends on if the Black population in Canada keeps growing like it has."

Basketball didn't need much help to become accessible for Black athletes, but football and hockey had to go out of their way. Both sports are considerably more expensive to play than baseball yet Black America has elevated football and Black Canada is making its mark on hockey.

So what's baseball doing about it?

Enter the Urban Youth Academy.

Chapter 6: The Unfinished Business of Major League Baseball's Urban Youth Academy

I learned of the Urban Youth Academy initiative in 2004 while scouting for the San Diego Padres. I was living in Rancho Cucamonga, just 60 miles northeast of the proposed site in Los Angeles.

I peppered Jimmie Lee Solomon and Thomas Brasuell with e-mails offering my time and effort on behalf of the original site. I was proud to hear of my beloved game's renewed commitment to the inner city.

As a fan, I was quite familiar with L.A.'s lost legacy of great Black ballplayers. There were a handful of Black inner city players drafted out of L.A. during the three years (2004-2006) I scouted the area, but the L.A. City Section was embarrassingly weak overall. Scouts rarely went into Los Angeles during that decade and when they did, they often returned with horror stories.

I remember going to Los Angeles High School to scout an outfielder named Jermaine Williams in the spring of 2005. It was hard to scout Jermaine because they never faced any good pitching in the L.A. City Section. Once they went up against a 5'4" pitcher who carried upwards of 160 pounds and it was hardly muscle. In fact, this pitcher couldn't throw the ball the required 60 feet, six inches to get it to the plate. Jermaine and his teammates were literally standing in front of the batter's box so they could make solid contact before his pitches hit the ground like a cricket bowler's would.

One of the scouts started calling him "El Guapo" in reference to a notoriously bad-bodied MLB relief pitcher named Rich Garces. It was only a superficial comparison, of course, because Garces threw bullets when he came up with the Red Sox. Nevertheless, El Guapo Jr. pitched the entire game (shortened by mercy rule) which only led us to wonder how bad their other pitchers must have been.

Williams still ended up a 7th-round pick of the Philadelphia Phillies that June. The year before that, I'd actually signed a 4th-rounder out of L.A.'s Westchester High School for the San Diego Padres; an African-American first baseman named Daryl Jones.

It was similarly difficult trying to scout Daryl and I couldn't help but daydream what it would have been like to evaluate Eric Davis and Darryl Strawberry in 1980, or any number of future big leaguers (Bob Watson, Willie Crawford, Dan Ford, Bobby Tolan, George Hendrick, Chet Lemon, etc.) who came out of the Fremont High School program built by Phil Pote in the 1960s.

To my disappointment, MLB's Jimmie Lee Solomon never returned or acknowledged my letters over the course of two years. Tom Brasuell's only response was limited to a single dismissive sentence, rather a fragment, informing me that he was not the one to contact.

As the months went by into 2005, I learned that retired major league catcher and former Angels farm director Darrell Miller would be heading up the program. Miller grew up in Riverside and went on to play five seasons for the hometown California Angels in the 1980s. It was hardly an inner city upbringing for him in the Inland Empire, but Miller is a fairly visible and experienced African-American in the sport. He also happens to be part of an iconic basketball family as the brother of both Reggie and Cheryl Miller.

(Reggie was one of the NBA's best guards through the 1990s and early 2000s while sister Cheryl is considered among the greatest woman basketball players of all-time. Unfortunately her prime came well before the WNBA came into existence, so the nation's mainstream never got to see her play on a regular basis. Both are still quite visible in the sport as commentators for Turner Network Television (TNT).)

I toured the facility as it was built and looked forward to it coming together in early 2006. I recall meeting Mr. Miller for the first time, handing him my St. Louis Cardinals business card (the team I switched to in 2005), and asking Mr. Miller to call me if I could ever be of assistance.

Teaching cows and chickens how to play baseball

I moved to Florida early in 2007, so I was in southern California just long enough to see the UYA go through the early stages. When I read in 2009 that MLB was breaking ground on a second UYA in Miami, I again took great interest in the endeavor.

By this point, the summer of 2009, I had been out of scouting for almost a year and couldn't help but dream about working at the new UYA in Miami. Though I live in Jupiter, some 80 miles north of the city, I was excited for any opportunity to use both my baseball and academic background to teach the game and life itself to Miami's inner city youth.

I agreed that Miami was a great destination for the second Urban Youth Academy. While it is, overall, a very productive baseball city, it's clearly divided along racial lines. Simply put, the Cuban areas have great baseball but the sport is virtually nonexistent in the parts of town that are predominantly African-American. You could run off the names of a litany of present-day Miami major leaguers like Alex Rodriguez, Alex Gonzalez, Gaby Sanchez, and others, but none of them are Black.

Even going back 50 years, the only African-American big leaguers I can find are Mickey Rivers (Northwestern HS), Warren Cromartie (Jackson HS), Lenny Harris (Jackson HS), Andre Dawson (Southwest Miami HS), and Shannon Stewart (Southridge HS). Danny Tartabull (Northwestern HS) is also Black but of Dominican descent.

Stewart is the most recent Miami African-American, having played his last game in 2008. Those are very good ballplayers, but they pale in numbers to all the Caucasian and Latino stars (add in Bucky Dent, Steve Carlton, Charlie Hough, Nick Esasky, etc.) who've come out of Miami in the last half century.

Meanwhile for the NFL, inner city Miami is their little version of the Dominican Republic. It's the greatest football factory in the world. The city once again topped all hometowns in the 2011 NFL Census (released by NFL Media) with 27 players, the heavy majority of whom came out of the inner city. Houston placed second (24) and Los Angeles a more distant third (18). (Note: I counted 30 Miami players (29 Black) in reviewing the NFL Media census.)

Many of those football players are coming out of a northwest corridor of Miami, just off Interstate 95, that includes areas like Liberty City, Carol City, Opa-Locka, Miami Gardens, and Miami Lakes.

My head was spinning when I considered the possibilities with MLB endorsement. It's a community that is short on money but big on athletes.

Darrell Miller remembered me from Los Angeles and responded to my inquiry; we spoke briefly on the phone over the late summer of 2009. He accepted my resume, was cordial, and said he'd keep me in mind but to sit tight because it would take another year for the academy to complete construction.

In early September, I decided to take a drive to the proposed site, which actually had a Hialeah address. Hialeah is adjacent to the west end of Miami.

Imagine my horror as I went through catacombs of lightly traveled, discontinuous streets, then 4-5 miles of dirt roads before arriving at the future site of the "Urban" Youth Academy.

I saw cows and I saw chickens. Then I circled a swamp and heard the rumbling of an alligator. The only creation of mankind was an old wooden sign that someone wrote "pigs for sale" on.

I didn't see any Black kids. Or White kids. Or anything besides chickens that could walk on two feet.

I was so upset that I grabbed my cell phone to vent to my friend Muzzy Jackson, who was at the time a scout for the Arizona Diamondbacks. Muzzy, an African-American raised in rural Georgia, is also very passionate on the issue.

Muzzy was about to get an earful, but there was another problem.

I couldn't get cell service!

No bars! That's how far into the swamps I had gone. And this was Major League Baseball's idea for the site of an Urban Youth Academy?

About 12 miles southeast is the heart of the inner city and two empty baseball fields on the campus of Miami Dade-North College. Not far from that is Florida Memorial University, which also has a baseball field. Northwestern and Carol City High Schools both have little-used fields and lots of land That little corridor was putting out Black NFL stars by the bushel but no Black MLB players since Mickey Rivers left Northwestern HS in 1966.

Youth baseball is almost nonexistent in that area. The Marlins RBI press release claims to have 400 participants, but there's no tangible evidence as such and few of the area baseball people I've spoken to are familiar with their efforts or with the person in charge. There is no website for the Marlins RBI program. I've inquired with the organization to little avail; they've never returned my calls. One of my letters was forwarded within the Marlins office with a note claiming I was "Singaya's cousin" in reference to a recent American Idol contestant of Indian descent whose name is actually "Sanjaya".

There are no publicized schedules, tryout dates, or rosters to be found anywhere in regard to the league. The main RBI link on the MLB.com website has no specific information on the Miami chapter aside from the contact number.

Meanwhile, the Pop Warner Football League in the exact same Miami community boasts 5,000 players and cheerleaders. A visit to their website (www.MiamiPopWarner.org) reveals an elaborate program that is clearly propped from the community, by both the children and the parents.

Major League Baseball had a golden opportunity to make a difference, to accomplish the very goal that is so dear to my heart but they went to the swamp instead. They decided to pour $3.3 million dollars into a facility that has little chance of reaching the intended population who, even if the children had transportation, would need at least a half hour to drive to a place they could have otherwise ridden their bikes to.

Why? Why would MLB do this? Why would they take such a philanthropic idea, a wonderful initiative, and throw it away? Why would they choose both to underserve the community and shoot themselves in the foot in the ongoing struggle for Black athletes?

I finally did get cellular service when I returned to the more civilized part of Hialeah and called Muzzy with emotions still running high. We laughed about the chickens and cows, but there was a palpable ache inside us both.

It wasn't long before I started hunting for answers and as I trolled the local media, I'd discovered that the Urban Youth Academy was a mere political pawn both for the city of Miami and Major League Baseball. An MLB press release on January 7th, 2009 stated as such in the first paragraph that the Urban Youth Academy would be built "as a component of the new Marlins stadium project."

Then-Hialeah mayor Julio Robaina had been adamant towards having the new Florida Marlins stadium built on the very same land. Such a proposition seemed almost as ridiculous, given the location's inaccessibility from the masses required to support a major league franchise.

In the end, the city of Miami was awarded the $640 million Marlins Ballpark and they broke ground near downtown on the site of the old Orange Bowl. As part of the "pork", Bud Selig and Major League Baseball awarded the losing site, Hialeah, with the Urban Youth Academy. In order to get the stadium deal finalized with the city and Marlins owner Jeffrey Loria, the UYA had to go to Hialeah.

"With other cities, we picked our location," Jimmie Lee Solomon told me in a recent conversation. "In Hialeah, we had no latitude on the location. We had to do what the city told us to do."

So in effect, Commissioner Selig used the UYA as a consolation prize to help Loria get a new stadium built with taxpayer dollars. If it had anything to do with reviving baseball in inner city Miami, it wouldn't be built in the Hialeah landfills.

In an MLB press release on March 23rd, 2009 (*Marlins Ballpark Vote Passes*), then-Mayor Robaina was quoted with, "My goal is to have it ready by the end of 2010, the beginning of 2011. There is a lot of infrastructure that has to be done. We're hoping to have it done by that time frame."

On September 3rd, 2009, I wrote Darrell Miller an e-mail regarding my visit, asking if he cared to hear my "two cents" on the location. I did so while gritting my teeth, without revealing my knowledge of the stadium deal.

Five days later, Miller responded and told me to "Feel free to give me any input and observations when you have a chance."

Later that evening, on September 8th, 2009, I wrote a full-page letter expressing my concerns with the location and my greater enthusiasm for putting the academy at Miami Dade-North or somewhere else in the epicenter of the football factory. I stopped short of mentioning the chickens, cows, and lack of cellular service, but I made my point (see Appendix I for the letter).

Mr. Miller never acknowledged it. He ignored several other unrelated e-mails I'd sent over subsequent months, including my application for a full-time position at the up-and-coming Houston UYA the following summer.

Meanwhile, four years later in 2013, the site of the Miami Urban Youth Academy remains a horrific wasteland despite Robaina's goal to have it completed by beginning of 2011. Not a brick has been laid nor has a pitcher's mound been raised. The Houston UYA that was supposed to be the third academy was already completed in April of 2010.

The excitement and hoopla of 2009 was replaced by silence from Major League Baseball. Not only was I not getting a direct response from MLB, but the stories disappeared from the paper and nobody explained what was going on.

On June 7th, 2010, *Miami Today* writer Jacquelyn Weiner published an article (*Youth Baseball Academy Pitched in Stadium Deal Sits on Bench*) that stated the Miami-Dade County Department of Environmental Resources Management had not even received an application from the city of Hialeah or Major League Baseball to use the site for their academy. Luis Espinosa, the communication manager, added: "There are some environmental concerns that need to be addressed at this location, and we look forward to working closely with the City of Hialeah on their plans for this site as soon as we receive their application."

This was 18 months after MLB announced the Miami site and they hadn't received approval for the site? They hadn't even applied for it?

Jacquelyn Weiner added in her article that "a representative of Major League Baseball did not facilitate multiple interview requests." So neither Jimmie Lee Solomon nor Darrell Miller nor anyone else at MLB even thought it worthwhile to address the issue with her, either.

On September 22nd, 2010, MLB announced their plans for a fourth Urban Youth Academy to go up in Philadelphia. An article written eight months later in the May 18th, 2011 *Philadelphia Inquirer* by Stan Hochman (*Why Are Plans for Urban Youth Academy Stalled?*) revealed many of the same frustrations shared by Weiner in south Florida.

Hochman's third paragraph:

"Hey, it could be worse. They announced an Urban Youth Academy for Hialeah, Fla., in January 2009 and 28 months later, all they have is a set of blueprints gathering dust."

Jimmie Lee Solomon did respond to Hochman, if only by e-mail: "Since there was no timetable," Solomon wrote, "we can neither claim to being on time, ahead of schedule, nor admit to being delayed. In addition to our diligent planning, weather has played a factor in our ability to move things along at a quicker pace."

To which Hochman responded:

"That is pure nonsense. We could have had a tropical heat wave in December and it would not have impacted the start of construction. First, you have to put the project out for bids, and that can be done even if you're up to your armpits in snow. Is the nearly $3 million from MLB, Baseball Tomorrow, the city and state still there?"

"The money," Solomon wrote, "that was allocated for the Urban Youth Academy is still available and has remained unchanged."

At the end of the article, Hochman asked Jimmie Lee Solomon through e-mail for an update on the Miami site:

Solomon wrote: "The proposed Academy in Hialeah was not stand alone, it was part of a huge project that suffered when the recession hit nationwide a couple years ago. We will get it back on track at the appropriate time. Our money to build this Academy is also still allocated."

Of course the recession hit well more than two years before this article. The economy has, if anything, improved since that day in January, 2009. The "huge project" that Solomon states was a part of the Miami academy was the Marlins Ballpark, which was built and open for the 2012 season in April.

Back to 2011, there was still no progress on either the Miami or the Philadelphia site. Jacquelyn Weiner published another *Miami Today* article on September 8th (*Major League Baseball's Youth Academy in Florida Marlins Stadium Deal Still Just a Dream*).

A telling passage:

"Several outside events have delayed the project," said Jimmie Lee Solomon, executive vice president of baseball development for Major League Baseball.

A key issue he cited: Hialeah may soon have new leadership as the mayor's post is up for election in November.

"We thought it was a little foolhardy... to try and move forward before next November's mayor's election," Mr. Solomon said.

Other factors included the economic downturn, during which "a lot of our priorities kind of shifted," and delays due to environmental approvals.

"The academy site sits on a 500-acre property owned by Flagler Development with unique environmental concerns, as it was previously a construction- and demolition-degree landfill," Rafael Rodon, an executive vice president with Flagler, has said.

The whole parcel must be cleared by the Miami-Dade County Department of Environmental Resource Management before any project on the land can move forward.

"Once the land is cleared for development and the November Hialeah election passes, the project can progress," Mr. Solomon said.

"We're ready to go forward with our part," he said.

In speaking with Solomon on the phone two years after this article, he maintains the mayoral transition as the cause of delay. "Mayor Robaina was our champion and when he was gone, it changed things. I haven't been there (in MLB) for more than a year so I can't say what's going on now, but when I was there, that's what was holding us up."

By this time in 2011, former city mayor Julio Robaina had stepped down to run for the mayoral office of the county; he was replaced in Hialeah by Carlos Hernandez. Robaina ended up losing the election after taking public criticism for his handling of the Marlins stadium. During the campaign trail, Robaina made statements regarding the stadium deal that were in clear contradiction to his published statements in 2008 and 2009. Robaina was concurrently investigated by federal authorities for loan sharking, mortgage fraud, and tax evasion.

Carlos Hernandez would successfully go up for re-election in November of 2011. But it did nothing to spur the development of the Urban Youth Academy despite Jimmie Lee Solomon's latest plea.

Robaina no longer holds office; he is long gone aside from having chosen his heir, Carlos Hernandez.

I must admit, I'm bewildered by MLB's failures to build the Miami academy, but not entirely disappointed. In fact, as someone who believed it was a terrible site to begin with, I hold out hope that MLB will reconsider. I continue to contact MLB decision-makers on its behalf.

Along with Hialeah's change in plans, there have been alterations in New York City. Jimmie Lee Solomon was dismissed by Major League Baseball in June of 2012. Frank Robinson is now listed as the MLB executive in charge of the endeavor. While Robinson is as respected as any man in the game it is a curious appointment for such a high-energy position that involves considerable legal and administrative experience. Frank Robinson is 78 years-old and has spent almost his entire adult life on the field as a player or as a coach. He is a wonderful presence for the sport, but one has to wonder what Bud Selig has in mind.

The misdeeds in Miami have brought damage, but nothing that is permanent. Here's hoping that the revamped MLB offices will recognize the power they have to right the wrongs and make decisions that are clearly in the interests of the game and not just to curry political favor.

Reading between the lines

Back in southern California, the Compton Urban Youth Academy is in its 7th year. Has it been successful in reviving the pipeline of inner city African-American baseball players?

Reading the press releases would lead you to think so. A June 16th, 2010 article in *Baseball America* (BaseballAmerica.com) was entitled *"MLB Urban Youth Academy Sees 25 Drafted"*. In the article, writer Conor Glassey lists 25 players drafted in 2010 "with MLB Urban Youth Academy experience"; a list he surely received from the UYA officials themselves.

Now to judge the veracity of the BA headline depends on what you consider the purpose of the UYA.

A look at the 25 drafted MLB Urban Youth Academy players reveals that:

*Only 7 of the 25 players are Black, while 13 are Caucasian and five Latino.

*Only one single player, Lejon Baker (Crenshaw High School), was from inner city Los Angeles.

*3 were drafted out of four-year colleges, meaning they couldn't have possibly been produced by an academy that was just brought into existence four years prior.

*5 players were actually raised in plush Orange County, 3 in the nearly-as-plush Los Angeles Valley, and 2 from the San Diego suburbs. Two more players were from regions that can only be described as desert.

Even if you take for granted that the Urban Youth Academy deserves credit for these players, only 28% are Black and just one (4%) is from the inner city. That one inner city Black player, Lejon Baker, did not sign a pro contract after being drafted in the 43rd round by the Atlanta Braves. So if the goal of the Urban Youth Academy was to reclaim Black inner city athletes, there's no way one could say "mission accomplished" in 2010.

And how much of a role did the UYA have in developing these players?

In most of the 25 cases, the only role played by the UYA is that these players participated in a showcase or tournament they hosted. The three college players (RHP Jacob Thompson from Long Beach State, 2B Joe Terry from Cal State-Fullerton, and 1B Jarred Frierson from UNLV) had long finished high school before they participated in a tournament that their coaches happened to schedule at the UYA.

"You can't put all the blame on the Urban Youth Academy," says Dave Perkin, the *Sports Illustrated* writer and former area baseball scout. "It's not realistic to expect

Los Angeles to be like the old days, the 1960s and 1970s. But it's fair to say they haven't changed it much, either. They can't take credit for those players."

I asked another southern California scout what he thought of the Compton Urban Youth Academy.

"Let me put it to you this way. Aaron Hicks went to Long Beach Wilson," he said. "I know they claim him. They also claim Trayce Thompson. Trayce Thompson went to Santa Margarita Catholic! And, I mean the kid from (suburban) Bellflower, Reggie Williams, I don't even know how he is doing anymore. He was already a junior when they opened up. Anthony Gose was a junior and he was from Downey or somewhere in that area.

"I can't think of one player they did. Trayvon Robinson and D'Arby Myers were drafted before they could have developed them. I'm racking my brain and I can't think of anyone they've developed. Certainly not one that's turned into a big leaguer, yet."

To claim that the UYA developed, produced, or provided scarce opportunity for these players is indeed a ridiculous assertion by MLB. Every one of these players mentioned would have played baseball regardless and been every bit as good whether or not the UYA existed. Even Lejon Baker, the one legitimate inner city Black player, was already in 8th grade by the time the academy began; they may have helped him hone his skills from that point, but it's not as if the UYA uncovered him and taught him baseball from scratch.

The MLB Urban Youth Academy releases such propaganda and unwitting reporters eat it up. On March 14th, 2011, Cork Gaines wrote an article for *Business Insider* entitled *After Five Years, MLB's Urban Youth Academy is a Resounding Success*. Gaines quoted Darrell Miller extensively and echoed MLB's claims that the UYA had 25 players drafted in 2010 and over 100 since the academy had opened in 2006.

Gaines closed his article with: "After five years, it is hard to argue with success."

Taylor Soper of MLB.com posted an article on August 18th, 2011 (*Robinson a Role Model as UYA Success Story*) that claimed the UYA had 11 more players drafted in 2011 without revealing who they were.

It also claimed then-Seattle Mariner Trayvon Robinson to be a success story simply because he came back to work out at the facility in 2009. Robinson, who is indeed Black and is indeed from the inner city of Los Angeles, was drafted and signed by the Los Angeles Dodgers in 2005. Considering the UYA wasn't built till 2006, how can he be a UYA success story? Simply for working out at the facility four years after he was drafted?

In that same article, Soper quotes Ike Hampton, the new Compton UYA director: "The idea was to create a facility in the U.S. to attract the inner city kids to continue to be involved in the game of baseball."

It surely was, but that doesn't stop them from taking credit for kids who grew up far from the inner city; who just happened to stop by for a cup of coffee along the way.

It's not to say the Compton Urban Youth Academy is worthless, because there's a lot that goes on there. The Breakthrough Tournament in February pits HBCUs (Historically Black Colleges and Universities) against Division I NCAA powers like UCLA; it's a great event for the sport. The Urban Youth Academy Showcase prior to the draft is also a strong event.

The UYA has been the site for clinics and umpire training in the past. Surely they've given some local kids more productive options for their time.

There is some value, but to say it is effectively winning back inner city baseball players is to be duped by propaganda. It is much more an event center than it is a player developmental program, or the "academy" that it bills itself.

While they occasionally run hitting clinics for local youth (often by former MLB outfielder Ken Landreaux), there's very little outreach to the community and the population the UYA was designed to attract.

"They haven't introduced baseball to one player who wouldn't have played otherwise," says Tommy Butler, a longtime scout for the Chicago White Sox who has lived in south central Los Angeles for more than 40 years.

"They all played for somebody else, they (Urban Youth Academy) just gave players freebies to bring them over. Not one player did they develop.

"They got some younger kids going to the clinics, but they're fat and they're not athletes. You need to go out in the neighborhood and get the good athlete kids.

"Some of these kids show up because they get a free cap and shirt, but hey, you have to look around the neighborhood.... If they had someone on their staff who knows what he's looking for and goes out and brings these kids in, that would really help."

Butler went further, questioning the dedication of the UYA staff.

"You're not going to get that with the administration there only three days a week, and they're looking at the clock at 3:00 and getting home to Orange County ahead of the rush hour traffic. Darrell's (Miller) hardly there. No, he's not there every day. Sometimes he's there three days a week, sometimes he might have not have been."

Another local area scout, who asked not to be named, also expressed his desire for the UYA leaders to be more proactive. "Each year has been more organized, I give them that. But Darrell, I mean he's late even to his own events. Even to events he's bringing his kid to, that doesn't show well.

"And to make a difference, they really need to go get 8-10 year-olds, 12-14 year-olds, not high school kids who are already good. They need to find young athletes and teach them baseball, that's their purpose.

"I don't see them doing that right now, not at all. And there's no way for kids in other parts of L.A., even inner city L.A. like Crenshaw and Inglewood, to get to Compton without a shuttle. I don't know how much money that would be, but they should have a shuttle get kids after school if they really want to make a difference.

"They haven't had any effect on increasing the numbers of Black baseball players so far, none at all."

I asked him if the other scouts ever expressed the same frustration.

"Oh yeah, scouts complain all the time! They're sick of the Academy bringing in Black players from the Inland Empire (50-100 miles east) when there are so many Black athletes right here and they're doing nothing to reach them."

Gerald Pickens is a local coach who started the Compton Baseball Academy Teams (CBAT) program for inner city youth some eight years before the UYA opened its doors. Pickens had been involved with youth baseball in Los Angeles since 1973 and is currently the coach at Centennial High School. He crossed paths in the development of many inner city baseball stars including both Darryl Strawberry and Eric Davis, whom Pickens coached as junior high kids back in the 1970s.

Pickens echoed the previous scout's opinions on the importance of recruiting athletes to play baseball.

"I have five guys on my varsity team right now who told me they didn't play baseball when I recruited them. I told them to give it a shot, I recruited them.

I asked Pickens if he had the same mission as the Urban Youth Academy.

"I don't want to get into a war of words, but yes. We have the same mission but they are not living up to the mission. Hopefully later we'll have a working agreement, there should be a good partnership and (former MLB executive) Jimmie Lee Solomon did say that. We haven't had one yet and I operate independently."

Pickens expressed frustration with their lack of production. "With the amount of money that they are given, there should be a drastic change in the amount of ballplayers drafted from this area. I'm referring to RBI, the Urban Youth Academy, the Los Angeles RBI and every program in the country where the director is making $125-$300 grand a year."

I asked him if he had even a tenth of the UYA budget at his disposal.

"A tenth of their money? I don't have that. If I had one-tenth of the budget they have, I'd have players coming out like you wouldn't believe. Because I'd have the budget to go out and get those football and basketball players and take them to the proper showcases and get them the proper training.

"You can quote that. If you put $50,000 in my bank account, I'd get it done!"

Unlike the stagnant Miami academy, the original UYA is in a sensible locale. It's certainly not in walking distance to Inglewood or Crenshaw, but Compton is an inner city all its own.

And it's possible the UYA has introduced some younger Blacks to the game; the small children who started going to the clinics in 2006 would now be getting into high school. But thus far, the effect is barely palpable. There were a number of good Black ballplayers coming out of the Southland for the 2012 Draft, but only one was from the inner city. His name is Ron Miller and he attended private Serra High School.

Miller was a powerfully built 5'11", 220-pound corner infielder who ended up signing as a 10th-round pick of the Miami Marlins in 2012. Right behind him at Serra was outfielder/lefthanded pitcher Dominic Smith, who also grew up in the inner city and became a 1st-round pick for the Mets the very next year.

Have Miller and Smith been helped by the Urban Youth Academy? It's definitely given them more opportunities to play. It's definitely made them better players. They are steps in the right direction.

Nevertheless, the clock has not been turned back to the 1960s in Los Angeles. MLB propaganda aside, we expected much more production out of the UYA after seven years.

And if this is the initial site, the model for which the others are built, it doesn't bode well for Houston, New Orleans, Cincinnati, Miami, or Philadelphia. It doesn't bode well unless there's a drastic change in strategy and implementation.

Back in Houston

Houston's Urban Youth Academy is located in Sylvester Turner Park in the northwest section of town. One local MLB scout I spoke to believes it's a good area, but other experts denounce the location including Martin Stringer.

Martin Stringer was the director of Houston's very successful RBI Program (see Chapter One).

While the Acres Homes area around Sylvester Turner Park is predominantly African-American, it has no track record of producing athletes. The region has been notoriously poor for baseball but not much better for football or basketball, either.

The local high school is Eisenhower, which does not have an NFL or NBA player to its credit and is not an athletic power in any of the big three sports. Their football team finished 5-6 in the Fall of 2011 and ranked 391st in the state of Texas by Maxpreps.com. Their basketball team went 5-17 the following winter before the baseball team went 13-13 in spring.

The next nearest high school is Waltrip HS, where Sylvester Turner himself attended many years before becoming the lawyer and Texas state representative he is today. It is somewhat competitive and has a current NFL player, but it's hardly a factory for athletes, Black or White.

It's possible there is untapped athletic baseball talent, but it is not evident in the caliber of the region's football and basketball.

Stringer has other issues.

"It's simply not a vibrant baseball area. You have Smokey Jasper Park on the northeast side, the field Jason Bourgeois and Michael Bourn grew up playing on. Lots of great baseball there, good history, lots of Black players. Then you have MacGregor Park on the south side. Carl Crawford grew up near there, Chris Young. We had our RBI games. There's plenty of land, plenty of room. Lots of athletes to cater to. Why did they pick Sylvester Turner? I wasn't consulted, that's for sure."

Beyond the lack of athletes, Stringer addressed the dangerous nature of the Acres Homes area. Stringer was once employed by the Houston Police Department as a gang expert and states he wrote the gang manual that the HPD uses to this day.

"I asked some of my friends on the force to look into the area, and they told me it was crime-ridden like I thought. One of the worst areas in the city. Lots of burglaries, drug marketing."

If we were to look at the football factories, it would take us all over town. North Shore High School has five athletes who played in the NFL in 2011; it is located on the far east side of the city, more than 20 miles from the site of MLB's Urban Youth Academy, and closer to the Smokey Jasper Park that Stringer spoke of. James Madison High School (two NFL players) is on the southwest side and also more than 20 miles away, in the other direction near MacGregor Park.

Forest Brook High School is due east, ten miles from the academy, not far from Smokey Jasper. FBHS has two notable Black pro athletes: Jason Bourgeois is a 2000 graduate and Lawrence Vickers, a veteran NFL backup fullback, came out of Forest Brook a year later.

So while there isn't really a catch-all location for Black athletes in Houston like there is in Miami or Los Angeles, there are clearly more advantageous locations than what MLB chose. And similar to Miami and L.A., Houston is strong in both baseball and football, yet highly segregated in their distribution of athletes. Likewise, the schools that are strong in basketball are also notoriously weak in baseball.

The explanation for the chosen site has much to do with the fact that Sylvester Turner and Jimmie Lee Solomon were in communication for many years prior. Turner and Solomon are friends and former Harvard Law School classmates from the early 1980s. "Sylvester contacted me even before we opened up in Compton," Solomon says, "but we decided to start in Compton first.

"Sylvester had some of it assembled in Houston, on his own. He started clearing the trees. He agreed to put the field in. By the time we got there, he had raised over seven million bucks. He had exactly the footprint we needed, all he needed was a show field. We put it in and then we expanded the clubhouse. That's how we got the academy in Houston. So our investment was about $1.5 million."

As it was built, Martin Stringer pushed hard for the Houston UYA director position and earned an interview; in the end, Darrell Miller and Jimmie Lee Solomon settled on Daryl Wade. Wade worked previously as the athletic director for the Houston Interscholastic School District, but had little to no baseball experience. He's African-American and from the area, having attended Waltrip High School like Sylvester Turner. Wade graduated from Waltrip in 1976, three years after Turner.

"I'm disappointed, yes. But if you're not going to hire me," said Stringer, "okay. But don't go out and hire a non-baseball guy.

"I interviewed with Darrell Miller and provided him an 18-page program of what worked at RBI and told him how I would implement it for the academy. I gave out my secrets. It's proven to work, it has worked. I was on a mission with RBI and I wanted to bring what I and Irvin Hall did to the academy. It hurts that I'm not involved at all. I didn't have to be in charge, but to not be involved at all for all I know about the pulse of Houston baseball, that's really disappointing."

New Orleans

On August 10th, 2011, MLB held a groundbreaking ceremony for yet another Urban Youth Academy in New Orleans despite the deadlock situations with Miami and Philadelphia. They chose to rebuild Wesley Barrow Stadium and Ponchartrain Park on the north end of town. It is clearly an underserved area for baseball and a location that can draw inner city Black athletes.

Ron Washington was among the faces at the ceremony. The Texas Rangers manager and longtime MLB infielder grew up just minutes from Barrow Stadium and praised the efforts to rebuild a once proud facility that had been ravaged by Hurricane Katrina. Barrow Stadium was for decades a meeting place of Black baseball players and anyone who played prep ball in the Crescent City knows all about it.

The neighborhood around Barrow Stadium is best described as middle-class Black. The true inner city Blacks are a long walk, bike-ride, or short drive away. The schools that are prolific for NFL and NBA talent are scattered around the city; none are necessarily within the immediate area, but within a reasonable commute. The New Orleans baseball experts I've spoken with believe MLB picked a viable location. It is more advantageous than Houston's locale and much more so than Miami's.

In yet another MLB.com article written by Alden Gonzalez on its 2012 opening day (*MLB, New Orleans Break Ground on UYA*), it was stated that there were now 115 participants from the Compton UYA who'd been drafted. Again, the list was surely given to Gonzalez by MLB and accepted as fact. MLB officials, like Solomon and Miller, were willing to talk with Gonzalez despite their refusals to respond to the writers in Philadelphia (Stan Hochman) and Miami (Jacquelyn Weiner). Gonzalez, of course, is also on the MLB payroll; MLB.com has never written anything truly critical of the league.

This New Orleans UYA cost $5.3 million to build, according to Gonzalez's article.

The legacy of the Kansas City Royals Academy

All of the academies have potential, but they must be well-managed to accomplish the mission.

The academy concept is nothing new; it's been proven to work.

Domestically, the Kansas City Royals were the academy pioneers back in 1970. Under then-owner Ewing Kauffman and farm director Syd Thrift, the Royals created an academy in Sarasota, Florida, that invited premium athletes who were unselected in the baseball draft. The Royals had tryouts all over the country, seeking the finest athletes in the land; putting a premium on size, speed, and arm-strength. Most of the athletes had little to no baseball experience, but the Royals didn't care. They were in the market for raw material that they believed they could harness.

The late Syd Thrift wrote quite fondly of the Kansas City Royals Academy in his 1990 autobiography, *The Game According to Syd* (Simon and Schuster). Thrift, who would later go on to executive roles with the Oakland A's, Pittsburgh Pirates (as general manager), and Baltimore Orioles, was the director of the academy for the first two of its three years of existence.

The Royals were an expansion team, having joined the American League in 1969; owner Ewing Kauffman was quite open-minded about finding new avenues for talent.

Jim Thrift, Syd's son and now a veteran scout for the Baltimore Orioles, has equally fond memories of his father's endeavor. It has clearly influenced his scouting career and the way he looks at players.

"I can't begin to tell you all the things I saw at the Royals academy," Thrift said. "What Ewing Kauffman asked my father was, right at the conception of the Royals, 'can you take an athlete and make him a baseball player?' My dad said, 'Sure!' Because you know at that time the best athletes weren't playing baseball, they were playing other sports.

"So in order to get this off the ground, they wrote 10,000 letters to high school and Legion coaches across the country, held 50 tryout camps, and took about a year. I think the tryout camp in Chicago had 482 players at it, that's what Art Stewart (Royals executive and former scouting director) told me. And they narrowed it down and narrowed it down until they brought the final fifty to Kansas City to work out. And that's how they sorted them out, the first 40-50 they boarded on the plane and flew to Sarasota."

According to Syd Thrift's book, the Royals had 16-month programs that involved not only instruction from topflight professional coaches, but classes from a local community college, weight training (which was in its infancy in the early 1970s), and psychological analysis.

"My dad put together a group of guys that I called mad scientists," said Jim Thrift. "Between Steve Boros, Joe Tanner, Chuck Stobbs…. Jack McKeon had his time there.

"Wes Santee, the famous track star from Kansas State, came in to teach people how to run. Bill Harrison's intro to vision training was there. Nutritionists were brought in to design the food. Olympic size pool for recovery work in 1970. They had psychologists, they were testing players long before they were doing that for the draft.

"I still have the video of Ted Williams coming to speak about hitting in street clothes!"

The academy was loaded with big-time athletes. "All the guys were monsters, they were all men. I shagged, I was a batboy. I couldn't believe what I would see there."

By far the most successful graduate was Frank White, an African-American who went on to become one of the game's great second basemen over the 1970s and 1980s.

White was a local kid from Kansas City who attended Lincoln High School. He was a tremendous athlete, a star in both high school football and basketball. White played summer baseball, but his inner city high school didn't even have a team.

White was by this time 20 years-old, married, and working for a local plating company as described in his autobiography, *One Man's Dream* (Ascend Books, 2012). At

5'11", 170 lbs., he was blessed with loads of athleticism; speed and arm-strength to die for and some serious line-drive power from the right side of the plate. But White was a raw talent with little experience.

Frank White and the Royals Academy were made for one another. After two years in Sarasota, White moved up the ladder to High-A Ball and then reached the major leagues in 1973. White grew into a 7-time All-Star, earning eight gold glove awards for fielding excellence. He ranks among the all-time greatest defensive second baseman and he ended up developing home run power late in his career, averaging 20 HR a season from 1984 to 1987.

Frank White singlehandedly made the academy a rousing success for the Kansas City Royals. The club won consecutive division titles from 1976 to 1978, losing the American League Championship Series to the hated New York Yankees on all three occasions. They won the division again in 1980 and finally beat the Yankees in the ALCS only to fall to the Philadelphia Phillies in the World Series. They won a share of the division title in the strike-shortened 1981 season and another A.L. Central crown in 1984 before going all the way to their only World Series Championship in 1985. In all, they made seven postseasons over a 10-year span.

Frank White wasn't their best player; those honors went to Hall of Fame third baseman George Brett. Nevertheless, White was a vital contributor and it's safe to say the franchise would have a few less flags without him. He's even received some Hall of Fame support for his all-around talent.

Aside from White, the academy can take at least partial credit for a couple of other long-term major leaguers both named "Washington".

Ron Washington came out of New Orleans as a skinny, raw athlete. It took 12 minor league seasons before he finally established himself as a big league backup at age 30 for the Minnesota Twins, but he also got his professional start in the Kansas City Royals Academy.

U.L. Washington was undrafted out of Stringtown High School in Oklahoma and signed as a free agent late in 1972 just as the academy was about to close. Washington would end up spending 11 seasons in the big leagues with four as a starting shortstop for the strong Royals teams of the early 1980s.

One player the Royals didn't get to the academy was Andre Dawson. Dawson was undrafted out of Southwest Miami High School in 1972 and attended the local academy tryout that summer. As described in his autobiography, *If You Love This*

Game... (with Alan Maimon, Triumph Books, 2012), Dawson made it to the final six but was cut in the end, told his 60 yard-dash wasn't fast enough; in retrospect, at least, he seemed the perfect academy prospect. Dawson wound up walking on at Florida A&M in Tallahassee before embarking on his Hall of Fame big league career.

Ewing Kauffman was forced to cut the academy out of the budget in 1973. The Royals were losing money and he seemed to be fighting an uphill battle with others on the board. They continued to look for raw athletes and operate the academy on a smaller scale, even inviting Martin Stringer fresh off the University of Wisconsin campus in the late 1970s. The memory of his two weeks at the scaled-down Kansas City Royals Academy played a part in his inspiration to lead RBI in Houston twenty years later.

Kauffman expressed regret in later life for cutting off the academy, but even three years of it brought tangible results with Frank White, Ron Washington, and U.L. Washington. Because Thrift's and Kauffman's operation was treated as a laboratory experiment and isolated from the rest of the organization, it drew considerable enmity from GM Cedric Tallis and farm director Lou Gorman, who were less than willing to share or give credit (according to both Thrifts).

One could only wonder how many more big league players could have been produced had the Royals allotted more time to work out the kinks and invite more premium athletes. The Royals Academy proved what could be done with the right coaches and a wholesale commitment to developing raw talent. These were athletes learning baseball from scratch out of high school, what if they had been reached as small children instead?

Essentially, that is what happens in the Dominican Republic. Children are invited to the academies as early as 11 years-old. It's an all-day program and most are taken out of school altogether just to play baseball.

Roughly 20% of major league players are from the D.R. in a given season and though the dynamics are changing, it is clear the academy concept has worked to this point in the Dominican. They were also quite prevalent and successful in Venezuela prior to recent political instability that has led a number of teams to pull out and send their Venezuelan prospects to the Dominican Summer League.

"Teams won't invest in players that they aren't going to get."

Major league clubs are willing to invest heavily into the Latin American academies, yet they've done little to develop ballplayers within their own cities.

"Not a compelling urgency to develop inner city players in this country," says Martin Stringer. "And many people don't know that. I saw it when I traveled to the Dominican Republic, it was an eye-opener for me.

"It doesn't make sense to put an academy in Waterloo and bring a kid into the system when someone else can draft them. Doesn't make sense to run a domestic urban academy because someone else can take your player! That's the sticking point to me."

Stringer's referring to the fact that the MLB draft does not extend to the D.R. nor any other country outside of the U.S., Canada, and Puerto Rico. So teams can sign international kids at age 16 whereas domestically they have a 1-in-30 shot of signing any player they might develop in such a hypothetical academy.

The Atlanta Braves are praiseworthy for their donations to the inner city baseball program at the Carver YMCA in downtown Atlanta; the Cincinnati Reds have done much to refurbish old fields throughout the Queen City and are promising an active role in the Urban Youth Academy under construction on the east side. But not even these organizations are willing to foot the entire bill because it doesn't make the business sense it does in the Dominican Republic.

Jeff Spelman founded the Team One Baseball Showcases near Cincinnati in 1992 and has been heavily involved with high school baseball and draft coverage over the last two decades. He agrees with Stringer's assertions, but adds a historical perspective from the National Basketball Association.

"Teams won't invest in players that they aren't going to get," Spelman said. "In the old NBA, they actually had a territorial draft where teams had first dibs on the elite college players in their city. That's how the Cincinnati Royals ended up with Oscar Robertson (All-American from the University of Cincinnati)."

The brilliant concept was begun in 1949 when they were still known as the BAA for Basketball Association of America. From 1949 to 1965, the league held not only a conventional draft for college talent but also a preliminary round for teams to select elite players within a 50-mile radius of their city. Any team choosing to take part in the territorial draft would lose their 1st-round pick from the regular phase in exchange for selecting a local boy sans competition.

Oscar Robertson was just one of the local stars selected as such. According to the NBA draft logs on www.basketball-reference.com, there were 22 players selected in the territorial draft from 1949-1965. Eleven of those 22, exactly half, went on to be inducted into the Basketball Hall of Fame in Springfield, Massachusetts.

Among the big names were Tommy Heinsohn (Holy Cross College, Boston Celtics), Wilt Chamberlain (Philadelphia Overbrook HS, Philadelphia Warriors), Dave DeBusschere (Detroit Austin Catholic Prep HS/University of Detroit, Detroit Pistons), Jerry Lucas (Ohio State, Cincinnati Royals), Walt Hazzard (UCLA, Los Angeles Lakers), Bill Bradley (Princeton, New York Knicks), and Gail Goodrich (UCLA, Los Angeles Lakers).

This was clearly an attempt to play off the popularity of NCAA Basketball. At the time, professional basketball was struggling at the gate but college stars were household names. The NBA believed correctly that Oscar Robertson would be that much bigger in Cincinnati and that Wilt Chamberlain would be a boon to fan interest in his hometown of Philadelphia.

In such an environment it would have made sense for teams to invest in their local players; had the NBA continued its territorial draft beyond 1965, I believe such investment would have persisted.

Coincidentally, 1965 is the same year the MLB draft began and it also represents a turning point in the number of hometown baseball players. Territorial preference wasn't institutionalized as it had been for 16 years in the NBA, but the nature of the times led to its occurrence nonetheless.

In that time, scouting departments were small (often just a few scouts) and travel budgets minimal. Travel means were archaic and the immediate communication possible through internet and cell phone today was nonexistent in 1965. So teams tended to own their home areas and skewed their signings towards local players.

A quick comparison of the 1968 World Champion Detroit Tigers to the 2006 American League Champs provides a glimpse. There were many games during the 1968 season that the Tigers played an All-Michigan bred outfield of Willie Horton (Detroit Northwestern HS) in left, Mickey Stanley (Grand Rapids Ottawa Hills HS) in center, and Jim Northrup (St. Louis HS, Alma College) in right field. Their starting catcher was All-Star Bill Freehan, who was also raised in the Detroit area despite attending a catholic high school in St. Petersburg, Florida.

By comparison, the 2006 Detroit Tigers did not have a single appearance from a Michigan-bred player for the entire season.

You can perform this exercise for just about any team and find similar differences between the eras. Teams today may prefer local players when all else is equal; the Minnesota Twins, for example, went out of their way to draft local high school catcher Joe Mauer first overall in 2001 and then to sign him to an 8-year contract prior to 2011.

But it's rare when "all else is equal"; Major League Baseball has become thirty organizations who are simply trying to get as much talent as cheaply as possible regardless of where the players come from. The current operation is nearly the opposite of the old NBA. The cash-strapped Florida/Miami Marlins never made a push for superstar Miami product Alex Rodriguez and Alex Rodriguez had no qualms ignoring them to sign unprecedented contracts with both the Texas Rangers and New York Yankees.

So as Stringer and Spelman elucidated, there's no compelling financial reason for individual major league teams to rebuild their inner city baseball programs.

And that's exactly where the institution of Major League Baseball could have come in and saved the day. That was the motive behind the creation of both RBI and the UYA; noble ventures that have yet to produce.

But don't think for a second that this game is rained out. The flame may be flickering but it's hardly extinguished.

Chapter 7: Three Reasons Black Kids Will Play Baseball

There are many who don't think it's a problem.

Then there are those who think it's hopeless.

I emphatically disagree with both camps. I've explained *what* baseball has lost, now let me explain *why* baseball can win.

1. Baseball is a fun game

Playing the devil's advocate over dinner in the summer of 2010, I asked then-Arizona Diamondbacks professional scout Muzzy Jackson why baseball shouldn't give up on luring Black athletes.

"Because it's such a great game. It brought so much to my life, it's fun, and it will sell itself."

I asked former MLB commissioner Fay Vincent a similar question, whether we could win back the African-American population.

"We can because the game is so glorious."

Manny Upton?

"Once I expose the game to the Black kids in Norfolk, they love baseball. It's not a lack of desire, it's a lack of exposure."

Some things are so simple we forget. Baseball is a great game, one that can compete head-to-head for people's affections against football, basketball, and everything else.

And that is my greatest argument for why Blacks will play baseball. Why baseball has a chance.

There's nothing like hitting a baseball. It's a guilty pleasure that combines grace with sheer violence. The thrill of catching a fly ball, throwing a strike, and taking an extra base are not far behind.

What does one have to do to get Black kids to enjoy the game?

"It's just about exposure," says Virginia Beach-area youth coach Manny Upton. "The desire and interest is there. I've worked a lot with Black communities in Norfolk, you should see how excited they are about baseball. They love the gloves we give them, they come back and they're so proud of them. They listen to what I say. Once they start playing it, they love it. Just most of them are never exposed to begin with."

Manny Upton knows a thing or two about producing Black major leaguers as the father of both B.J. and Justin Upton. The Atlanta Braves teammates have been two of the most exciting power/speed outfielders in the game. They are precious and rare examples of exceptional Black athletes who developed a love for baseball because they played from an early age and stuck with it.

"My dad loved baseball," said the paternal Upton. "My heart was always in baseball. But I believe there are things to gain from playing every sport. I didn't push baseball over the others, though it was my favorite and I made sure it was available. It just turned out it was their best."

The Uptons are clearly among a handful of exceptional athletes in major league baseball today. B.J. was the #1 talent coming out of the 2002 Draft; he went second overall to the Tampa Bay Devil Rays after the Pittsburgh Pirates inexplicably selected Ball State righthanded pitcher Bryan Bullington. Three years later, Justin went first overall to the Arizona Diamondbacks in one of the strongest drafts in history.

Nobody doubts that both of them could have played other sports. B.J. played basketball all the way through high school and was very good, though not nearly as dominant on the hardwood as on the diamond. For a time he was dominant, however, on the gridiron.

"B.J. didn't even play football as a senior," says father Manny. "But he still had a lot of big college offers. He went to visit Florida State for baseball. Mike Martin (baseball coach) introduced him to Bobby Bowden (football coach) and he ended up with a football scholarship."

The ramrod 6'3", 175-pound B.J. Upton had such exceptional speed and athleticism that elite football schools considered him worth the gamble.

Justin Upton was an inch shorter and more thickly built at 6'2", 190 lbs., when he was a high school senior. Both future big league outfielders were drafted as high school shortstops. Justin was slightly faster than B.J. and even farther advanced as a righthanded hitter. Justin played football his freshman and sophomore years at Hickory High before attending the famed Nike Combine the following summer.

After the combine, Manny was told that Justin was among the ten best rising junior football players in the nation. A tremendous high school quarterback, some of the football experts in attendance believed Justin had an even brighter future as a free safety.

Nevertheless, the Nike Combine proved the end of Justin's football career; he decided shortly thereafter to concentrate on baseball. Having already attended a number of national showcases and baseball tournaments, it was clear by sophomore year that the younger Upton was going to be an early 1st-round pick just like B.J. More importantly, Justin liked baseball better.

So what's the difference between the Uptons and the legions of other great Black athletes who don't choose baseball?

"My boys were exposed to it. That's it."

And of course, the Uptons had both mom and dad behind them. Manny exposed them to baseball early and his wife Yvonne, a physical education teacher, was right there with him. Few of the nation's great Black athletes have such parental support or exposure to baseball, which so often go hand in hand.

The Uptons are a best case scenario. They represent what can happen when you combine great athleticism with exposure to baseball and highly involved parents.

They could have easily played in the NFL, but they chose baseball. Baseball is a great game and it will compete for the best athletes head-to-head with football and basketball when put on equal ground. There's no excuse for baseball's inferiority complex.

The Uptons are living proof.

<u>2. The Black talent pool is gigantic</u>

Baseball has never achieved its potential among the Black population. For one reason or another, African-American athletes have always been cast aside by the Grand 'Ol Game. In the beginning it was racism that kept the Josh Gibsons and Satchel Paiges out of the big leagues and now it's the prohibitive filters of desire, access, and opportunity.

Nevertheless, the pool of outstanding Black athletes continues to expand. The United States counted roughly 38.9 million African-Americans in the 2010 U.S. Census, which was 12.3% higher than ten years prior. Thanks to hard-fought advances in civil rights and integration, Blacks have easier access to play sports than ever before.

There's a reason that African-Americans represent 78% of the NBA, 67% of the NFL, and at least 12,000 of the NCAA Division I basketball and football scholarships; because they earned it. The number of talented athletes among African-Americans is disproportionately higher than every other racial group.

An otherwise intelligent man, who'd been a farm director and a general manager over six decades in baseball, told me he saw no need to attract Black ballplayers because "Black tools don't play in baseball" as they do in football and basketball. Such an argument is quickly refuted not only on principle but from history itself.

The "Black tools" of Willie Mays and Hank Aaron did just fine and so do those of current African-American stars like Prince Fielder and Andrew McCutchen. Furthermore, look at the nations where Black kids do play, where baseball is actually considered a "Black sport" in the words of Pittsburgh Pirates international scout Rene Gayo.

According to the Central Intelligence Agency Factbook, the Dominican Republic has more Whites (16%) than Blacks (11%) with the remaining population racially mixed (73%). The Dominicans who make it to the major leagues are almost exclusively Black; there hasn't been one White Dominican who's made an impact. In a nation where everybody plays ball, it's the Blacks who dominate. Blacks dominate baseball in the Dominican Republic every bit as much as they dominate basketball in the United States.

The same is seen in Cuba, a nation that is approximately 65% White and only 10% Black (with the remaining 25% mulatto, according to the CIA Factbook in 2002). Baseball is the unquestionable national sport and Cuba has dominated the international scene for decades. Many scouts believe that Cuba plays the best baseball in the world but its Fidel Castro dictatorship has made it nearly impossible to escape the country. Despite the dangerous obstacles of defection and a population lower than Ohio's, the island nation is the birthplace of 17 current major league baseball players at the 2013 All-Star break (see Appendix J).

Among those 17 players, twelve are Black, or Afro-Cuban. That's 70.6% from a nation that is 15% Black.

Further revealing is that three of the five non-Black Cubans weren't raised in Cuba. Jose Fernandez (Miami Marlins), Yonder Alonso, and Yasmani Grandal (both of the San Diego Padres) moved to Florida as children. (They would best be described as "mulatto" rather than White, regardless.) So of the 14 Cuban major leaguers actually raised in Cuba, 12 (85.7%) are Black!

So why should America be any different? If Blacks and Whites had equal desire, access, and opportunity in baseball, why wouldn't Blacks dominate the sport here like they do in the Caribbean? The Caribbean Blacks have the same genetic ancestry of those in the U.S. As a former African-American minor leaguer once expressed to me, "The only difference between Sammy Sosa and me is that his boat dropped him off at a different port."

The Black Latinos have significantly raised the talent, athleticism, and entertainment value of the league. Multi-dimensional Toronto Blue Jays shortstop Jose Reyes has electrified major league ballparks for a decade. Robinson Cano of the Yankees may end up among the greatest second baseman of all-time. Dodgers shortstop Hanley Ramirez is one of the game's most gifted hitters and athletes. David Ortiz is the face of the Red Sox. Then there's slugging Blue Jay third baseman Edwin Encarnacion and Yankee power/speed threat Alfonso Soriano. Seattle Mariners ace righty Felix Hernandez won the 2010 Cy Young Award and remains a dominant pitcher for a lowly club. The Texas Rangers went to two consecutive World Series (2010, 2011) and are perhaps the game's most exciting team; they can thank a number of Black Latinos including Elvis Andrus, Adrian Beltre, Nelson Cruz, Alexi Ogando, and flame-throwing closer Neftali Feliz.

The sport would be downright dull if you took out the Black Latinos. Who would still pay money to watch what's left?

Add to the Dominicans and Venezuelans an influx of Black Cubans. Livan Hernandez was very good as were fellow pitchers Orlando Hernandez and Jose Contreras. Shortstop Alexei Ramirez is an exciting player for the Chicago White Sox. In recent years, Oakland A's centerfielder Yoenis Cespedes and Cincinnati Reds closer Aroldis Chapman have brought their exceptional skill-set to the big leagues.

But perhaps no Afro-Cuban has come over and shown the talent and upside of Yasiel Puig. The 6'2", 220-pound rightfielder burst on the scene in June of 2013, flashing a sculpted physique and a five-tool package to rival any in the game. Puig has done the impossible; he's out-tooled both Matt Kemp and Carl Crawford in the same outfield.

But Cuba has less people than the Buckeye State and only 10% of them are Black. Isn't it possible there are a whole lot of Yasiel Puigs running around America on a football field?

"Do I think there's a lot like Yasiel? No, he's special," says Logan White of the L.A. Dodgers. "I think there are guys as strong as him and as physical and as athletic as he is, yeah. There's no question."

Those who say that Black tools don't play in baseball surely refer to the jumping ability of NBA stars like Russell Westbrook and Blake Griffin. Or perhaps the incredible cuts and moves displayed by any number of NFL wide receivers and defensive backs. The ability to jump and cut is helpful but admittedly not as critical to playing baseball as it is to basketball and football. Nevertheless, as shown by Dominicans, Cubans, and African-American baseball stars of the past, their athletic contributions go well beyond jumping and cutting to hitting, throwing, and fielding. What further evidence is required to prove what history has already confirmed?

The other sports are all too pleased to step in for baseball. In addition to the 12,000+ going to college on NCAA basketball and football scholarships, there are another 1,500 elite Black athletes playing in the NBA and NFL. Still, the demographic is so dense with athletes that there are many other young Black men who could still make it in baseball. "There are a lot of 9th and 10th men on a high school basketball team who would make good baseball players," then-Detroit Tigers scout Nathan Durst used to tell me in the 1990s.

With such a pool of exciting, untapped potential, baseball can't possibly fail if they put in any effort at all. Baseball should be getting more Matt Kemps and Andrew McCutchens just by accident. Negligence is the only road to failure.

3. Major league baseball provides the best career and you don't have to do steroids*

"The all-Black high schools in Baton Rouge don't even have baseball teams," says Southern University baseball coach Roger Cador. "Their administrators only care about football and basketball and the parents aren't making any outcry about it.

"That's because everyone is telling these kids to play football and basketball and they don't look at the injuries and longevity. Baseball, you can have a much longer career. The injuries are nowhere near as bad as football. These are things that should encourage Black kids to play baseball, but I don't see people telling them that and the kids don't know."

To Coach Cador's point about longevity, Detroit Lions kicker Jason Hanson was the NFL's only 40 year-old in 2012. He retired after the season.

The NBA had three 40 year-olds in 2012-2013: Grant Hill, Juwan Howard, and Jason Kidd. All three have also since retired.

By comparison, the 2012 major league baseball season featured 14 players over the age of 40.

The NFL Players Association has claimed the average NFL career length to be 3.2 years for a rookie who makes the team for the first time. The average NBA career is 6.07 years according to research done by basketball website *Weakside Awareness* (www.Weaksideawareness.blogspot.com).

The last major study on MLB career length was done by the University of Colorado in 2007, who came up with 5.6 years which makes it close to the NBA and 75% longer than the NFL.

Salary? A November 12th, 2011 article by Joe Dorish in Yahoo! Sports showed that NBA players averaged $5.15 million, MLB $3.31 million, and the NFL a mere $1.9 million. Even NHL players ($2.4 million) edged the professional footballers.

While the NBA salaries are decidedly higher than baseball's, keep in mind there are only 15 roster spots per team; or 60% as many as there are in major league baseball (450 versus 750). And though basketball players have professional options overseas, baseball offers many more quite livable salaries for major league "call-downs" playing in the upper levels of minor league ball.

The NFL has the most roster spots (1,696); that's 29% more than MLB and NBA combined; more than twice the number of major league baseball players.

Still, NFL players get paid much less ($1.9 million versus $3.1 million) and have barely half the career length (3.2 versus 5.6 years) of major leaguers.

When you consider salary, career length, and job opportunities, baseball is every bit as good a professional option as football and basketball if not better.

But what further separates baseball from football, at least, is the toll it takes on a body. Football has become an incredibly violent sport. While padding and helmets have improved by leaps and bounds, they haven't kept pace with the increasing size, speed, and aggressiveness of the athletes.

Injuries are inherent to baseball but not nearly to the extent of football. They aren't as common, they aren't as serious, and they aren't nearly as life-shortening as the inevitable head trauma for a pro football player.

An incredulous article written by Gregg Doyel of CBSsports.com (*NFL is Killing its Players*, 12/23/10) stated that 280 NFL players had already suffered season-ending injuries for that year. That makes for a whopping 16.5% of the roster spots! A typical baseball season may see 30-40 (an educated guess), or about 5%.

But the long-term effects are even more disturbing. Concussions and mental health are the topic du jour among football people in 2013. In fact, there are hundreds of pending lawsuits against the NFL from former players and families concerning their head injuries. One class action suit in particular claims to have 4,200 plaintiffs.

The NFL Players Association became so alarmed that they granted Harvard University $100 million to perform a 10-year study on the health of its retirees. Harvard will have at least 1,000 subjects and the results are greatly anticipated by 2023.

The NFLPA has publicized studies proving the average life expectancy of a four-season NFL veteran to be 55; a good twenty years less than the average American.

The explanation for such goes beyond injuries and head trauma all the way to performance enhancing drugs (PED).

While Major League Baseball took the brunt of the media and congressional persecution against steroids, the NFL managed to slip behind the scenes during the 2000s. Any sports fan with common sense can conclude that whatever percentage of PED use exists in baseball is multi-fold more prevalent in the NFL.

"Here's what they do in the NFL," says a major league baseball executive with connections in the other league. "We're going to have testing four times a year, here are the dates. They give them the dates they're going to have testing! If anybody in the NFL gets caught doing something like that, they are an idiot! And they still do!

"All I know is that their drug policy is a joke. They all know that."

Those who believe alleged steroid users like Barry Bonds (#1), Alex Rodriguez (#5), Sammy Sosa (#8), and Mark McGwire (#10) should be stricken from the all-time home run list must likewise view the NFL leaderboards as entirely irrelevant.

It is my contention that the same criteria of excluding drug-users would negate nearly every NFL record. The career rushing leader might be Walter Payton or even Tony Dorsett, who's #8 and 5,614 yards behind. No telling who'd have the most receptions; only Redskins legend Art Monk (#13) played his prime in the 1980s while the rest of the top-21 receivers are products of the steroid-ridden decades that followed.

It's not just running backs and receivers by any means. Linemen are much bigger and stronger than ever before and anyone who thinks it's entirely natural is kidding themselves. The 260-pounders of the late 1970s have become 330-pound behemoths in the 2010s. Mean Joe Greene would get pushed around on the D-line today.

I am suspicious that many quarterbacks and even kickers have enhanced their careers with PEDs. It may not show up in the NFL's "Mickey Mouse" drug testing, but it is made obvious in their un-natural muscular development, their inhuman tolerance to sub-freezing temperatures, the changes in their facial structure, and the long-term complications that follow their career.

You have to use performance enhancing drugs to compete in the NFL. You have to cheat; you have to compromise your organs and your long-term health. It is nearly impossible to play clean in a league that depends so much on being bigger, faster, and stronger.

I consider myself a football fan, but my interest has faded for the very same reason others have lost interest in baseball. I enjoy watching sports because I want to see human beings do incredible things. When you're jacked up on 'roids, you're super-human. And it punishes those who wish to stay clean because they can't compete on a level playing field. I'd just as much watch a bunch of super robots than 22 "'roided out" football players crashing helmets. The humanity is what makes a sport worth watching.

Why the NFL has thus far escaped scrutiny is beyond my explanation, but one thing is clear; the media is scared to death to go after them.

I found it particularly disturbing in 2008 when the press largely ignored a steroid dealer's suicide just as he was about to release the names of his NFL clients. David Jacobs of Plano, Texas, had already been convicted of dealing. But in early June of that year, both he and his live-in girlfriend were found dead from gunshot wounds. Seeing how the media jumped on every word of baseball whistle-blowers like Brian McNamee, it's puzzling that David Jacobs' death didn't raise their eyebrow.

Perhaps the difference is in the media power of the leagues. The scandals of Major League Baseball became low-lying fruit once congress went after them in 2003. The media had Bud Selig on the ropes from that point. By comparison, an attack on PED use in the NFL would have required a little more investigation on the part of a journalist.

Nevertheless these are issues to be encountered by any young man, Black or White, who decides to pursue a football career. He may very well be forced to do steroids and compromise the rest of his life and health if he wants to play in the NFL.

Not that steroids aren't a problem in baseball. Though it's cleaned up considerably in recent years, there are undoubtedly those who beat the tests just like they do in the NFL. But it's much easier for a clean athlete to compete in major league baseball than the NFL because not only is PED use less rampant, but the sport itself depends much more on skills like hand-eye coordination that PEDs don't affect.

To Commissioner Selig's credit, baseball has taken great strides to clean up its league since 2003. Now they need to trumpet this advantage to its prospective athletes.

"Baseball has faced the problem," says Joe McIlvaine, assistant GM of the Seattle Mariners. "They haven't eradicated it, but they've certainly taken major steps towards eliminating it.

"But at least baseball has acknowledged it. It has hurt their draw at this point in time. But I think ten years from now, if the NFL and NBA haven't done anything, parents may say, 'hey kids, let's play baseball!' because there is less opportunity to get in trouble there if it's so well policed.

"All those things, you're saying and I'm saying, are the same thing. If I'm a parent, I'd certainly like him to go into something where he's not corrupted."

Another "lifestyle" advantage of baseball is their College Scholarship Plan (CSP). Not every player will get one, but it's designed to cover four years for a kid who signs out of high school and cover whatever remaining time for one who signs early out of college.

I administered the CSP to a number of players I signed. There are restrictions; it punishes anybody who decides to go part-time in school and there are qualifying dates for both beginning and finishing the program. The compensation is determined by the current tuition and does not account for inflation.

Nevertheless, it does give players the option of going to college without shelling out their own cash. I don't know for sure what the use percentage is, but the Padres and Cardinals organization would tell their scouts only 3% when I worked there.

These are clear edges for baseball over football, but I question how many kids, particularly African-Americans, have a true understanding of what lies ahead.

Baseball provides a much better life in every way.

And you don't have to do steroids.

Chapter 8: The Surefire Plan- Three Actions for Major League Baseball

The ball is figuratively in the hands of Major League Baseball. No one else can shape the future of the sport as effectively as its ultimate governing body. Nobody else has the money or the influence, but do they have the will? If the commissioner's office is motivated, there's no reason they can't reach the Black population the way the NFL and NBA have.

Before getting into what MLB can control, let's look at what factors they can't:

1. The number of single mother households among the Black population.

2. The faster pace of football and basketball.

3. The more aggressive nature of football and basketball.

4. The 23,308 available NCAA Division 1 football and basketball scholarships compared to 3,463 for baseball.

5. The fact that pick-up baseball is costlier and requires more participants than basketball.

There is little Major League Baseball can do to affect these realities. They won't be able to keep fathers from leaving home. While MLB can speed it up, it will never be a game on par with the pace and aggressiveness of the others. The NCAA controls the scholarship limits and as long as college baseball is a money drainer, those numbers won't change. And by the nature of the sport, it will always require more participants and equipment than basketball.

Major League Baseball can't worry about what it can't do. They must focus on what they *can* do to attract Black players. We've established three filters from Chapter 5: desire, access, and opportunity. Major League Baseball is fully capable of expanding all three.

I would start simple and local. There's a "magic city" that will by itself make baseball a much stronger game if MLB retraces their steps and adjusts their plan.

1. Fix the Urban Youth Academy, starting in Miami!

Major League Baseball had the right idea. Academies can work in the inner cities and bring out strong Black ballplayers like there's no tomorrow. They worked for the Kansas City Royals in the early 1970s and they're mainstays in Latin America.

They work not only because of expert instruction, but because money is not an issue for its participants; it makes the game accessible. The NFL does well with inner city Blacks because they have made it cheap to play an expensive sport. Baseball is inherently less expensive than football; there's no reason whatsoever that MLB can't do the same given motivation and structure.

Of all the inner cities in America, none have the powder keg potential of Miami. The "Magic City" can do wonders for MLB as it has already for the National Football League.

There were 29 African-American NFL players from Miami during the 2011 season but zero in major league baseball. Many of the NFL players were from the northwest corridor surrounding Liberty City. Miami Dade College's North Campus is right in the heart of it, with two unused baseball fields and plentiful adjacent land. It's just a few hundred feet from Nathaniel "Traz" Powell Stadium, the facility where many of the aforementioned NFL players played high school football.

Yet Major League Baseball instead chose a wasteland twelve miles west.

Still, there is hope for those who care about the mission.

Because of political and bureaucratic handcuffs, MLB has yet to break ground on the wasteland in Hialeah. It isn't too late to move to Liberty City! Miami Dade College's North Campus would make for an ideal site. Florida Memorial University is an option if MLB could attain more of the land surrounding their baseball field. The high schools are in prime locations with plenty of room, particularly Northwestern and Carol City. Any one of these sites would cater to the premium Black athletes that baseball has lost.

The same little area that typically produces 10-15 NFL players at a time hasn't put out a Black major leaguer since Mickey Rivers in 1966. This little area with a 5-mile radius can change baseball by itself!

So how many more Mickey Rivers and Andre Dawsons and Shannon Stewarts are there?

"The number is…" starts Jimmie Lee Solomon. "You couldn't count them with a calculator! They're going to football and basketball and the rest of them are falling to the wayside."

So why not move the academy to an area where so great Black athletes reside?

"It's not as easy as it sounds," says Jimmie Lee Solomon. "To just move locations, you have to make sure you have a facility, have the land, have an agreement with the people involved. You can't just pick up and move."

Regardless, the potential reward is extraordinary and I contend that Major League Baseball must absolutely find a way to make it work.

Think of the impact Los Angeles had on baseball in 1981; as described in Chapter One, inner city L.A. had 20 major leaguers including two Hall of Famers and a load of All-Stars. The Black community of one city was able to drastically affect an entire league.

Miami can do that for baseball, right now! Though the city is only 19% Black, that subset produces some of the best athletes in the nation.

The NFL has a near monopoly on those athletes. While MLB is completely shut out, the NBA was limited to three Black Miamians themselves in 2013: Raja Bell, Udonis Haslem, and James Jones, the latter two of whom were able to win a championship ring playing for the hometown Miami Heat.

The Miami Pop Warner youth football league is an outstanding feeder to the local high schools. They are exceptionally organized and the parents highly involved. Their regular season extends from late August to mid-October with the playoffs going through November.

I find it hard to believe that the same parents who support Miami Pop Warner wouldn't be interested in a youth baseball league during the spring and summer. Pop Warner is great, but what about the other 9-10 months of the year? Right now, they have minimal baseball options. The Miami RBI program hasn't made the inroads. Most of these elite athletes endure entire childhoods without picking up a bat or a glove.

Let's give them the option. Open up the academy, give these kids a place to play baseball, offer their parents another outlet, and just see what happens. It's my belief that many more will take it up and continue to play in high school whether or not they prefer football. At some point, you're going to end up with Andre Dawsons and Mickey Rivers and a lot more than ever before.

The benefits are great for both baseball and community.

For me, any plan for MLB to revitalize Black baseball should begin right here in Miami. They have so much in place already, including an earmarked $3.3 million. See it through and the results will come. A hugely successful program in Miami will jumpstart the nation.

They must not make the same mistakes they've made in other cities. The right people must be put in place and they absolutely have to storm local schools to recruit their kids and parents. They can't expect kids to just show up on their porch.

"What I didn't want Major League Baseball to do was put up a facility and then let it sit," says Solomon. "You can't just come in, fix it, and leave. You need brick-and-mortar but you must also maintain a presence through coaches and people to run the academy.

"You can have a garden, but if you don't water it, it won't do you no good."

"An old college football teammate of mine named Reggie Williams had a similar role with the NFL. He ran the NFL YET program (Youth Education Towns) that refurbished fields in Super Bowl cities every year. It was a nice gesture, but if you go back to those fields a few years later, a lot of them got run down.

"I didn't want that. That's why we started the academy."

Major League Baseball simply can't fail if it acts accordingly. Miami has everything: the athletes, the climate, the desire, and the land. An academy in the right location with the right staff will put out Black players like there's no tomorrow.

Urban Youth Academies in Los Angeles, Houston, and New Orleans are already built. Cincinnati is close while Philadelphia is mired in the same bureaucracy as Miami. They all have great potential if they are managed adeptly. But it's Miami, the proclaimed Magic City, that can release the spark to set them all off.

2. Speed up the game!

Fixing the game's pace is a centralized measure that will immediately affect the sport and its image from coast to coast.

The universal complaint about baseball is that it's too slow. The young Black athletes I surveyed overwhelmingly cited the slow pace behind their decision to pursue other sports. But it's not just Black kids; it's White kids, Latino kids, Asian kids, you name it. With millions of Americans calling the game 'dull', it's a wonder that MLB has never taken decisive and corrective action.

Just the opposite, they've made the game even slower. An average major league game was less than 2 ½ hours as recently as thirty years ago. It was less than two hours long for much of the 20th century.

Today, major league games are over three hours long with even less action; the additional time is in pitchers standing on the mound and hitters stepping out of the box to readjust their batting gloves. It's even worse in the playoffs and World Series where games take at least another half hour longer. The World Series is supposed to be baseball's grandest stage, its best foot forward, but it's usually slower-paced and less exciting than the regular season. The television ratings of World Series games are now lower than run-of-the-mill regular season NFL games.

Wisely, the NFL, NBA, and NHL have done everything in their power to speed up their play. Their respective commissioners must laugh to themselves over baseball's inability to keep pace in a faster society. Baseball remains the only sport where there are no penalties for excessive timeouts or delays of game.

It's almost as bad at the minor league level and it is actually much worse in college. When I scouted in California, I had to accept the fact that normal 9-inning games including schools like UCLA, Cal State-Fullerton, and Long Beach State were going to last at least four hours and sometimes over five. The College World Series games are excruciatingly long which explains why its television ratings have been stagnant despite increased exposure to the mainstream. What started in the big leagues has infected the sport below.

The purists wax poetic of how baseball is "timeless" and the only game without a clock. But the major league rulebook has long stated that pitchers are permitted only 12 seconds between pitches. Umpires haven't enforced it and commissioners long before Bud Selig have looked the other way. It wasn't entirely necessary until the 1990s; pitchers used to get the ball and throw it. But now pitchers abuse the loophole to the point where the game becomes cumbersome to watch for even its most devout fans.

In 1995, MLB Commissioner Bud Selig responded to post-strike backlash by asking former umpire Steve Palermo to investigate methods of improving the pace. In the final months of the season, Selig implemented Palermo's recommended restrictions on pitching changes and time between pitches. It worked quite well in 1995, but come opening day of 1996 they were no longer enforced.

After forming another committee, the league attempted to enforce a higher strike zone in the late 1990s, but it was short-lived and quickly forgotten. More "pace of game" committees were set up during the 2000s to no avail. The games continued to get longer and slower.

The strategy of Selig has been to publicly address complaints and set up a committee or task force, but not to actually solve the problem. People forget about it for a while, then it comes up again and he repeats his course of action.

Meanwhile, generations of fans are lost because they'd rather watch multiple football and basketball drives than wait a full minute for the next pitch.

The best advertisement to play baseball is major league baseball. If it's appealing to watch on television, kids will grow up wanting to play the sport just as they had for more than a century. If it's slow and boring and unappealing to watch, who's going to want to play it?

As a scout and a coach, I am shocked by how many young players don't watch major league baseball. When I ask what got them into baseball, it is usually their father and not the major leagues.

If we want kids to play baseball, we can't rely solely on the father-son pipeline. With many African-American households, the father-son pipeline is not even an option. Their best exposure to baseball is what's on TV. We can't allow baseball to be subordinated into the niche of suburban White kids whose dads force them to play.

Whether it's enforcing the 12-second rule, bringing a clock to baseball, limiting timeouts, limiting pickoff throws, or eliminating pitching mound conferences, MLB must do whatever it takes! Baseball has no chance to reclaim its title as national pastime unless Bud Selig or a future commissioner fixes this problem. Society has become faster paced, baseball must follow.

The game will never be as fast-paced as, say, hockey or basketball, but as long as the little white ball is flying around, the fans will pay attention and they will be on the edge of their seat waiting to see what happens next. It's a wonderful game when it's played on its toes. But it's a hellacious bore when the pitcher holds onto the ball for sixty seconds only to make a half-hearted pickoff throw. Try getting an inner city kid to choose baseball over basketball after sitting through that!

3. MLB funding of select Reviving Baseball in the Inner Cities (RBI) chapters

RBI began with the noblest intentions. John Young had a great idea in 1988. He started in Los Angeles with dreams it would spread through the country. Today, RBI exists in over 200 cities.

It's just not the way Young planned it.

It exists in name, but it hasn't come close to accomplishing the mission John Young put forth. The number of Black major leaguers has been cut in half since RBI was created. The individual chapters are mostly floundering and the talent level is poor.

Furthermore, a majority of its players are neither Black nor from the inner city. RBI has become little more than propaganda for Major League Baseball; they are quick to use it as evidence of philanthropy, but have done almost nothing to make it work.

The fact it's in 200 cities makes for a good press release, but the reality is that none of them are productive.

Though some, like Harlem and Los Angeles, have done well to procure donations, they receive very little funding from Major League Baseball. They are left to fend for themselves financially; MLB lends their name and some baseballs and that's not enough.

In the rush to give the public an appearance of progress, Major League Baseball has somehow managed to build a forest without growing trees. The RBI program is simply spread too thin to be effective.

"It's going to take money, but baseball is rolling in money," says Fay Vincent, who preceded Bud Selig as MLB commissioner from 1989-1992. "You're paying the commissioner $50 Million in two years and you can say, well, ask him if we can't get $10 million of that back and use it for this... I mean, I don't mean to be rude to him, he deserves it, but it would be hard for us to say that wouldn't be a very good use of some of the money.

"Baseball has enough to pay him and do this other thing as well. It's going to take money and leadership. I'd get somebody like Len Coleman and somebody who's really committed to it. I'd give him a 10-year contract and we won't even begin to worry about results for seven years. Pay them a lot of money, get some smart people, and get it under way."

MLB has money, but it's not feasible or productive to bankroll 200 RBI chapters.

What baseball needs to do is to start small, to focus on a few particularly high-yield cities, and make sure they work. Big cities like Miami, Oakland, Los Angeles, Dallas, Detroit, Atlanta, New York, Indianapolis, Houston, Tampa, Birmingham, Orlando, and Chicago produce so many outstanding Black athletes that their RBI programs should be prioritized. By putting MLB money and manpower into any number of those cities, baseball would make a tremendous impact.

Like the Urban Youth Academy, RBI can bring baseball to those who can't otherwise afford to play. MLB must take that mission seriously and make sure the objective is accomplished.

"If we really, really want to attract Black players as an industry," says Logan White of the Dodgers, "Major League Baseball is going to have to get involved with youth baseball. Because what's happening is that with the travel and select ball, Anup, the money excludes a lot of Black kids.

"Maybe it got a little bit better with the RBI program, but I think unless MLB really takes into heart the youth programs, they won't change the numbers. Instead of one big complex, they need to have more facilities. I think there has to be; they have to spend more money and have batting cages in multiple locations. Maybe we can hire people to run those and things like that, but that's a whole other issue. But I do think they are going to need to change youth baseball to change the numbers of Blacks."

Investing in RBI is one big change. But the money will go nowhere without quality administration and instruction. Former Cincinnati Reds and Kansas City Royals farm director Muzzy Jackson has a great idea on where to get coaches.

"There are at least 600, maybe 800 players released every single year. Minor leaguers who don't get invited back. You could easily post RBI or Urban Youth Academy coaching jobs and find some very qualified ex-pro players. Just pay them $1,000 a month. It doesn't sound like much, but they'll jump at it. Especially those who want to take college classes on the side. Or if they'd like to go into coaching, this is a start for them. These are players who don't have many options outside of baseball but they have pro experience and a lot to offer the kids of RBI and the academies."

The NFL has been involved in youth football for years. The success of football factories like Miami's Liberty City is partly attributed to USA Football, the NFL partner that donates to youth programs around the nation. The NFL has invested in their future athletes and they are reaping the rewards as the most popular, athletically competitive, and financially profitable sports league in the land.

Jimmie Lee Solomon agrees that no one can make this change for our sport except Major League Baseball.

"I think they're going to have to because who else is going to have a stake? And that's the issue. Who else has the reach to do that besides Major League Baseball? You're not just creating players, you're creating fans. Consumers for your sport... It works in so many ways for MLB to do this. It's a no-brainer for me. No doubt.

"And I think that there are men who are still in baseball who believe that and want to push it forward."

These are three immediate steps with which Major League Baseball would make a tremendous impact towards improving the sport's appeal to legions of outstanding Black athletes. They don't involve ridiculous money or time, just a coordination of effort. It will take further time and effort from the grassroots to advance the cause, but these actions are the spark.

Only the commissioner's office can light it.

Chapter 9: The South is Rising! Georgia Leads a Black Baseball Revival

Amid the doom and gloom of Blacks and baseball comes a ray of revival from an unexpected place. It comes from a state notorious for its football and infamous for its role in the struggle for racial equality.

While Black baseball is going backwards most everywhere else, it's coming on strong in Georgia.

In the 2011 season, California led the fifty states with a total of 16 Black big leaguers. Georgia and Florida were tied for second with 10 while Texas was fourth with 9.

Georgia's total population is barely half of Florida, a quarter of California, and less than 40% of Texas. But it's comparable to the bigger states in its sheer number of African-Americans. According to the 2010 U.S. Census, Georgia (3.05 million) actually has more Blacks than California (2.69 million) and just a little less than Florida (3.2 million) and Texas (3.17 million).

Georgia hasn't always been such a big player. California was a runaway leader in 1981 with an astounding 53 Black MLB players. Back then, Texas had 7 Blacks and was tied for third. Florida had five (tied for 6th place) and Georgia was well down the list with only three.

Who could have guessed in 1981 that thirty years later California would drop from 53 to 16 while Georgia would rise from 3 to 10?

And this is just the beginning in Georgia. Major league scouts have noticed a tremendous increase in baseball talent coming out of the Peach State in recent years. While the on-field success of the Atlanta Braves led to a surge of baseball interest in the 1990s, the more recent bump is attributed to its African-American sub-segment.

Georgia is becoming the king of Black baseball.

"Yeah, I definitely agree with you," says San Diego Padres east coast crosschecker Chip Lawrence. "Georgia is doing a good job with their youth programs. Kids are growing up wanting to play baseball. They have older kids to point to, Brandon Phillips, Jason Heyward, players they can look to and set their sights on."

Brandon Phillips' high school coach, Greg Goodwin, plays no small role in the region's revival. Redan High School has made itself quite a presence on the Black baseball scene.

"Somehow I've been able to build something in here and maintain the program," said a proud Goodwin. "The kids have bought into it. They understand the tradition of our baseball team. They respect the players who came before them. They respect the game. They know it's a game of failure and they accept it. It's a way of life at Redan High School.

"I haven't coached for 14 years but I'm still involved. The kids support one another. The alumni supports the program. It's been a blessing. It didn't just happen, we had to do a lot to build it and maintain it."

The area demographics have shifted since major league All-Star Wally Joyner graduated from Redan High in 1980, but strong baseball has been a constant. "I started coaching in 1988 and the school was 90% White. Now it's 98% Black. It didn't matter what color we were, we won when we were all White and we won when we became all Black."

Redan made Georgia sports history in the spring of 2013 by defeating perennial powerhouse Marist Academy for the state championship under Coach Marvin Pruitt. This made Redan the first all-Black baseball team to win the state championship since integration.

The school has three alums in the big leagues today: Phillies outfielder Domonic Brown, Reds second baseman Brandon Phillips, and Rockies infielder Chris Nelson. No other American high school has more than one current Black big leaguer (since the Upton brothers graduated from different schools). Both Brown and Phillips have become All-Stars to boot.

Redan's the best, but not the only Georgia school to come up big with Black ballplayers.

Over the nine drafts between 2000 and 2008, Georgia produced three Black players who were true 1st-rounders; they were a distant second to Florida (6), and tied with three other states. (See Appendix K)

In the five most recent drafts between 2009 and 2013, among 161 true 1st-round picks, there were 21 Black players (13%) selected. Five of them grew up in Georgia while four were raised in California, three in Florida and two in Texas. Georgia was #1.

Georgia area scouts will tell you this is no fluke; in fact, the state could have had even more Black 1st-rounders the last five years. Major league teams are hesitant to draft players in the first round they are unsure of signing; a handful of Black Georgians fell into that category. For example, the Boston Red Sox selected Parkview High School outfielder Brandon Jacobs in the 10th round in 2009 but spent 1st-round money to buy him out of a football scholarship to Auburn.

One can expect the number of Black major leaguers from Georgia to escalate in the coming years. I, for one, won't be shocked if they catch California.

So what happened? What are they doing right in Georgia?

Goodwin was one of the spearheads. Redan's former head baseball coach (1988-1999) has since become the school's principal as well as a part-time scout for the Los Angeles Dodgers. Not only did he take charge of baseball on the local scene, but he co-founded Mentoring Viable Prospects (MVP); an organization that runs a tournament every July to expose talented minority players from Georgia and five other states.

"Understand that baseball is prohibitive for a lot of inner city people. We know that Major League Baseball is trying with the RBI program, but we don't think MLB is doing enough. So we did this and we've been very successful.

"We can sit down and think they are not doing that and not doing this, but until you go out and do something you're not part of the solution."

Can the rest of the country do what Goodwin has done?

"We are willing to be duplicated!"

Goodwin attributes much of Redan's success to their ability to keep Black kids playing baseball between the ages of 12 and 14.

"The parks were always full with African-American kids playing little league baseball. When they get to be teenagers, that's when they go to football and basketball. Parents here, they keep them in baseball, but in the majority of towns they go on to play football and basketball."

Goodwin believes the stature of Redan baseball and the visibility of Domonic Brown and Brandon Phillips motivates kids and parents to stick with the sport through their early teens. He also credits James Phillips, Brandon's father. In 2007, James built the Phillips Baseball Center which Goodwin feels has been a boon in promoting the sport within the 12-14 year-old demographic.

Also effusive in praise for James Phillips is Los Angeles Angels scout Chris McAlpin, who drafted and signed youngest son P.J. as a 2nd-round pick in 2005.

"Apparently James is the luckiest man alive with those kids or he's doing something right; Brandon, two kids in the minors, and then (daughter) Porsha who is a big-time basketball player in the WNBA. He and his wife did a tremendous job with those kids. And James runs a great hitting facility."

The success of the academy is not just a matter of 'build it and they will come'.

"Those kids who come over there, from 8 to 18, as soon as they walk in that door they work. He's up on them, by the book, and it's a sweat box. They get after it. If they want to have an attitude, they leave. If they don't work, they don't stay."

McAlpin sighs and then adds, "James Phillips and Greg Goodwin have touched a lot of lives."

It's not about Friday night lights in the summer

What's great about the Black revival in Georgia is that it's coming from all over the state. While most of their present big leaguers hail from suburban Atlanta, there are many more coming from the sticks. Byron Buxton is the marquee talent among a contingent of rural Blacks. The Twins phenom was the second overall pick of the 2012 Draft; he hails from Baxley, a southeastern Georgia town with a population of 4,400.

So what's in the water in Georgia?

Local observers agree that summer baseball programs have only hastened the development of Black players. Travel ball has grown considerably in Georgia. East Cobb Baseball (based in Marietta) is the largest and perhaps most successful such program in the nation with more than 80 teams spread between the ages of 8 and 18. Their facilities and their instruction are topnotch. Over the years, East Cobb Baseball has accumulated a mountain of trophies and championship banners.

Through the leadership of Guerry Baldwin, East Cobb has both recruited and developed countless African-American athletes including present major leaguers Dexter Fowler, Jason Heyward, Chris Nelson, and Marlon Byrd. This is in addition to Caucasian All-Stars such as Braves catcher Brian McCann, Giants catcher Buster Posey, and Orioles outfielder Nick Markakis, all of whom played their youth ball for East Cobb.

The Atlanta Blue Jays have burst on the scene as one of the few travel programs run by an African-American. Anthony Dye had coached for East Cobb prior to starting the Blue Jays in 2003 and his website lists 35 draft picks who have since come through the program.

The Blue Jays are not nearly as extensive as East Cobb, they feature just three teams: a 15-under, 16-under, and 17/18 year-old squad. Dye has developed a number of promising African-American players most notably shortstop Tim Beckham, the first overall pick by Tampa Bay in the 2008 draft.

"I think they're just great athletes," said Coach Dye, "and with Tim Beckham getting drafted, and Jay Austin, Xavier Avery, and Delino DeShields who've gone high in the draft recently, more people are trying to play baseball or focusing more on baseball instead of trying to play basketball and football.

"A lot of African-American kids play baseball in the Atlanta area. When you get into high school now, a lot of kids are becoming one-sport athletes instead of two or three-sport athletes. Because now the parents say, well okay, my kid can get drafted out of high school if he's pretty good at doing this. And it's not about Friday night lights. It's not about being in the gym all the time."

Summer baseball has certainly exploded in Georgia. There are other powerful programs throughout the state that are must-see for scouts including Team Elite, Team Georgia, and the Homeplate Chili Dogs.

"East Cobb is very good and you have to say the Atlanta Blue Jays are getting to that category," says McAlpin. "They just do a good job going out and getting those athletes. What's good for us is that these kids are getting to play for so long and develop.

"I know when we took Chevez Clarke (Angels' 1st-round pick in 2010), Chevy played at the highest level you could possibly play at as an amateur. He was at Under Armour (showcase) to East Cobb to East Coast Showcase and he probably averaged playing 200 games a year. You kind of get a feel for how the body is going to hold up for a pro schedule.

"I definitely think those programs helped in turning a lot of those kids towards baseball."

Life of Byron

In Chapter 5, I identified desire, access, and opportunity as components of a three-part filter separating African-Americans from baseball. In that light, it's easy to see how baseball has become more inclusive in Georgia.

In terms of desire, there is simply much more passion for baseball among Blacks in the Peach State than there is in any other. Manny Upton says his sons B.J. and Justin were pleasantly surprised when they joined the Atlanta Braves prior to the 2013 season.

"The Atlanta Braves have gone out of their way to attract Black fans. Lots of Black fans in the stands there, the club told us there were 10,000 on opening day!"

Such a figure would mean that more than 20% of the fans in attendance were African-American, a percentage that may very well be a high for a major league baseball game.

Though there are no official statistics as such, it is clear as day to anyone who turns on a game that the Atlanta Braves have more Black fans in their stands than any other team.

That wasn't always the case in Atlanta. I went to many a Braves games at old Fulton County Stadium between 1989 and 1993 as an undergraduate at Emory University. Even after the Braves' remarkable worst-to-first 1991 season that preceded 16 consecutive division titles, it was a running joke how lily-white the stands were.

I remember a young and vociferous Black man sitting next to me behind home plate in the famous "when Sid slid" game to clinch the 1992 National League Championship Series against Pittsburgh. It dawned on me that he and his friend were the only African-American fans in the vicinity.

My educated guess would put the Braves' Black fan percentage over 10% today with the rest of the league less than half of that. (Simmons Market Research claimed a league-wide rate of 7.5% in 1999, but it's visibly less in 2013.)

The popularity of the Braves helps Black youth baseball, but don't forget the ever-important father factor. We've well established the importance of a strong father figure for a young baseball player. Do the Black baseball prospects in Georgia have that advantage?

"With most of them, that would be the case," says Chris McAlpin. "Even when there is not a father directly there, there's basically somebody with them who has been a major father figure."

Byron Buxton has yet to play a day of big league baseball, but he may be the most exciting prospect ever to come out of Georgia. The hyper-talented 6'2", 190-pound outfielder from Baxley could have played any sport he wanted and he excelled in football, basketball, and baseball while at Appling County High School. But baseball was his favorite and that's what he chose, signing with the Minnesota Twins as the second overall pick of the 2012 Draft.

Buxton is exactly the type of athlete baseball has been losing to other sports. Did he, perhaps, have paternal influence that helped steer him to baseball?

"Yeah, he had a strong father," responded McAlpin. "No question. His father played a big part in his life."

I then asked McAlpin about other Black players he'd signed and scouted.

"Chevez Clarke, his father Ken was at every game. He was a businessman himself. He was very supportive. Going back to Calvin Johnson (prep baseball star who now plays for the NFL Detroit Lions), his dad's right there in the picture. Jay Austin (Astros' 2nd-round pick in 2008), his father is right there in the picture."

Anthony Dye felt like he stepped in for a lot of his Atlanta Blue Jay players who didn't have involved fathers. But he noted some of the dads started showing up later. "When a kid looks like he's going to get a million dollars, he gets all the family support in the world!"

Down in south Georgia, Larry Greene was a 2011 1st-round sandwich pick of the Philadelphia Phillies, taken out of Berrien High School in tiny Nashville.

"My father was a big part of me, he's the reason I'm here, why I got so good," said Greene. "I've played baseball since I was like three.

"I was actually smaller than everybody," says the rock-solid leftfielder who now stands 6'0" and weighs 240 lbs. "I didn't get big until 9th grade. I wasn't very good in little league. I worked my butt off when I was little and I got better and better. My dad worked with me a lot!"

Greene says he was recruited as a linebacker by several SEC schools prior to a season-ending injury his junior year. He decided he loved baseball more and chose to focus on it from that point.

Then there's Delino DeShields Jr., the Astros' 1st-round pick in 2010. And Dwight Smith, the Blue Jays' 1st-round sandwich pick in 2011. Their namesake fathers are ex-big leaguers who were much involved in their boys' careers.

Such a pattern is easy to explain. It's no different than it is with Caucasian and Latino families; baseball is a father-son sport and the closer the dad, the better chance for the son.

Given these results, one might expect their single parent household rate to be considerably less than the national average. But according to the Kids Count project of the Annie E. Casey Foundation, it is only slightly lower: 65% of Georgia's Black children are from single parent households compared to the national rate of 67%. Yet, as we see, most every Black baseball player has dad in the house or at least in the picture.

Inner city Atlanta has improved somewhat in the last ten years. It's better than most inner cities, but nowhere near as productive as the rest of the state. Martin Luther King High School had an outfielder named Trey Griffin drafted in 2010 but there's been little else over the last five years. The difference with the inner city, when compared to suburbs and the country, is surely related to its much higher rates of poverty and single mother households.

It's encouraging that Black-populated areas like Stone Mountain, Griffin, and Tyrone are putting out baseball players without the safety cushion of money. They are proving that desire and a father's dedication can take them a long way in baseball.

"Tim Beckham wasn't in the inner city but it was bad where he lived," says Coach Dye. "Xavier Avery wasn't from the inner city but it was a bad neighborhood. Jay Austin wasn't inner city, but it was a not-so-good neighborhood, either. They were all able to come out of it through baseball."

"If you listen to me and let me coach you, I'll get you a million dollars."

Tim Beckham was truly a breakthrough for the sport. It's not every day that an exceptional Black athlete from a prestigious football school ends up choosing baseball.

Griffin High School has been a football powerhouse for decades. According to an ESPN.com story by Paula Lavigne (*Top Football Talent Shifts to the South*, 2/1/12), Griffin has produced 15 NFL players since 1970; a list that includes former Chicago Bears wide receiver Willie Gault and ex-Falcons linebacker Jesse Tuggle. Dallas Cowboys Hall of Famer Rayfield Wright was also a Griffin grad, in 1963.

At the same time, Griffin baseball was hardly on the map. They had a player drafted in 1968 and another in 2000, but the years in between were barren. Baseball scouts didn't have much reason to visit Griffin until Tim Beckham showed up.

Beckham attracted hordes of scouts before becoming the first overall pick in the 2008 draft. The following year, his former teammate Telvin Nash was taken in the 3rd round by Houston and signed as an outfielder.

Nash was a powerfully built and surprisingly nimble 6'1", 230-pound defensive end who could have definitely played high Division I college football. His father Ray has been on the Griffin football coaching staff for years. But dad was also involved and supportive of Nash's baseball career and that's the direction he chose.

Baseball has gotten off the bench and finally busted into this town of talented Black athletes.

The crazy thing is, Beckham was just inches away from being just another great Black athlete who slipped through the cracks.

Beckham played little league but had long given up baseball by junior high. Blessed with quickness and exceptional hands, he was sure to become a Division I hoops player despite his lack of height.

But older brother Jeremy was a baseball player who would go on to play for Georgia Southern. While playing travel ball for the Atlanta Blue Jays, Jeremy told Coach Dye about little brother Tim.

Dye drove over to watch Tim play an AAU basketball tournament in Suwanee and was stunned by his athleticism at age 13. He had no doubt that it would play extremely well on a baseball field.

"I said, 'if you listen to me and let me coach you, I'll get you a million dollars'. He said, 'a million dollars?' I said 'when you turn 18, if you let me coach you and you answer to me and do everything I tell you and do pushups and sit-ups, I can get you a million dollars. I know I can get you drafted because I believe in my coaching ability.'"

Beckham got drafted all right. As the first overall pick in 2008, Beckham didn't just get a million dollars, he got $6.15 million. The 6'0", 190-pound shortstop reached the majors in 2013 and he remains a prospect for the Tampa Bay Rays.

Where have you gone, Willie Mays? Hank Aaron? Satchel Paige?

Georgia has the advantages of a good baseball climate and abundant parks.

Georgia also has an inordinately high African-American population. They rank 4th in the U.S., trailing only New York, Texas, and Florida, and not by much. Per capita, only Mississippi (37.6%) and Louisiana (31.8%) are more densely populated with Blacks than Georgia (31.5%).

While the Black population is largely urban in the Midwest, Northeast, and West Coast, a high number of Georgia's African-Americans reside in the country where they comparatively have more income and a stronger family unit than in the inner city.

Despite these advantages, there's no reason Georgia can't be duplicated or at least paralleled by other states, especially by those in the Deep South.

The other Deep South states have slightly improved in recent years; it hasn't become evident at the big league level, but in traveling the southeast I've witnessed some impressive Black talent coming out of Mississippi and the Carolinas. Louisiana and the panhandle of Florida have also had some talented Black prospects. (Mainland Florida is "deep south" in geography but no longer Deep South in culture!)

The state that's slumped for decades is Alabama, which had seven Black big leaguers in 1981 and only two in 2013.

This is despite having two major cities with tremendous baseball heritage.

Birmingham produced Willie Mays and was home to the Negro league Birmingham Black Barons. Mobile's native sons include four Hall of Famers: Hank Aaron, Billy Williams, Willie McCovey, and Satchel Paige.

But it was tough luck getting a Black Alabama kid to play baseball in the 1990s and 2000s. The only two 2013 big leaguers are both Tampa Bay Rays: middle reliever Wesley Wright and outfielder Desmond Jennings. Desmond Jennings was serendipitous; he fully intended to play football for Nick Saban at the University of Alabama, but fate and poor grades got in his way.

Mobile and Birmingham are now in the football business. Mobile produced 4 Black NFL players in 2011 while Birmingham contributed 9 (see Appendix E). But Alabama football might be even stronger in the sticks. The state as a whole produced 46 NFL players that year, at least 35 of whom are African-American.

In addition to their 35+ NFL contributions, Alabama contributed 8 Black athletes to the 2011-2012 NBA.

Let that sink in: 35+ Black NFL players, 8 Black NBA players, and two Black men playing major league baseball.

The state did have two Blacks selected in the 1st round of the 2013 MLB Draft; college draftees Phillip Ervin and Tim Anderson both grew up in Alabama. Shades of Tim Beckham, Anderson actually quit baseball for basketball as a child only to pick it up again as a high school junior.

Baseball can only hope there is more behind them. Alabama has Georgia-like potential. The bordering states have the same latitudes and climate and a similar culture. Alabama's population is 26.8% Black, ranking it sixth per capita among 50 states, with an overall population about half of Georgia's.

Both states are crazy about their college football, but the state of Alabama has become an asylum as such. They've won the last four NCAA National Championships between Auburn (2010) and Alabama (2009, 2011, 2012).

Nevertheless, baseball and football can coexist because the Deep South is blessed with plenty of Black athletes to share.

No need for a knockout

What's scary about the Georgia revival is that they might just be scratching the surface. Baseball has reclaimed a load of Black kids from the Peach State, but there are still so many more.

Larry Greene played baseball, football, and basketball growing up in south Georgia before signing with the Phillies in 2010.

"It was me and one other kid, only two of us Black kids on the baseball team. Football team was half Black. There was a lot more Black players in football growing up than baseball."

Two Black kids on Larry's baseball team, 15-20 on his football, and this is supposed to be a Black baseball hotbed?

Football is still taking their pick of the litter in Georgia.

"Especially where I'm from in south Georgia," agrees Chris McAlpin. "And even at Lassiter and Parkview and all the schools up in the Atlanta area. Football is king."

Baseball gets a few of the do-everything athletes like Jason Heyward and Byron Buxton, but hardly the lion's share.

And while more Black kids than ever are playing baseball in Georgia, it's still nowhere near the number and athletic quality of those who are playing football.

Paula Lavigne's ESPN.com article provides convincing evidence that the Deep South is the greatest football region in America. Football expert Tom Lemming believes the South took over in the 1970s, coinciding with advances in civil rights and the abandonment of spring football in other regions.

Lemming goes as far as to say, "... Then you got a lot more, better athletes who are playing down there and not really concentrating on baseball and basketball, but football."

It puts things into perspective. Baseball made these great gains in Georgia and it hardly put a dent into football. It proves that football is a stronghold but it also proves that it doesn't matter because there are so many Black athletes to choose from.

Baseball is not even close to having the whole peach pie to themselves, but they're plenty pleased with what they've gained. Major league baseball will take their Dexter Fowlers and Jason Heywards and Brandon Phillips along with the Byron Buxtons who are on the way. It shows that by just winning over a portion of the Black population, you can change the face of the league.

Baseball doesn't have to score a knockout in Georgia or anywhere else. Cam Newton can still play football and Dwight Howard can go shoot hoops and baseball will still gain a treasure trove as long as they provide access and opportunity to the rest.

Chapter 10: Glass Walls, Broken Hearts, and Final Thoughts

It's not a glass ceiling so much as a glass wall.

When I peer through the wall, I see more beautiful athletes than I can count. They look like Josh Gibson and Bob Gibson and Hank Aaron but they wear different uniforms and play on different fields. The coach in me wants to bust through the wall to hit them fungos and throw batting practice.

But we can't touch them. They are not their grandfathers or great grandfathers. Josh Gibson and Oscar Charleston? What we'd do to have them now.

Some of them grow up to play in the NFL or NBA, but many more do not. How many of those blessed athletes could have reached fame and fortune and enriched their own lives had someone handed them a baseball as kids?

Sometimes we get tantalized on this side of the wall. Matt Kemp, they call him "Bison". He excites us by charging after fly balls in Dodger Stadium, with his tremendous power, and the way he wins games all by himself. Andrew McCutchen hits laser shots and flies around the bags hardly touching ground with his cleats. He's brought nothing but energy to the Pirate faithful at PNC Park.

And then we see the Black Cubans who've come to our side. There's Yasiel Puig playing next to Matt Kemp, running and throwing and hitting like he's a bigger and stronger Roberto Clemente. And we see a muscular 5'9" Yoenis Cespedes of the Oakland A's. He wins the Home Run Derby; generating incredible bat-speed and hitting them farther over the fence than even the big guys. We turn on a Cincinnati Reds game and watch lefty Aroldis Chapman uncoil his long, sinewy arms and legs and whip the most frightening fastballs and sliders we've ever seen.

Great athletes are exhilarating to watch. They change the game and you can't take your eyes off them.

Yet my eyes do wander, through the glass wall, and I become nauseous, thinking of the ones we don't have for there are so many more McCutchens and Puigs on the other side. I desperately extend an olive branch but the glass bends it back.

Come. Bless our game.

Only Major League Baseball can break that glass. Major League Baseball can take a ramrod and obliterate the glass wall into 39 million pieces. It's up to the men and women on Park Avenue to decide on where to take their sport. They can invigorate or they can choose to let die.

After all my research and years in the game, it is no longer a mystery why there are so few Black kids playing baseball. It is no longer a mystery why the NFL and NBA are rewarded while our sport has blacked itself out. I think of what must have gone through Josh Gibson's mind before his heart broke forever on that cold winter day in 1947. That's when it becomes perfectly clear how our game went from a source of African-American pride to almost complete irrelevance.

They've been riding this road for decades.

We can't go back in time and get LeBron James and Robert Griffin III to play baseball.

Nor do we want to.

Baseball may never claim the lion's share of Black athletes like we did in the first half of the 20th century. We don't need the lion's share, we just need to get more.

Accusations and regret become futile at this point; it is time for action. Whatever is broken between baseball and Black America must be fixed.

There is no doubt to me that this is attainable. There's no doubt in my mind that baseball will be better for it in every way. Society, especially African-American society, will collectively reap the rewards. On a business end, the added excitement that rides from better athletes will translate into dollars.

The long-term health of baseball depends on many things, many of which MLB is powerless to change.

But Major League Baseball can change this. More importantly, they are the only entity that can. I call on them to serve not only their sport but their nation. I am certain that our "surefire plan" is exactly that; it will work and it will work big.

Now who's going to help me carry out this ramrod?

Extra Innings: Baseball's Ultimate Fantasy Team-Ten Black Athletes Who Could Have Been Hall of Fame Baseball Players

Do you ever wonder how different major league baseball would look if it were the only game in town?

For the early 20th century, that was the case. It was unfortunate baseball was so racist because God only knows how loaded the league would have been.

Can you imagine Josh Gibson and Biz Mackey competing with Mickey Cochrane and Bill Dickey for a berth as the All-Star catcher? How about Black outfielders Oscar Charleston and Cool Papa Bell playing with or against Joe DiMaggio and Ted Williams? How much would fans pay to watch Satchel Paige, in his prime, go up against Bob Feller?

"Every Black athlete played baseball back then," says longtime scout and baseball executive Muzzy Jackson. "Buck O'Neil was my mentor when I worked with the Kansas City Royals and he said it all the time. Imagine an age where Shaquille O'Neal is playing baseball. You've got Magic Johnson on the mound. Barry Sanders in center field. That's what it was like then. That was Negro league baseball!"

Football and basketball were around but with hardly the stature they hold today. The best athletes played baseball first, the other sports were fallbacks. Football legends like Jim Thorpe and George Halas were baseball players before. Even the iconic George Gipp was attending Notre Dame for baseball and The Gipper would have played it professionally if not for his untimely death. Blacks were every bit as skewed to baseball and then some.

What if that were still the case and there were no other options? Can you picture Lawrence Taylor and Clyde Drexler as baseball players in the 1980s? What if Randy Moss and Allen Iverson chose the diamond in the 1990s? Michael Vick and Chris Paul in the 2000s? Not every one of these exceptional Black athletes would have transferred their gifts to baseball, but surely some would. How exciting would major league baseball be?

If nothing else, the sport would have gained considerable speed. There's no question that the NFL and NBA have taken the fastest runners. Just about every NBA guard and NFL skill player would grade out as an above-average major league runner. Many would be considered burners and base-stealers.

But speed is not just about running the basepaths. As Branch Rickey famously declared, foot-speed is the common denominator of both offense and defense in baseball. Quick feet help an infielder range for a ball on the ground and an outfielder gallop after one in the air. With the loss of speed and athleticism, most scouts agree that today's baseball players have less defensive range than they did 30 years ago. It doesn't show up statistically, but anyone who watched Frank White and Lou Whitaker knows that today's second sackers (outside of Brandon Phillips) have nowhere their quickness; this applies all over the field.

But Black athletes would bring a lot more than speed. The other tools could only be enhanced by their increased presence in the game. There are plenty of African-American athletes with strong throwing arms; the NFL has a number of well-gunned Black quarterbacks including Robert Griffin III and Cam Newton. A couple of former baseball draft picks, Colin Kaepernick and Russell Wilson, have good arm-strength themselves. There are other athletes with great arms, but nobody notices because they play positions where throwing is not involved.

Power? You don't think some of those big NFL and NBA guys could crush a baseball? I've heard the story of Lawrence Taylor, the iconic New York Giants linebacker of the 1980s, taking batting practice with the University of North Carolina baseball squad when he was in college. Though he hadn't played baseball in years, L.T. destroyed the ball with brute strength until blisters sent him home. Current Detroit Lions franchise wide receiver Calvin Johnson has put many out of Comerica Park before Tiger games.

I remember a Detroit Tigers scout named Rob Guzik tell me in the 1990s how well the ball jumped off of Randy Moss's bat when he played baseball for DuPont High School in West Virginia. Combined with his tremendous speed and athleticism, Guzik raved, "He could have been the greatest to ever play the game!" comparing his all-around skills to those of a righthanded Ken Griffey Jr. Unfortunately, Moss's last baseball season was cut short by an arrest and he proceeded to focus on football and basketball from that point. (He wound up winning West Virginia's Mr. Basketball award two years in a row ahead of DuPont teammate and future NBA star Jason Williams.)

Logan White was dying to draft and sign another future NFL star while working as a scout for the San Diego Padres in the mid-1990s. Lawyer Milloy played both sports for the University of Washington before becoming a 4-time All-Pro safety.

"I wrote him up huge as a baseball player, but he was going to be a #1 pick in football. I have no doubt in my mind that Lawyer Milloy would have been an All-Star in baseball. Because he could fly and he had all the skills. He could throw, play defense, and hit for power."

I'm a huge sports fan, but I'll always be a baseball man first; I see the other sports through the lens of a baseball scout. I often envy athletes of other sports because I wonder what they could have been had they played baseball. In some cases (see the Donte Robertson story in Chapter 4) I have even acted on it.

It is perhaps pointless and impractical, but still fun to create such an imaginary world. What if everybody played baseball? What if there was complete access, desire, and opportunity for all the great athletes in America? As a baseball fan, would there be anything more fun to watch?

For this exercise, I'm choosing Black athletes from the NFL, NHL, and NBA. I'm basing this on my scouting experience with insight from others around baseball. As you'll see, most of these gifted athletes didn't play the game at all.

Nevertheless, here is Anup Sinha's fantasy league baseball team. I believe these athletes had the physical tools to become not just major league players, but Hall of Famers.

Top-10 Black Athletes with Hall of Fame Baseball Tools

1. Calvin Johnson, Wide Receiver, Detroit Lions (NFL)

Baseball Experience: played through high school   Projected MLB Position: CF/RF

"To this day, 14 years of scouting, Calvin Johnson is the greatest athlete I've ever seen," said longtime Los Angeles Angels scout Chris McAlpin. "He looked like a young Dave Winfield. He was just a freak athlete, but with him he actually had baseball skills."

Known affectionately as "Megatron", Johnson is a game-breaking 6'5", 235-pound wide receiver with tremendous speed, soft hands, excellent strength, and the vertical leap of a dunk champ. His size and vertical is so impressive that in a *Sports Illustrated* poll, NBA players picked Megatron as the pro athlete most capable of joining their league (May 21st, 2013). The 121 participants voted him #1 and by a mile.

Funny thing is, Johnson didn't play basketball for Sandy Creek High School. His second sport was actually baseball and scouts like Chris McAlpin, Chip Lawrence, and Jim Thrift wished it was his first.

Johnson loved baseball and he's revealed to Detroit reporters that he would have pursued it if not for football. Johnson was also an outstanding student (surprised?) and had decided with his parents that he would play only one sport in college to best maintain his studies. MLB scouts made inquiries out of high school, but no one was quite willing to pay the prodigious bonus request to sign him out of Georgia Tech.

There's no question Johnson's speed would have made an impact in baseball. Despite his size, he could have been the very fastest player in the league. Think of a big-time basestealer (50+) with excellent range in the outfield.

Size doesn't always convert to power, but Johnson hit them far as a 215-pounder in high school and he still puts them out when he takes batting practice with the Detroit Tigers. His righthanded swing is a bit stiffer from football training, but as a scout it's easy to see how he could have developed a fluid stroke had he worked on it out of high school.

Johnson's throwing arm? "He had a 70 arm," said Chip Lawrence, referring to the 20-80 scouting scale where 50 is average and 70's well above. For some perspective, of the 90 starting outfielders in the big leagues, it's likely that only 15-20 have throwing arms that would grade out 70 or higher.

Megatron's intangibles are topnotch as well. He's a great competitor who is very intelligent and a ridiculously hard worker.

One could only dream of the kind of baseball player Johnson would have been. Would he have been even better than local rival Domonic Brown, as Chip Lawrence suggested? Could he have been Dave Winfield the way Chris McAlpin envisioned? Matt Kemp at his best? The Black Mike Trout?

Calvin Johnson is simply a special athlete, a transcendent one at that. It's a pleasure to watch him perform; as a long-suffering Detroit Lions fan, I'm a direct beneficiary of his career decision. Still, I can't help but dream what could have been had he chosen to play my favorite sport instead.

2. Chris Paul, Point Guard, Los Angeles Clippers (NBA)

Baseball Experience: none noted Projected MLB Position: SS/2B

"Chris Paul, you know him?" asked longtime major league scout Phil Pote. "Basketball player? I'll tell you, if I would have seen him at age 17 and I was a scout, I wouldn't have had to have seen him play baseball. I'd sign him right there on athleticism! That speed and body control, wow!"

The chiseled 6'0", 190-pound Paul is likened to a mix of Isiah Thomas and John Stockton on the basketball court. He led the New Orleans Hornets from the point for six seasons before joining the up-and-coming Los Angeles Clippers in 2011. His outstanding all-around basketball game employs athletic skills that would have made him quite a baseball player. An excellent dribbler and ball handler, Paul has the quick, soft hands that could have worked well as an infielder. He has the strong forearms of a good hitter and the blazing speed to steal bases.

Among baseball players, Paul would grade out as a well above-average runner, at least a 70 on the 20-80 scale. The quick feet and exceptional body control could have made him a gold glove second or third baseman; Paul could surely learn the difficult off-balance plays that made highlight reel heroes out of Roberto Alomar and Frank White.

Think of Frank White, Bobby Grich, or perhaps a Ryne Sandberg-type. Then add a large dose of leadership; Chris Paul makes his teammates better and he's the primary reason the Clippers have a chance to win the NBA Finals in the near future.

Despite possessing such impressive tools, there's no mention of ever playing baseball in any of Paul's biographies. His late maternal grandfather was greatly influential to his basketball career and his father coached him in both basketball and football growing up in rural North Carolina.

3. Cam Newton, Quarterback, Carolina Panthers (NFL)

Baseball Experience: played till age 14 Projected MLB Position: RF/RHP

"I quit baseball at 14 because I was afraid of the pitches," Cam Newton told *ESPN The Magazine* writer Carmen Thompson for the website's *My Path to the Pros* series (June 26th, 2013).

"The kids started getting better and throwing faster, and it would've hurt getting hit by that ball, so I stopped playing."

Later in the interview, Newton tried to address what had to be on everybody's mind.

"My mom always wondered how I could be afraid of a little baseball when I always had these huge guys chasing me. It's a good question."

The 6'5", 230-pound NFL quarterback is built almost as well as Florida Marlins' slugging rightfielder Giancarlo Stanton and I can't help but compare their physical tools. Stanton himself was a tremendous high school football player (Notre Dame HS in Sherman Oaks, California) who nearly went to the University of Southern California to play tight end.

Newton may run a little better than Stanton. Judging from how well he throws a football, Newton would likely have a good rightfielder's arm. If Newton's bat didn't develop, he would probably have a chance as a pitcher.

Newton even has the sloped shoulders which, as a scout, I loved to see in hitters. Don Mattingly and Carlos Baerga are exaggerated examples. It is my belief that it makes their hands looser, their swings shorter to the ball, and it improves their extension after contact.

Strength? Come on! Leadership ability? You can't be a national championship quarterback without it.

After a tremendous rookie season, Newton struggled as a second-year NFL player. He has a bright future but despite his Heisman Trophy and NCAA championship at Auburn, I can't help but wonder if he'd have been even better in baseball.

4. P.K. Subban, Defenseman, Montreal Canadiens (NHL)

Baseball Experience: none noted Projected MLB Position: 3B/C

The first hockey player on the list, Subban is a tremendously aggressive defenseman for the NHL's most storied franchise. He hits one of the hardest slap shots you'll ever see.

His actions on the rink are more powerful than graceful. The 6'0", 210-pound Subban has plenty of fast twitches and much strength throughout his body. His iron hands and forearms would make him a heavy righthanded hitter. I would love to see Subban take batting practice, I bet the ball would absolutely jump off his bat.

He shows considerable athleticism on skates. I pick third base for his body-type and his ability to finish hockey plays off-balance. If he can throw, I'd try him behind the plate. Subban's criticized often by opponents for his over-aggressive play but there's no questioning his desire.

Subban was born in Toronto and grew up in Ontario. I find no record of him playing baseball or any other sport. Many young athletes from that region learn to skate as soon as they walk and proceed to play hockey all year-round.

5. Robert Griffin III, Quarterback, Washington Redskins (NFL)

Baseball Experience: none noted Projected MLB Position: CF

"I only had a little exposure to him, but as far as I know, he never played baseball," says Mitch Thompson, who was an assistant baseball coach at Baylor University for 18 years.

That's baseball's loss. There may not be a more electrifying athlete in sports today. The NFL has seen its share of athletic quarterbacks but Griffin takes it to another level. A world class hurdler, Griffin can still make touch passes and throw the long ball.

RG3 falls into that exclusive group of athlete who could excel at any sport he wanted. It doesn't take a genius to see how he could have been special in baseball, too. The 6'2", 220-pounder would be the fastest player in MLB and I'd like his chances to hit, given all the upper-body twitches and coordination. The football arm should translate to a plus baseball arm. He would be fun to watch, that's for sure. Maybe a faster Andre Dawson?

Griffin wasn't a big recruit out of high school but he sure blossomed at Baylor, reviving their football program almost single-handedly. Prior to that, Griffin ran track and played basketball for nearby Copperas Cove High School.

6. Brandon Marshall, Wide Receiver, Denver Broncos (NFL)

Baseball Experience: none noted Projected MLB Position: RF/3B

This is the kind of "kid" baseball should never whiff on. Brandon Marshall is 6'4", 230 lbs., with a great baseball body, plus speed, great aggressiveness, and a good throwing arm. He also grew up in a baseball hotbed, outside of Orlando, Florida.

Yet he played and excelled in every sport but baseball for Lake Howell High School: football, basketball, and track. When the NFL imposed a lockout before the 2011 season, he set his sights on professional basketball.

I watched Brandon Marshall as a Miami Dolphin and he was a beast. Any coach in any sport would love his toughness and determination. Marshall's strong hands would have helped him become a good hitter and perhaps a sure infielder had he ever played baseball. The size and strength give him big power potential and his upper body is loose enough to develop a smooth swing. Like most NFL wide receivers, Marshall would make a plus runner in baseball though not a burner to the extreme of Calvin Johnson.

Marshall has only attempted one pass in his NFL career, but I happened to watch it live on television. He looked like he'd have a gun in baseball and I can only imagine how strong his throwing arm would get if he actually used it with regularity.

7. Dwyane Wade, Guard, Miami Heat (NBA)

Baseball Experience: little league Projected MLB Position: 3B/CF

There's a whole lot to like about the future NBA Hall of Famer. Dwyane Wade is a chiseled 6'3", 220-pound guard with explosive athleticism. I'm sure he could have played in the NFL and had he grown up playing baseball, I have no doubt he would have been outstanding.

Wade is blessed with quick hands and quick feet. He'd surely be a plus fielder on the infield or in the outfield and I'd like his chances to hit. Best of all, Wade is a big money athlete and that transfers across sports. He does his best under pressure. I'll never forget Game 3 of the 2006 NBA Finals against the Dallas Mavericks; one of the greatest singular performances I've ever seen from an athlete. With six minutes left and Miami about to go down three games to none, Wade rallied the Heat from a 13-point deficit by providing 12 by himself.

Wade's father played a lot of baseball, but not Dwyane himself. He dabbled in football at Rickards High School in Chicago, but basketball was always the priority.

8. Shane Larkin, Point Guard, Dallas Mavericks (NBA)

Baseball Experience: little league | Projected MLB Position: SS

"Oh, he could play baseball all right," said Joe Logan, the Orlando Reds youth baseball coach and Larkin family friend. "But basketball took over when he was about ten."

No one on this list has the pedigree of Shane Larkin, who happens to be the son of Hall of Fame shortstop Barry Larkin. And one can see a lot of resemblance both facially and in his athletic actions. But Larkin chose basketball, had an outstanding career at the University of Miami, and will try to make it as an undersized 5'9" point guard for the Dallas Mavericks.

There aren't many little guys in the NBA, but Larkin has the exceptional athleticism and smarts to make it happen. His hands and feet are lightning quick. He would have been an infielder all the way and probably would have developed a quick righthanded bat, too.

Of course, the lack of size that will hurt him in basketball wouldn't be nearly as much an issue in baseball.

9. Charles Tillman, Cornerback, Chicago Bears (NFL)

Baseball Experience: none noted | Projected MLB Position: 3B/2B/OF

Charles "Peanut" Tillman attended the same high school (Copperas Cove HS in Texas) as Robert Griffin III. He's a wiry strong 6'2" cornerback with very quick feet and hands, notorious for his ability to force fumbles.

Tillman also has the sloped shoulders and strong forearms of someone who could really swing a bat.

I find no record of Tillman ever trying the Grand Ol' Game.

10. Wayne Simmonds, Right Wing, Philadelphia Flyers, (NHL)

Baseball Experience: none noted | Projected MLB Position: CF

Simmonds is a rangy 6'2", 200-pound righthanded shooter with athleticism to die for. He starred as a centerfielder at a charity softball game in London, Ontario in 2010, and flashed all the tools to have been something special.

Few can handle the puck like Simmonds, showing the exceptional hand-eye coordination that would serve him well hitting a baseball. His speed-skating would likely translate to speed-running. I have no idea if he can throw, but I'd take a chance on the rest of the package!

Simmonds grew up in Scarborough, Ontario, and was likely tied up with hockey from an early age.

The truth is that these ten are just the tip of the iceberg. There are literally hundreds of other Black athletes who could have been outstanding baseball players. Most NFL quarterbacks would have had at least a fighting chance to play in the majors. And those who play the speed positions in football (i.e. wide receivers, running backs, defensive backs) would have had at least that tool in their favor and possibly much more. Just about every NBA guard would have a chance to become a very good defender somewhere on the diamond with any throwing arm at all.

I picked ten who made me drool (figuratively) as a scout. If any one of them would have tried on a mitt, someone would have paid them a lot of money.

During my scouting career, I was able to watch a number of kids who wound up making a name for themselves in other sports. These three African-Americans didn't make the Top-10 for one reason or another, but they were interesting to scout and I wanted to share my observations. They are listed in alphabetical order:

Shane Battier, Small Forward, Miami Heat (NBA): *Battier went to the same suburban Detroit school as I, but eight years later (graduating in 1997). I got to see him play a lot of basketball. He didn't play baseball as a freshman or sophomore but was a little league phenom and decided to give it a whirl his junior year.*

Battier looked rough coming late off of basketball and he sat the bench. But the first time I got him running home-to-first, he did it from the right side slightly faster than big league average (4.25 seconds). To see a 6'8", 220-pound kid do that was not an everyday occurrence on the Michigan high school baseball scene. As the year went on, Battier ended up becoming Detroit Country Day's starting first baseman and one of their best hitters.

He wasn't a pro baseball prospect, but had he focused on it younger? You never know because his makeup was extraordinary. He was a team player who was very respectful to adults and an outstanding student. If he wants to become an NBA general manager when he's done playing, I'd give Shane Battier a good chance to make it in the front office as well.

Battier's swing was too long to hit against really hard throwers and he would have had to work very hard to become a good defender at first base or the outfield. Still, he was fun to watch. At the time I thought he was a "freak" athlete which is ironic because on the Miami Heat, he's carved a niche as the industrious over-achiever while LeBron James and Dwyane Wade wear the freak label. That really puts the NBA's athleticism into perspective.

Desean Jackson, Wide Receiver, Philadelphia Eagles (NFL): *As far as tools are concerned, Jackson was my kind of player. He was undersized (about 5'9", 155 lbs as a Long Beach Poly HS senior in 2005), but there was line-drive strength in his righthanded swing and incredible speed. He was an 80 runner, top of the scale, with a base-stealer's aggressiveness. Jackson was going to be a pure centerfielder and I envisioned his ultimate upside to be like Rickey Henderson's without the power*

But Jackson's intangibles put me off. He wasn't a good teammate or a hard worker and I just didn't see the requisite attitude to improve his skills. He was benched from a game I was going to for showing up late. I didn't think he had the right day-to-day approach for baseball though he does just fine getting up for one game a week to play football. I'd imagine his attitude has changed much for the better since his teenage days.

Colin Kaepernick, Quarterback, San Francisco 49ers (NFL): *I saw Kaepernick pitch in two different baseball showcases during the summer of 2005. He was a northern California high school kid who stood a very skinny 6'5", 170 lbs. What's funny is that I had no idea what kind of speed he had; he worked out as a pitcher only and nobody thought to run him. Now he's setting NFL rushing records for a quarterback.*

When I saw Kaepernick, he was in between his junior and senior year. He was a "follow" as a pitcher but not at the time a top prospect; too physically undeveloped, but because of his height it was clear he had the potential for much improvement. Kaepernick threw in the mid-to-high-80s at the end of the summer and had a good bite on his curveball. But the arm-action was rough; he couldn't repeat his delivery because he was so weak in his core and lower half, and there wasn't much command of any of his pitches.

The great athleticism you see on the football field today? It wasn't evident in the summer of 2005. I'd imagine if he'd have stuck with baseball, he'd be throwing a lot harder than 88 MPH now. His body has really developed since then and he's become quite physical.

Appendix A: Census of 1975 Major League Baseball Players

Overall African-American Representation of Top-600: 115, 19.2%

African-American Position Players among Top-350 in at-bats: 99, 28.3%

(Listed in decreasing number of at-bats.)

Over 600 AB (7): Dave Cash, Al Oliver, Ralph Garr, George Scott, Mickey Rivers, Willie Horton, Lenny Randle

500-599 AB (23): Reggie Jackson, Claudell Washington, Ken Singleton, Lee May, Jim Rice, Chris Chambliss, George Hendrick, Dave Parker, Roy White, John Mayberry Sr., Ron LeFlore, Derrel Thomas, Rod Carew, Bobby Bonds, Lou Brock, Don Baylor, Billy North, Billy Williams, Willie Davis, Bill Madlock, Dave Winfield, Von Joshua, Bobby Tolan

400-400 AB (23): Joe Morgan, Dusty Baker, Bob Watson, Hal McRae, Reggie Smith, Larvell Blanks, Pat Kelly, Amos Otis, Hank Aaron, George Foster, Ken Griffey Sr., Willie Stargell, Tommy Davis, Carlos May, Paul Blair, Dan Ford, Leroy Stanton, Garry Maddox, Gary Matthews, Dick Allen, Bake McBride, Willie McCovey, Jimmy Wynn,

300-399 AB (20): Wilbur Howard, Earl Williams, Willie Crawford, Andre Thornton, Lyman Bostock, Bobby Darwin, Rowland Office, Tommy Harper, Al Bumbry, Enos Cabell, Oscar Gamble, Charlie Spikes, Cliff Johnson, John Briggs, Ben Oglivie, Al Cowens, Vada Pinson, Lee Lacy, Cecil Cooper, Frank White

200-299 AB (11): Larry Hisle, Nate Colbert, Tony Solaita, Bobby Mitchell, John Milner, Jerry Hairston Sr., Elliott Maddox, Dan Driessen, Gene Clines, Dave May, Bill Robinson

97-199 AB (15): Walt Williams, Jack Pierce, Larry Milbourne, Larry Lintz, Ollie Brown, Rich Coggins, Tony Scott, Cito Gaston, Tim Hosley, Buddy Bradford, Jim Holt, Alex Johnson, Frank Robinson, Tony Taylor, Jerry White

African-American Pitchers Among Top-250 in Innings Pitched: 16, 6.4%

(Listed in decreasing number of innings pitched.)

200+ IP (6): Vida Blue, Fergie Jenkins, Lynn McGlothen, Ray Burris, Rudy May, J.R. Richard

100-199 IP (6): Jim Bibby, Dock Ellis, John Candelaria, Jesse Jefferson, Larry Demery, Bob Gibson

48-99 IP (4): Blue Moon Odom, Al Downing, Tom Hall, Grant Jackson

Appendix B: Census of 1981 Major League Baseball Players

Overall African-American Representation Among Top-700: 134, 19.1%

African-American MLB Position Players Among Top-400 in At-Bats: 116, 29%

ID	At-Bats	First Name	Last Name	Pos	HS City	State	Environment
1	451	Jim	Rice	OF	Anderson	SC	Rural
2	450	Ozzie	Smith	SS	Los Angeles	CA	Inner City
3	439	Willie	Wilson	OF	Summit	NJ	Suburban
4	423	Rickey	Henderson	OF	Oakland	CA	Inner City
5	421	Al	Oliver	1B	Portsmouth	OH	Rural
6	416	Cecil	Cooper	1B	Brenham	TX	Rural
7	414	George	Foster	LF	Los Angeles	CA	Inner City
8	410	Bump	Wills	2B	Spokane	WA	Suburban
9	404	Chris	Chambliss	1B	Oceanside	CA	Suburban
10	401	Tony	Scott	OF	Cincinnati	OH	Inner City
11	400	Dusty	Baker	OF	Sacramento	CA	Suburban
12	400	Ben	Oglivie	OF	New York	NY	Inner City
13	399	Mickey	Rivers	OF	Miami	FL	Inner City
14	397	Ruppert	Jones	OF	Oakland	CA	Suburban
15	396	Enos	Cabell	3B	Los Angeles	CA	Inner City
16	396	Ken	Griffey	OF	Donora	PA	Suburban
17	394	Andre	Dawson	OF	Miami	FL	Inner City
18	394	George	Hendrick	OF	Los Angeles	CA	Inner City
19	393	Gene	Richards	OF	Monticello	SC	Rural
20	392	Al	Bumbry	OF	King George	VA	Rural
21	390	Ken	Landreaux	OF	Los Angeles	CA	Inner City
22	390	Dwayne	Murphy	OF	Lancaster	CA	Suburban
23	389	Hal	McRae	DH	Avon Park	FL	Rural
24	388	Dave	Winfield	OF	Minneapolis	MN	Suburban
25	378	Lloyd	Moseby	OF	Oakland	CA	Inner City
26	378	Eddie	Murray	1B	Los Angeles	CA	Inner City
27	377	Don	Baylor	DH	Austin	TX	Suburb
28	375	Dan	Ford	OF	Los Angeles	CA	Inner City
29	372	Amos	Otis	OF	Mobile	AL	Suburban
30	369	Rod	Carew	1B	New York	NY	Inner City
31	364	Larry	Herndon	OF	Memphis	TN	Inner City
32	364	Frank	White	2B	Kansas City	MO	Inner City
33	363	Ken	Singleton	OF	New York	NY	Suburb
34	359	Gary	Matthews	OF	Los Angeles	CA	Suburb
35	358	Hubie	Brooks	3B	Los Angeles	CA	Inner City
36	358	Warren	Cromartie	OF	Miami	FL	Inner City
37	357	Willie	Randolph	2B	New York	NY	Inner City
38	349	Willie	Aikens	1B	Seneca	SC	Rural

39	339	Mike	Easler	1B	Cleveland	OH	Suburban
40	339	U.L.	Washington	SS	Stringtown	OK	Rural
41	337	Ron	LeFlore	OF	Detroit	MI	Inner City
42	336	Rodney	Scott	2B	Indianapolis	IN	Inner City
43	335	Lou	Whitaker	2B	Martinsville	VA	Rural
44	334	Reggie	Jackson	OF	Philadelphia	PA	Suburb
45	333	Garry	Templeton	SS	Los Angeles	CA	Suburb
46	328	Leon	Durham	1B	Cincinnati	OH	Inner City
47	328	Chet	Lemon	OF	Los Angeles	CA	Inner City
48	328	Mookie	Wilson	OF	Bamberg	SC	Rural
49	323	Gary	Maddox	OF	Los Angeles	CA	Suburb
50	320	Claudell	Washington	OF	Oakland	CA	Suburb
51	319	Jerry	Mumphrey	OF	Tyler	TX	Rural
52	313	Tim	Raines	OF	Orlando	FL	Suburb
53	308	Joe	Morgan	2B	Oakland	CA	Inner City
54	295	Gary	Ward	OF	Los Angeles	CA	Inner City
55	290	John	Mayberry	1B	Detroit	MI	Inner City
56	288	Al	Woods	OF	Oakland	CA	Inner City
57	287	Steve	Henderson	OF	Houston	TX	Inner City
58	280	Harold	Baines	OF	Easton	MD	Rural
59	278	Bill	Madlock	3B	Decatur	Il	Rural
60	273	Cliff	Johnson	1B	San Antonio	TX	Inner City
61	273	Lenny	Randle	2B	Los Angeles	CA	Inner City
62	270	Ron	Jackson	1B	Birmingham	AL	Suburban
63	264	Hosken	Powell	OF	Selma	AL	Rural
64	264	Broderick	Perkins	1B	Pittsburg	CA	Rural
65	253	Al	Cowens	OF	Los Angeles	CA	Inner City
66	245	Ellis	Valentine	OF	Los Angeles	CA	Inner City
67	240	Dave	Parker	OF	Cincinnati	OH	Inner City
68	233	Dan	Driessen	1B	Hardeeville	SC	Rural
69	230	Billy	Sample	OF	Salem	VA	Rural
70	226	Andre	Thornton	1B	Phoenixville	PA	Rural
71	221	Bake	McBride	OF	Fulton	MO	Rural
72	218	Derrel	Thomas	2B	Los Angeles	CA	Inner City
73	213	Lee	Lacy	OF	Oakland	CA	Inner City
74	208	Gary	Gray	1B	New Orleans	LA	Inner City
75	207	Ricky	Peters	OF	Los Angeles	CA	Inner City
76	189	Oscar	Gamble	OF	Montgomery	AL	Suburban
77	176	Lonnie	Smith	OF	Los Angeles	CA	Inner City
78	174	Lynn	Jones	OF	Meadville	PA	Rural
79	163	Bobby	Bonds	OF	Los Angeles	CA	Suburban
80	163	Larry	Milbourne	SS	Port Norris	NJ	Suburban
81	156	Shooty	Babitt	2B	Oakland	CA	Suburban
82	156	Bob	Watson	1B	Los Angeles	CA	Inner City
83	151	Danny	Goodwin	C	Peoria	IL	Suburban
84	145	Jeff	Leonard	OF	Philadelphia	PA	Inner City
85	135	John	Milner	DH	Atlanta	GA	Suburban

86	135	Joe	Pittman	2B	Houston	TX	Inner City
87	134	Lamar	Johnson	1B	Birmingham	AL	Suburban
88	134	Eddie	Miller	OF	Richmond	CA	Suburban
89	131	Billy	North	OF	Seattle	WA	Suburban
90	126	Dave	Henderson	OF	Dos Palos	CA	Rural
91	125	Darryl	Motley	OF	Portland	OR	Suburban
92	119	Tito	Landrum	OF	Joplin	MO	Rural
93	119	Jerry	White	OF	San Francisco	CA	Inner City
94	112	Dave	Edwards	OF	Los Angeles	CA	Inner City
95	111	Willie	Upshaw	1B	Blanco	TX	Rural
96	105	Thad	Bosley	OF	Oceanside	CA	Suburban
97	102	Johnny	Ray	2B	Chouteau	OK	Rural
98	96	Dick	Davis	1B	Los Angeles	CA	Suburban
99	95	Jesse	Barfield	OF	Chicago	IL	Suburban
100	93	Jerry	Royster	3B	Sacramento	CA	Inner City
101	92	Mitchell	Page	DH	Los Angeles	CA	Inner City
102	88	Bill	Robinson	1B	Pittsburgh	PA	Suburban
103	87	Larry	Hisle	DH	Portsmouth	OH	Rural
104	84	Ron	Washington	SS	New Orleans	LA	Inner City
105	75	Pat	Kelly	2B	Philadelphia	PA	Inner City
106	73	Terry	Harper	OF	Atlanta	GA	Suburban
107	73	Greg	Wells	1B	McIntosh	AL	Rural
108	71	Tye	Waller	3B	San Diego	CA	Inner City
109	62	Bobby	Brown	OF	Eastville	VA	Rural
110	68	Willie	Stargell	OF	Oakland	CA	Suburban
111	58	Marshall	Edwards	OF	Los Angeles	CA	Inner City
112	55	Jerry	Manuel	2B	Sacramento	CA	Suburban
113	55	Lee	May	1B	Birmingham	AL	Inner City
114	52	Darryl	Sconiers	1B	Los Angeles	CA	Suburbs
115	47	Gary	Alexander	1B	Los Angeles	CA	Inner City
116	47	Kelvin	Moore	1B	Leroy	AL	Rural

African-American MLB Pitchers Among Top-300 in Innings Pitched: 18, 6%

ID	IP	First Name	Last Name	Hand	HS City	State	Environment
1	172	Mike	Norris	RHP	San Francisco	CA	Inner City
2	147	Rudy	May	LHP	Oakland	CA	Inner City
3	141	Juan	Eichelberger	RHP	San Francisco	CA	Inner City
4	135	Ray	Burris	RHP	Duke	OK	Rural
5	127	Eddie	Solomon	RHP	Perry	GA	Rural
6	124	Vida	Blue	LHP	Mansfield	LA	Rural
7	106	Fergie	Jenkins	RHP	Chatham	ONT	Rural
8	100	Al	Holland	LHP	Roanoke	VA	Suburban
9	93	Jim	Bibby	RHP	Franklinton	NC	Rural
10	76	Lynn	McGlothen	RHP	Grambling	LA	Rural
11	66	Lee	Smith	RHP	Castor	LA	Rural
12	62	Roy Lee	Jackson	RHP	Opelika	AL	Rural

13	54	Odell	Jones	RHP	Los Angeles	CA	Inner City
14	43	Dave	Stewart	RHP	Oakland	CA	Inner City
15	43	Grant	Jackson	LHP	Fostoria	OH	Rural
16	40	John	Candelaria	LHP	New York	NY	Inner City
17	32	Darrell	Jackson	LHP	Los Angeles	CA	Inner City
18	26	Larry	Bradford	RHP	Chicago	IL	Inner City

Appendix C: Census of 2011 Major League Baseball Players

Overall African-American Representation out of Top-850: 75, 8.8%

African-American MLB Position Players Among Top-450 in At-Bats: 65, 14.4%

(Listed in order of decreasing at-bats (AB). Pos= position, Amat= amateur level prior to signing pro contract (HS= high school, JC= junior college, C= college), Rd= round drafted, HS City=hometown as amateur, MLB Dad= whether player had father who played in MLB)

#	AB	First	Last	Pos	Team	Amat	Rd	HS City	State	Environment	MLB Dad?
1	656	Michael	Bourn	OF	ATL	C	4	Houston	TX	Inner City	No
2	639	Juan	Pierre	OF	CHW	C	13	Alexandria	LA	Rural	No
3	610	Brandon	Phillips	2B	CIN	HS	2	Atlanta	GA	Suburban	No
4	602	Matt	Kemp	OF	LAD	HS	6	Midwest City	OK	Suburban	No
5	592	Justin	Upton	OF	ARI	HS	1	Virginia Beach	VA	Suburban	No
6	591	Austin	Jackson	OF	DET	HS	8	Denton	TX	Rural	No
7	584	Ian	Desmond	SS	WAS	HS	3	Sarasota	FL	Suburban	No
8	583	Curtis	Granderson	OF	NYY	C	3	Chicago	IL	Suburban	No
9	580	Torii	Hunter	OF	LAA	HS	1	Pine Bluff	AR	Rural	No
10	572	Andrew	McCutchen	OF	PIT	HS	1	Fort Meade	FL	Rural	No
11	569	Prince	Fielder	1B	MIL	HS	1	Melbourne	FL	Suburban	Yes
12	567	Adam	Jones	OF	BAL	HS	1	San Diego	CA	Inner City	No
13	567	Jimmy	Rollins	SS	PHI	HS	2	Oakland	CA	Suburban	No
14	567	Chris	Young	OF	ARI	JC	16	Houston	TX	Inner City	No
15	560	B.J.	Upton	OF	TB	HS	1	Virginia Beach	VA	Suburban	No
16	556	Ryan	Howard	1B	PHI	C	5	St. Louis	MO	Suburban	No
17	546	Derek	Jeter	SS	NYY	HS	1	Kalamazoo	MI	Suburban	No
18	537	Howie	Kendrick	2B	LAA	JC	10	Jacksonville	FL	Suburban	No
19	531	Coco	Crisp	OF	OAK	JC	7	Los Angeles	CA	Inner City	No
20	531	James	Loney	1B	LAD	HS	1	Houston	TX	Suburban	No
21	516	Cameron	Maybin	OF	SD	HS	1	Asheville	NC	Rural	No
22	506	Carl	Crawford	OF	BOS	HS	2	Houston	TX	Inner City	No
23	505	Vernon	Wells	OF	LAA	HS	1	Dallas	TX	Suburban	No
24	481	Dexter	Fowler	OF	COL	HS	14	Atlanta	GA	Suburban	No
25	473	Delmon	Young	OF	DET	HS	1	Los Angeles	CA	Suburban	No
26	453	Rickie	Weeks	2B	MIL	C	1	Orlando	CA	Suburban	No
27	451	Michael	Brantley	OF	CLE	HS	7	Fort Pierce	FL	Suburban	Yes
28	450	Ben	Revere	OF	MIN	HS	1	Lexington	KY	Suburban	No
29	446	Marlon	Byrd	OF	CHC	JC	10	Atlanta	GA	Suburban	No
30	435	Derrek	Lee	1B	PIT	HS	1	Sacramento	CA	Suburban	No
31	417	Russell	Martin	C	NYY	JC	17	Montreal	QU	Suburban	No

32	406	Jemile	Weeks	2B	OAK	C	1	Orlando	FL	Suburban	No
33	398	Orlando	Hudson	2B	SD	JC	43	Darlington	SC	Rural	No
34	396	Jason	Heyward	OF	ATL	HS	1	Atlanta	GA	Suburban	No
35	378	Nyjer	Morgan	OF	MIL	JC	33	Edmonton	AB	Suburban	No
36	370	Will	Venable	OF	SD	C	7	San Francisco	CA	Suburban	Yes
37	368	Corey	Patterson	OF	STL	HS	1	Atlanta	GA	Suburban	No
38	362	Eric	Thames	OF	TOR	C	7	San Jose	CA	Suburban	No
39	337	Jerry	Hairston	UT	SD	C	11	Chicago	IL	Suburban	Yes
40	312	Tony	Gwynn	OF	LAD	C	2	San Diego	CA	Suburban	Yes
41	288	Chone	Figgins	UT	SEA	HS	4	Tampa	FL	Suburban	No
42	284	Denard	Span	OF	MIN	HS	1	Tampa	FL	Inner City	No
43	267	John	Mayberry	OF	PHI	C	1	Kansas City	KS	Suburban	Yes
44	250	Ben	Francisco	OF	PHI	C	5	Los Angeles	CA	Suburban	No
45	247	Desmond	Jennings	OF	TB	JC	10	Birmingham	AL	Suburban	No
46	243	Xavier	Paul	OF	PIT	HS	4	New Orleans	LA	Suburban	No
47	240	Willie	Harris	UT	NYM	C	24	Cairo	GA	Rural	No
48	239	Jason	Bourgeois	OF	HOU	HS	2	Houston	TX	Inner City	No
49	237	Mike	Cameron	OF	FLA	HS	18	LaGrange	GA	Rural	No
50	224	Dee	Gordon	SS	LAD	JC	4	Avon Park	FL	Rural	Yes
51	198	Eric	Young	2B	COL	HS	30	Piscataway	NJ	Suburban	Yes
52	195	Josh	Harrison	2B	PIT	C	6	Cincinnati	OH	Suburban	No
53	185	Bill	Hall	UT	HOU	HS	6	Nettleton	MS	Rural	No
54	184	Domonic	Brown	OF	PHI	HS	20	Atlanta	GA	Suburban	No
55	183	Fred	Lewis	OF	CIN	C	2	Wiggins	MS	Rural	No
56	180	Chris	Nelson	2B	COL	HS	1	Atlanta	GA	Suburban	No
57	175	Brandon	Allen	1B	OAK	HS	5	Montgomery	TX	Rural	No
58	170	Kyle	Blanks	1B	SD	JC	42	Moriarty	NM	Rural	No
59	157	Darnell	McDonald	OF	BOS	HS	1	Denver	CO	Suburban	No
60	143	Trayvon	Robinson	OF	SEA	HS	10	Los Angeles	CA	Inner City	No
61	137	Emman.	Burris	2B	SF	C	1	Washington	DC	Inner City	No
62	132	Scott	Hairston	OF	NYM	JC	3	Tucson	AZ	Suburban	Yes
63	107	David	Sappelt	OF	CIN	C	9	Graham	NC	Rural	No
64	101	Milton	Bradley	OF	SEA	HS	2	Los Angeles	CA	Suburban	No
65	99	Dewayne	Wise	OF	TOR	HS	5	Chapin	SC	Rural	No

African-American MLB Pitchers Among Top-400 in Innings Pitched: 10, 2.5%

(Listed in decreasing order of innings pitched (IP). LHP= lefthanded pitcher, RHP= righthanded pitcher)

#	IP	First	Last	Hand	Team	Amat	Rd	HS City	State	Environment	MLB Dad?
1	237.1	C.C.	Sabathia	LHP	NYY	HS	1	Oakland	CA	Suburban	No
2	224.1	David	Price	LHP	TB	C	1	Nashville	TN	Suburban	No
3	199.2	Edwin	Jackson	RHP	STL	HS	6	Columbus	GA	Suburban	No
4	171	James	McDonald	RHP	PIT	JC	11	Los Angeles	CA	Suburban	No
5	75.2	Dontrelle	Willis	LHP	CIN	HS	8	Oakland	CA	Suburban	No

6	51	Darren	Oliver	LHP	TEX	HS	3	Sacramento	CA	Suburban	Yes
7	48.1	Latroy	Hawkins	RHP	MIL	HS	7	Gary	IN	Inner City	No
8	39.2	Cory	Wade	RHP	NYY	C	10	Indianapolis	IN	Suburban	No
9	36	Tyson	Ross	RHP	OAK	C	1	Oakland	CA	Suburban	No
10	33	Arthur	Rhodes	LHP	STL	HS	2	Waco	TX	Rural	No

Appendix D: Census of 2011-2012 National Basketball Association Players

African-American NBA Players Among Top-435: 346, 79.5%

Inner City NBA Players Among Top-435: 95, 21.8%

Top-435 NBA Players Listed by State

Last Name	First Name	Race	Hometown	State	Environment	College
Boozer	Carlos	Black	Juneau	AK	Suburban	Duke
Chalmers	Mario	Black	Anchorage	AK	Suburban	Kansas
White	D.J.	Black	Tuscaloosa	AL	Suburban	Indiana
Bledsoe	Eric	Black	Birmingham	AL	Inner City	Kentucky
Carroll	DeMarre	Black	Birmingham	AL	Inner City	Missouri
Moon	Jamario	Black	Rockford	AL	Rural	Merdian JC
Wallace	Ben	Black	Hayneville	AL	Rural	Virginia Union
Wallace	Gerald	Black	Childersburg	AL	Rural	Alabama
Gladness	Mickell	Black	Sylacauga	AL	Rural	Alabama A&M
Cousins	DeMarcus	Black	Mobile	AL	Suburban	Kentucky
Fortson	Courtney	Black	Montgomery	AL	Suburban	Arkansas
Johnson	Joe	Black	Little Rock	AR	Suburban	Arkansas
Fisher	Derek	Black	Little Rock	AR	Suburban	Arkansas-Little
Brewer	Ronnie	Black	Fayetteville	AR	Rural	Arkansas
Evans	Jeremy	Black	Crossett	AR	Rural	Western
Anderson	James	Black	Junction City	AR	Rural	Oklahoma State
Bayless	Jerryd	Black	Phoenix	AZ	Suburban	Arizona
Bibby	Mike	Black	Phoenix	AZ	Suburban	Arizona
Jefferson	Richard	Black	Phoenix	AZ	Suburban	Arizona
Frye	Channing	Black	Phoenix	AZ	Suburban	Arizona
Nash	Steve	White	Victoria	BC	Suburban	Santa Clara
Hamilton	Jordan	Black	Los Angeles	CA	Inner City	Texas
Fields	Landry	Black-White	Los Alamitos	CA	Suburban	Stanford
Farmar	Jordan	Black-White	Woodland Hills	CA	Suburban	UCLA
DeRozan	DeMar	Black	Los Angeles	CA	Inner City	Southern
Thompson	Klay	Black-White	Santa Margarita	CA	Suburban	Washington State
Hayes	Chuck	Black	San Leandro	CA	Suburban	Kentucky
Higgins	Cory	Black	Danville	CA	Suburban	Colorado
Budinger	Chase	White	Carlsbad	CA	Suburban	Arizona
Harden	James	Black	Lakewood	CA	Suburban	Arizona State
Pendergrap	Jeff	Black	Rancho	CA	Suburban	Arizona State
Smith	Greg	Black	Fresno	CA	Suburban	Fresno State
Davis	Baron	Black	Los Angeles	CA	Inner City	UCLA

Prince	Tayshaun	Black	Los Angeles	CA	Inner City	Kentucky
Pondexter	Quincy	Black	Fresno	CA	Suburban	Washington
Pierce	Paul	Black	Los Angeles	CA	Inner City	Kansas
Daye	Austin	Black	Irvine	CA	Suburban	Gonzaga
Childress	Josh	Black	Lakewood	CA	Suburban	Stanford
Stephenson	DeShawn	Black	Easton	CA	Rural	
Chandler	Tyson	Black	Los Angeles	CA	Inner City	
Stone	Julyan	Black	Goleta	CA	Rural	Texas-El Paso
Hollins	Ryan	Black	Pasadena	CA	Suburban	UCLA
Collison	Darren	Black	Rancho	CA	Suburban	UCLA
Smith	Craig	Black	Los Angeles	CA	Inner City	Boston College
Collins	Jason	Black	Northridge	CA	Suburban	Stanford
Gooden	Drew	Black	El Cerrito	CA	Suburban	Kansas
George	Paul	Black	Palmdale	CA	Suburban	Fresno State
Jennings	Brandon	Black	Los Angeles	CA	Inner City	
Lee	Malcolm	Black	Riverside	CA	Suburban	UCLA
Leonard	Kawhi	Black	Riverside	CA	Suburban	San Diego State
Ariza	Trevor	Black	Los Angeles	CA	Inner City	UCLA
Kidd	Jason	Black-White	Oakland	CA	Suburban	California
Holiday	Jrue	Black	North Hollywood	CA	Suburban	UCLA
Arenas	Gilbert	Black	Van Nuys	CA	Suburban	Arizona
Johnson	Amir	Black	Los Angeles	CA	Inner City	
Anderson	Ryan	White	El Dorado Hills	CA	Suburban	California
Barnes	Matt	Black	Sacramento	CA	Suburban	UCLA
Westbrook	Russell	Black	Los Angeles	CA	Inner City	UCLA
Lin	Jeremy	Asian	Palo Alto	CA	Suburban	Harvard
Afflalo	Aaron	Black	Los Angeles	CA	Inner City	UCLA
Williams	Derrick	Black	La Mirada	CA	Suburban	Arizona
Wright	Dorell	Black	Los Angeles	CA	Inner City	
Tyler	Jeremy	Black	San Diego	CA	Suburban	
Dudley	Jared	Black	San Diego	CA	Suburban	Boston College
Honeycutt	Tyler	Black	Sylmar	CA	Suburban	UCLA
Brackins	Craig	Black	Palmdale	CA	Suburban	Iowa State
Young	Nick	Black	Reseda	CA	Suburban	Southern
McGuire	Dominic	Black	San Diego	CA	Inner City	Fresno State
Morris	Darius	Black	Los Angeles	CA	Inner City	Michigan
Miller	Andre	Black	Los Angeles	CA	Inner City	Utah
Lopez	Robin	White	Fresno	CA	Suburban	Stanford
Walton	Luke	White	San Diego	CA	Suburban	Arizona
Lopez	Brook	White	Fresno	CA	Suburban	Stanford
Jackson	Reggie	Black	Colorado	CO	Suburban	Boston College
Billups	Chauncey	Black	Denver	CO	Inner City	Colorado
Amundson	Lou	White	Louisville	CO	Suburban	UNLV
Smith	Jason	White	Kelsey	CO	Rural	
Blatche	Andray	Black	South Kent	CT	Rural	
Williams	Jordan	Black	Torrington	CT	Rural	Maryland
Gomes	Ryan	Black	Waterbury	CT	Suburban	Providence

Camby	Marcus	Black	Hartford	CT	Suburban	Massachusetts-
Smith	Nolan	Black	Washington	DC	Suburban	Duke
Durant	Kevin	Black	Washington	DC	Inner City	Texas
Young	Sam	Black	Washington	DC	Inner City	Pittsburgh
Sanders	Larry	Black	Port St. Lucie	FL	Suburban	Virginia
Evans	Reggie	Black	Pensacola	FL	Suburban	Iowa
Jones	James	Black	Miami	FL	Suburban	Miami
Parsons	Chandler	White	Winter Park	FL	Suburban	Florida
Knight	Brandon	Black	Fort Lauderdale	FL	Suburban	Kentucky
McGrady	Tracy	Black	Auburndale	FL	Rural	
Jones	Dominique	Black	Lake Wales	FL	Rural	South Florida
Gee	Alonzo	Black	Riviera Beach	FL	Suburban	Alabama
Haslem	Udonis	Black	Miami	FL	Inner City	Florida
Stoudemire	Amar'e	Black	Orlando	FL	Suburban	
Daniels	Marquis	Black	Orlando	FL	Inner City	Auburn
Carter	Vince	Black	Daytona Beach	FL	Suburban	North Carolina
Dooling	Keyon	Black	Fort Lauderdale	FL	Inner City	Missouri
Wilkins	Damien	Black	Orlando	FL	Suburban	Georgia
Barea	Jose	Latino	Miami	FL	Suburban	Northeastern
Blake	Steve	White	Miami	FL	Suburban	Maryland
Speights	Marreese	Black	St. Petersburg	FL	Suburban	Florida
Bell	Raja	Black	Miami	FL	Suburban	Florida
Smith	Josh	Black	Powder Springs	GA	Suburban	
Brooks	Marshon	Black	Stone Mountain	GA	Suburban	Providence
Brown	Kwame	Black	Brunswick	GA	Rural	
Hill	Jordan	Black	Atlanta	GA	Suburban	Arizona
Hickson	J.J.	Black	Marietta	GA	Suburban	North Carolina
Goudelock	Andrew	Black	Stone Mountain	GA	Suburban	College of
Thompkins	Trey	Black	Norcross	GA	Suburban	Georgia
Howard	Dwight	Black	Atlanta	GA	Suburban	
Leslie	Travis	Black	Atlanta	GA	Inner City	Georgia
Douglas	Toney	Black	Jonesboro	GA	Suburban	Florida State
Meeks	Jodie	Black	Norcross	GA	Suburban	Kentucky
Aminu	Al-Farouq	Black	Norcross	GA	Suburban	Wake Forest
Williams	Louis	Black	Snellville	GA	Suburban	
Singleton	Chris	Black	Canton	GA	Rural	Florida State
Favors	Derrick	Black	Atlanta	GA	Inner City	Georgia Tech
Hinrich	Kirk	White	Sioux City	IA	Suburban	Kansas
Collison	Nick	White	Iowa Falls	IA	Rural	Kansas
Korver	Kyle	White	Pella	IA	Rural	Creighton
Howard	Juwan	Black	Chicago	IL	Inner City	Michigan
Wade	Dwyane	Black	Oak Lawn	IL	Suburban	Marquette
Mohammed	Nazr	Black	Chicago	IL	Inner City	Kentucky
Turner	Evan	Black	Oak Park	IL	Suburban	Ohio State
Iguodala	Andre	Black	Springfield	IL	Suburban	Arizona
Liggins	DeAndre	Black	Chicago	IL	Inner City	Kentucky
Brown	Shannon	Black	Maywood	IL	Suburban	Michigan State

McGee	Javale	Black	Chicago	IL	Inner City	Nevada
Cardinal	Brian	White	Tolonto	IL	Rural	Purdue
Bynum	Will	Black	Chicago	IL	Inner City	Georgia Tech
Allen	Tony	Black	Chicago	IL	Inner City	Oklahoma State
Maggette	Corey	Black	Oak Park	IL	Suburban	Duke
Parker	Anthony	Black	Naperville	IL	Suburban	Bradley
Cook	Brian	Black	Lincoln	IL	Rural	Illinois
Curry	Eddy	Black	South Holland	IL	Suburban	
Shumpert	Iman	Black	Oak Park	IL	Suburban	Georgia Tech
Singleton	James	Black	Chicago	IL	Inner City	Murray State
Rose	Derrick	Black	Chicago	IL	Inner City	Memphis
Simmons	Bobby	Black	Chicago	IL	Inner City	DePaul
Pargo	Jeremy	Black	Chicago	IL	Inner City	Gonzaga
Livingston	Shaun	Black	Peoria	IL	Suburban	
Pargo	Jannero	Black	Chicago	IL	Inner City	Arkansas
Lee	Courtney	Black	Indianapolis	IN	Inner City	Western
McRoberts	Josh	White	Carmel	IN	Suburban	Duke
Harangody	Luke	White	Merrillville	IN	Rural	Notre Dame
Jeffries	Jared	Black	Bloomington	IN	Suburban	Indiana
Johnson	JaJuan	Black	Indianapolis	IN	Suburban	Purdue
Randolph	Zach	Black	Marion	IN	Rural	Michigan State
Hill	George	Black	Indianapolis	IN	Suburban	IUPUI
Gordon	Eric	Black	Indianapolis	IN	Inner City	Indiana
Conley	Mike	Black	Indianapolis	IN	Inner City	Ohio State
Teague	Jeff	Black	Indianapolis	IN	Inner City	Wake Forest
Hayward	Gordon	White	Indianapolis	IN	Suburban	Butler
Moore	E'Twaun	Black	East Chicago	IN	Suburban	Purdue
Alabi	Solomon	Black		INT		Florida State
Delfino	Carlos	Latino		INT		
Bargnani	Andrea	White		INT		
Erden	Semih	White		INT		
Diaw	Boris	Black		INT		
Eyenga	Christian	Black		INT		
Asik	Omer	White		INT		
Jordan	Jerome	Black		INT		Tulsa
Katner	Enes	White		INT		
Fernandez	Rudy	Latino		INT		
Barbosa	Leandro	Black		INT		
Ayon	Gustavo	Latino		INT		
Fesenko	Kyrylo	White		INT		
Gasol	Pau	White		INT		
Haddadi	Hamed	White		INT		
Calderon	Jose	Latino		INT		
Dragic	Goran	White		INT		
Duncan	Tim	Black		INT		Wake Forest
Gortat	Marcin	White		INT		
Casspi	Omri	White		INT		

Ginobili	Manu	White		INT		
Belinelli	Marco	White		INT		
Ibaka	Serge	Black		INT		
Jerebko	Jonas	White		INT		
Gasol	Marc	White		INT		
Ilyasova	Erson	White		INT		
Gallinari	Danilo	White		INT		
Biyombo	Bismack	Black		INT		
Biedrins	Andris	White		INT		
Beaubois	Rodrigue	Black		INT		
Batum	Nicolas	Black		INT		
Bogut	Andrew	White		INT		Utah
Udrih	Beno	White		INT		
Radmanovi	Vladimir	White		INT		
Pietrus	Mickael	Black		INT		
Vucevic	Nikola	White		INT		Southern
Vesely	Jan	White		INT		
Parker	Tony	Black		INT		
Vasquez	Greivis	White		INT		Maryland
Petro	Johan	Black		INT		
Varejao	Anderson	White		INT		
Splitter	Tiago	White		INT		
Turkoglu	Hedo	White		INT		
Turiaf	Ronny	Black		INT		Gonzaga
MbahAMout	Luc	Black		INT		UCLA
Milicic	Darko	White		INT		
Thabeet	Hasheem	Black		INT		Connecticut
Mills	Patty	Black		INT		St. Mary's (CA)
Pachulia	Zaza	White		INT		
Nene		Black		INT		
Pavlovic	Aleksandar	White		INT		
Nowitzki	Dirk	White		INT		
Scola	Luis	White		INT		
Sefalosha	Thabo	Black		INT		
Pekovic	Nikola	White		INT		
Seraphin	Kevin	Black		INT		
Yi	Jianlian	Asian		INT		
Mahinmi	Ian	Black		INT		
Rubio	Ricky	White		INT		
Mozgov	Timofey	White		INT		
Evans	Maurice	Black	Wichita	KS	Suburban	Texas
Watson	Earl	Black	Kansas City	KS	Suburban	UCLA
Rondo	Rajan	Black	Louisville	KY	Suburban	Kentucky
Mack	Shelvin	Black	Lexington	KY	Suburban	Butler
Monroe	Greg	Black	Harvey	LA	Suburban	Georgetown
Thornton	Marcus	Black	Baton Rouge	LA	Suburban	Louisiana State
Millsap	Paul	Black	Grambling	LA	Rural	Louisiana Tech

Duhon	Chris	Black	Slidell	LA	Suburban	Duke
Thomas	Tyrus	Black	Baton Rouge	LA	Inner City	Louisiana State
Davis	Glen	Black	Baton Rouge	LA	Suburban	Louisiana State
Granger	Danny	Black	Metaire	LA	Suburban	New Mexico
Bass	Brandon	Black	Baton Rouge	LA	Suburban	Louisiana State
Wafer	Von	Black	Lisbon	LA	Rural	Florida State
Kleiza	Linas	White	Rockville	MD	Suburban	Missouri
Greene	Donte	Black	Towson	MD	Suburban	Syracuse
Gay	Rudy	Black	Baltimore	MD	Inner City	Connecticut
Selby	Josh	Black	Baltimore	MD	Inner City	Kansas
Jarrett	Jack	Black	Fort Washington	MD	Suburban	Georgia Tech
Neal	Gary	Black	Aberdeen	MD	Rural	Towson
Lawson	Ty	Black	Upper Marlboro	MD	Suburban	North Carolina
West	Delonte	Black	Greenbelt	MD	Suburban	St. Joseph's
Hibbert	Roy	Black	Adelphi	MD	Rural	Georgetown
Beasley	Michael	Black	Frederick	MD	Rural	Kansas State
Miller	Brad	White	Pittsfield	ME	Rural	Purdue
Battier	Shane	Black-White	Birmingham	MI	Suburban	Duke
Benson	Keith	Black	Farmington Hills	MI	Suburban	Oakland
Horford	Al	Black	Grand Ledge	MI	Rural	Florida
Kaman	Chris	White	Wyoming	MI	Rural	Central Michigan
Chandler	Wilson	Black	Benton Harbor	MI	Rural	Depaul
Green	Willie	Black	Detroit	MI	Inner City	Detroit Mercy
Russell	Walker	Black	Rochester	MI	Suburban	Jacksonville
Harris	Manny	Black	Detroit	MI	Inner City	Michigan
Richardson	Jason	Black	Saginaw	MI	Inner City	Michigan State
Humphries	Kris	White	Minnetonka	MN	Suburban	Minnesota
Przybilla	Joel	White	Monticello	MN	Suburb	Minnesota
Aldrich	Cole	White	Bloomington	MN	Suburban	Kansas
Anderson	Alan	Black	Minneapolis	MN	Inner City	Michigan State
Leuer	Jon	White	Orono	MN	Suburban	Wisconsin
Harrellson	Josh	White	St. Charles	MO	Suburban	Kentucky
Lee	David	White	St. Louis	MO	Suburban	Florida
Rush	Brandon	Black	Kansas City	MO	Inner City	Kansas
Hansbrough	Tyler	White	Poplar Bluff	MO	Rural	North Carolina
Burks	Alec	Black	Grandview	MO	Suburban	Colorado
Tolliver	Anthony	Black	Springfield	MO	Suburban	Creighton
Outlaw	Travis	Black	Starkville	MS	Rural	
Williams	Mo	Black	Jackson	MS	Suburban	Alabama
Ellis	Monta	Black	Jackson	MS	Rural	
Jefferson	Al	Black	Prentiss	MS	Rural	
Dampier	Erick	Black	Monticello	MS	Rural	Mississippi
Paul	Chris	Black	West Forsyth	NC	Suburban	Wake Forest
Stackhouse	Jerry	Black	Kinston	NC	Rural	North Carolina
Haywood	Brendan	Black	Greensboro	NC	Suburban	North Carolina
Whiteside	Hassan	Black	Gastonia	NC	Rural	Marshall
Smith	Ish	Black	Concord	NC	Suburban	Wake Forest

West	David	Black	Garner	NC	Suburban	Xavier
Morrow	Anthony	Black	Charlotte	NC	Suburban	Georgia Tech
Wall	John	Black	Raleigh	NC	Suburban	Kentucky
Curry	Stephen	Black	Charlotte	NC	Suburban	Davidson
Howard	Josh	Black	Kennersville	NC	Rural	Wake Forest
Maynor	Eric	Black	Raeford	NC	Rural	Virginia
Jamison	Antawn	Black	Charlotte	NC	Suburban	North Carolina
Bonner	Matt	White	Concord	NH	Suburban	Florida
Watkins	Darryl	Black	Paterson	NJ	Inner City	Syracuase
Bynum	Andrew	Black	Plainsboro	NJ	Suburban	
Foye	Randy	Black	Newark	NJ	Inner City	Villanova
Clark	Earl	Black	Rahway	NJ	Suburban	Louisville
Thomas	Lance	Black	Scotch Plains	NJ	Suburban	Duke
Samuels	Samardo	Black	Newark	NJ	Inner City	Louisville
Faried	Kenneth	Black	Newark	NJ	Inner City	Morehead State
Dalembert	Samuel	Black	Elizabeth	NJ	Suburban	Seton Hall
Smith	J.R.	Black	Lakewood	NJ	Suburban	
Deng	Luol	Black	Blairstown	NJ	Suburban	Duke
Thompson	Jason	Black	Medford	NJ	Suburban	Rider
Irving	Kyrie	Black	West Orange	NJ	Suburban	Duke
Harrington	Al	Black	Roselle	NJ	Suburban	
Jones	Dahntay	Black	Hamilton	NJ	Suburban	Duke
Noah	Joakim	White	Lawrenceville	NJ	Suburban	Florida
Murphy	Troy	White	Morristown	NJ	Suburban	Notre Dame
Babbitt	Luke	White	Reno	NV	Suburban	Nevada
Watson	C.J.	Black	Las Vegas	NV	Suburban	Tennessee
Johnson	Armon	Black	Reno	NV	Suburban	Nevada
Odom	Lamar	Black	New York	NY	Inner City	Rhode Island
Ebanks	Devin	Black	New York	NY	Inner City	West Virginia
Harris	Tobias	Black	Dix Hills	NY	Suburban	Tennessee
Hayward	Lazar	Black	Buffalo	NY	Inner City	Marquette
Anthony	Carmelo	Black-Latino	New York	NY	Inner City	Syracuse
Fredette	Jimmer	White	Glens Falls	NY	Rural	Brigham Young
Ivey	Royal	Black	New York	NY	Inner City	Texas
Stephenson	Lance	Black	New York	NY	Inner City	Cincinnati
James	Mike	Black	Amityville	NY	Suburban	Duquesne
Tinsley	Jamaal	Black	New York	NY	Inner City	Iowa State
Jenkins	Charles	Black	New York	NY	Inner City	Hofstra
Brand	Elton	Black	Peeskill	NY	Rural	Duke
Villanueva	Charlie	Black	New York	NY	Inner City	Connecticut
Walker	Kemba	Black	New York	NY	Inner City	Connecticut
Telfair	Sebastian	Black	New York	NY	Inner City	
Flynn	Jonny	Black	Niagara Falls	NY	Suburban	Syracuse
Green	Danny	Black	North Babylon	NY	Suburban	North Carolina
Gaines	Sundiata	Black	New York	NY	Inner City	Georgia
Gaines	Francisco	Latino	New York	NY	Inner City	Louisville
Price	A.J.	Black	Amityville	NY	Suburban	Connecticut

Forbes	Gary	Black	New York	NY	Inner City	Massachusetts
World	Metta	Black	New York	NY	Inner City	St. John's
Gordon	Ben	Black	Mount Vernon	NY	Suburban	Connecticut
Gibson	Taj	Black	New York	NY	Inner City	Southern
Brown	Derrick	Black	Dayton	OH	Suburban	Xavier
Cole	Norris	Black	Dayton	OH	Suburban	Cleveland State
Redd	Michael	Black	Columbus	OH	Suburban	Ohio State
Koufos	Kosta	White	Canton	OH	Suburban	Ohio State
Mullens	Byron	Black-White	Canal	OH	Suburban	Ohio State
Martin	Kevin	Black	Zanesville	OH	Rural	Western Carolina
Wright	Chris	Black	Trotwood	OH	Suburban	Dayton
James	LeBron	Black	Akron	OH	Suburban	
Cook	Daequan	Black	Dayton	OH	Suburban	Ohio State
Boykins	Earl	Black	Cleveland	OH	Inner City	Eastern Michigan
Azubuike	Kelenna	Black	Tulsa	OK	Suburban	Kentucky
Orton	Daniel	Black	Oklahoma City	OK	Suburban	Kentucky
Williams	Shelden	Black	Midwest City	OK	Suburban	Duke
Udoh	Ekpe	Black	Edmond	OK	Suburban	Baylor
Henry	Xavier	Black	Oklahoma City	OK	Suburban	Kansas
Griffin	Blake	Black-White	Oklahoma City	OK	Suburban	Oklahoma
Magloire	Jamaal	Black	Toronto	ONT	Suburban	Kentucky
Thompson	Tristan	Black	Brampton	ONT	Suburban	Texas
Joseph	Cory	Black	Toronto	ONT	Suburban	Texas
Dunleavy	Mike	White	Portland	OR	Suburban	Duke
Love	Kevin	White	Lake Oswego	OR	Suburban	UCLA
Gray	Aaron	White	Emmaus	PA	Rural	Pittsburgh
Kennedy	D.J.	Black	Pittsburgh	PA	Inner City	St. John's
Bryant	Kobe	Black	Lower Merion	PA	Suburban	
Lowry	Kyle	Black	Philadelphia	PA	Inner City	Villanova
Blair	DeJuan	Black	Pittsburgh	PA	Inner City	Pittsburgh
Carroll	Matt	White	Horsham	PA	Rural	Notre Dame
Warrick	Hakim	Black	Wynnewood	PA	Suburban	Syracuse
Allen	Lavoy	Black	Morrisville	PA	Suburban	Temple
Morris	Marcus	Black	Philadelphia	PA	Inner City	Kansas
Hamilton	Richard	Black	Coatesville	PA	Rural	Connecticut
Evans	Tyreke	Black	Chester	PA	Suburban	Memphis
Morris	Markief	Black	Philadelphia	PA	Inner City	Kansas
Henderson	Gerald	Black	Merion	PA	Suburban	Duke
Ellington	Wayne	Black	Birdsboro	PA	Rural	North Carolina
Nelson	Jameer	Black	Chester	PA	Suburban	St. Joseph's
Salmons	John	Black	Plymouth	PA	Suburban	Miami
Anthony	Joel	Black	Montreal	QUE	Suburban	UNLV
Moore	Mikki	Black	Blacksburg	SC	Rural	Nebraska
Garnett	Kevin	Black	Mauldin	SC	Rural	
Allen	Ray	Black	Dalzell	SC	Rural	Connecticut
Felton	Raymond	Black	Latta	SC	Rural	North Carolina
Booker	Trevor	Black	Union	SC	Rural	Clemson

Sessions	Ramon	Black	Myrtle Beach	SC	Suburban	Nevada
Miller	Mike	White	Mitchell	SD	Rural	Florida
Williams	Shawne	Black	Memphis	TN	Inner City	Memphis
Brewer	Corey	Black	Portland	TN	Rural	Florida
Marion	Shawn	Black	Clarksville	TN	Rural	UNLV
Williams	Elliot	Black	Memphis	TN	Inner City	Memphis
Wright	Brandan	Black	Nashville	TN	Suburban	North Carolina
Hudston	Lester	Black	Memphis	TN	Inner City	Tennessee-
Young	Thaddeus	Black	Memphis	TN	Inner City	Georgia Tech
Johnson	Wesley	Black	Corsicana	TX	Rural	Syracuse
Maxiell	Jason	Black	Carrolton	TX	Suburban	Cincinnati
Williams	Deron	Black	The Colony	TX	Suburban	Illinois
Jordan	DeAndre	Black	Houston	TX	Inner City	Texas A&M
Lewis	Rashard	Black	Houston	TX	Inner City	
Randolph	Anthony	Black	Dallas	TX	Inner City	Louisiana State
Martin	Cartier	Black	Houston	TX	Inner City	Kansas State
Lucas III	John	Black	Houston	TX	Suburban	Oklahoma State
Augustin	D.J.	Black	Missouri City	TX	Suburban	Texas
Battie	Tony	Black	Dallas	TX	Inner City	Texas Tech
Martin	Kenyon	Black	Dallas	TX	Inner City	Cincinnati
Gibson	Daniel	Black	Houston	TX	Inner City	Texas
Okafor	Emeka	Black	Houston	TX	Inner City	Connecticut
Harris	Terrel	Black	Garland	TX	Suburban	Oklahoma State
Miles	C.J.	Black	Dallas	TX	Inner City	
Thomas	Kurt	Black	Dallas	TX	Inner City	Texas Christian
Andersen	Chris	White	Iola	TX	Rural	Blinn JC
Price	Ronnie	Black	Friendswood	TX	Rural	Utah Valley
Green	Gerald	Black	Houston	TX	Suburban	
Najera	Eduardo	White	San Antonio	TX	Suburban	Oklahoma
Bosh	Chris	Black	Dallas	TX	Inner City	Georgia Tech
Jackson	Stephen	Black	Port Arthur	TX	Rural	Butler County JC
Williams	Sean	Black	Mansfield	TX	Suburban	Boston College
Johnson	Ivan	Black	San Antonio	TX	Suburban	Cal State San
Sloan	Donald	Black	Dallas	TX	Inner City	Texas A&M
Silas	Xavier	Black	Austin	TX	Suburban	Northern Illinois
Arthur	Darrell	Black	Dallas	TX	Inner City	Kansas
Uzoh	Ben	Black	San Antonio	TX	Suburban	Tulsa
Pittman	Dexter	Black	Rosenberg	TX	Rural	Texas
Perkins	Kendrick	Black	Beaumont	TX	Suburban	
James	Damion	Black	Nacogdoches	TX	Rural	Texas
Aldridge	LaMarcus	Black	Seagoville	TX	Rural	Texas
Butler	Jimmy	Black	Tomball	TX	Suburban	Marquette
Redick	J.J.	White	Roanoke	VA	Rural	Duke
Crawford	Jordan	Black	Chatham	VA	Rural	Xavier
Cunningha	Dante	Black	Dumfries	VA	Suburban	Villanova
Macklin	Vernon	Black	Portsmouth	VA	Suburban	Florida
Harper	Justin	Black	Richmond	VA	Suburban	Richmond

Williams	Reggie	Black	Prince George	VA	Rural	Virginia Military
Davis	Ed	Black	Richmond	VA	Suburban	North Carolina
Diop	DeSagna	Black	Mouth of Wilson	VA	Suburban	
Hill	Grant	Black	Reston	VA	Suburban	Duke
Williams	Terrence	Black	Seattle	WA	Inner City	Louisville
Crawford	Jamal	Black	Seattle	WA	Inner City	Michigan
Hawes	Spencer	White	Seattle	WA	Suburban	Washington
Robinson	Nate	Black	Seattle	WA	Suburban	Washington
Scalabrine	Brian	White	Enumclaw	WA	Rural	Southern
Williams	Marvin	Black	Bremerton	WA	Suburban	North Carolina
Stuckey	Rodney	Black	Kent	WA	Suburban	Eastern
Terry	Jason	Black	Seattle	WA	Suburban	Arizona
Thomas	Isaiah	Black	University Place	WA	Suburban	Washington
Brockman	Jon	White	Snohomish	WA	Rural	Washington
Bradley	Avery	Black	Tacoma	WA	Suburban	Texas
Webster	Martell	Black	Seattle	WA	Suburban	
Ridnour	Luke	White	Blaine	WA	Rural	Oregon
Stiemsma	Greg	White	Randolph	WI	Rural	Wisconsin
Butler	Caron	Black	Racine	WI	Suburban	Connecticut
Harris	Devin	Black	Wauwatosa	WI	Suburban	Wisconsin
Novak	Steve	White	Brown Deer	WI	Suburban	Marquette
Matthews	Wesley	Black	Madison	WI	Suburban	Marquette
Landry	Carl	Black	Milwaukee	WI	Inner City	Purdue
Patterson	Patrick	Black	Huntington	WV	Suburban	Kentucky
Mayo	O.J.	Black	Huntington	WV	Rural	Southern
Johnson	James	Black	Cheyenne	WY	Suburban	Wake Forest

Appendix E: 2011 African-American NFL Players Produced by Selected City

This is based on the 2011 NFL Census as reported by USA Football. Players were attributed to cities depending on the location of their graduating high school. NOTE: this does not include every top city, just the ones researched for this book. For example, Houston would definitely rank near the top.

1. Miami (29, listed by high school)

Carol City HS (4): Ricky Jean Francois, Santana Moss, Kenny Phillips, Robert Sands

Christopher Columbus HS (1): Pat Lee

Gulliver Prep HS (1): Patrick Robinson

Miami HS (4): Atari Bigby, Jamaal Jackson, Andre Johnson, Roscoe Parrish

Miami Beach HS (1): Chad Johnson

Miami Central HS (2): Willis McGahee, Rod Issac

Miami Jackson HS (2) Elvis Dumervil, Stefan Logan

Miami Lakes HS (2): Thaddeus Lewis, Jamar Lattimore

Miami Northwestern HS (2): Vernon Carey, Anthony Gaitor

Miami Springs HS (1): Devin Aromashodu

North Miami Beach HS (2): E.J. Biggers, Louis Delmas

Pace HS (1): DeMarcus Van Dyke

Norland HS (4): Antwan Barnes, Dwayne Bowe, Antonio Brown, Richard Gordon

Washington HS (2): Antonio Dixon, Brandon Harris

2. Los Angeles (16)

Crenshaw HS (3): Dante Hughes, Brendan Mebane, Brian Price

Dorsey HS (4): Na'il Diggs, Christopher Owens, Jerome Boyd, Rahim Moore

Locke HS (1): Richard Marshall

Lynwood HS (1): Ashlee Palmer

Narbonne HS (2): Nnamdi Asomugha, Dashon Goldson

St. Bernard HS (1): Joselio Hanson

University HS (2): Steve Smith, Titus Young

Venice HS (1): Jonas Mouton

Verbum Dei (1): Akeem Ayers

3. Dallas (11)

Carter HS (3): Michael Crabtree, Jonathan Scott, DeMarcus Love

Kimball HS (2): Michael Adams, Phillip Tanner

Lake Highlands HS (3): Marshall Newhouse, Frank Okam, Wade Smith

St. Mark's HS (1): Sam Acho

W.T. White HS (1): Jason Smith

Woodrow Wilson HS (1): Sergio Kindle

4. Detroit (11)

Bishop Gallagher HS (1): Braylon Edwards

Cass Tech HS (1): Joe Barksdale

Crockett HS (1): Robert Eddins

DePorres HS (1): Alan Ball

Detroit Central HS (1): Antonio Gates

Martin Luther King HS (2): Anthony Adams, Kevin Vickerson

Mumford HS (1): Derrick Mason

Pershing HS (1): Larry Foote

Renaissance HS (1): Ron Bartell

Southeastern HS (1): Bart Scott

5. Birmingham, AL (9)

Birmingham HS: Mario Addison

Huffman HS (2): Andre Smith, Marcell Dareus

Minor HS (2): Brandon Johnson, Bryan Thomas

Phillips HS: Jerricho Cotchery

Wenonah HS: Joe Webb

West End HS: Earl Bennett

Woodlawn HS: Karlos Dansby

6. Chicago (8)

Carver HS: Jason Avant

DuSable HS: Jason Williams

Hubbard HS: Kelvin Hayden

Hyde Park HS: Joe Mays

Kenwood Academy: Quincy Black

Morgan Park HS: Fred Evans

North Chicago HS: Michael Turner

Simeon HS: Martez Wilson

7. Indianapolis (6)

Arlington HS: James Brewer

Ben Davis HS: Tandon Doss

Cathedral HS: Mathias Kiwanuka

Franklin Central HS: Donald Washington

North Central HS: Courtney Roby

Warren Central HS: Darren Evans

8. Mobile, AL (4)

B.C. Rain HS: Rodney Hudson

Murphy HS: Captain Munnerlyn

Vigor HS: San'Derrick Marks

Williamson HS: Nick Fairley

9t. Cincinnati (3)

Moeller HS (2): Greg K. Jones, Rico Murray

Woodward HS (1): Ray Edwards

9t. Oakland (3)

Bishop O'Dowd HS (1): Kirk Morrison

Oakland Tech HS (2): Josh Johnson, Marshawn Lynch

11t. New York City (2)

Cardinal Hayes HS: Willie Colon

Fort Hamilton HS: Jaiquawn Jarrett

11t. San Francisco (2)

Archbishop Riordan HS: Eric Wright

Sacred Heart Academy: Jason Hill

Appendix F: African-American Census of 1959 MLB

(Courtesy of Dave Perkin from *Sports Illustrated*)

Dave Perkin went through the entire 1959 MLB roster, team-by-team, and determined the racial makeup for each player. Here are his results by team:

NATIONAL LEAGUE (# of total players)

Chicago Cubs (39): 33 White, 6 Black, 0 Latino

Cincinnati Reds (39): 30 White, 6 Black, 3 Latino

Los Angeles Dodgers (37): 31 White, 6 Black, 0 Latino

Milwaukee Braves (37): 30 White, 5 Black, 2 Latino

Philadelphia Phillies (36): 30 White, 3 Black, 3 Latino

Pittsburgh Pirates (37): 30 White, 5 Black, 2 Latino

San Francisco Giants (34): 24 White, 9 Black, 1 Latino

St. Louis Cardinals (49): 41 White, 8 Black, 0 Latino

Out of 308 National League players, 37 were American Black (African-American) for a rate of 12%. Including the 11 Latino Blacks makes it 15.6%.

AMERICAN LEAGUE (# of total players)

Baltimore Orioles (41): 34 White, 5 Black, 2 Latino

Boston Red Sox (41): 37 White, 2 Black, 2 Latino

Chicago White Sox (40): 33 White, 4 Black, 3 Latino

Cleveland Indians (41): 36 White, 1 Black, 4 Latino

Detroit Tigers (37): 34 White, 2 Black, 1 Latino

Kansas City A's (43): 41 White, 1 Black, 1 Latino

New York Yankees (37): 35 White, 1 Black, 1 Latino

Washington Senators (40): 33 White, 1 Black, 6 Latino

Out of 320 American League players, there were 17 African-Americans (5.3%). Including the 20 Latino Blacks brings the number to 37 (11.6%).

OVERALL AFRICAN-AMERICAN REPRESENTATION: 8.6%

OVERALL BLACK (AFRICAN-AMERICAN AND LATINO) REPRESENTATION: 13.5%

Appendix G: Survey on Attitudes of African-American Athletes Towards Baseball

This was a two-sided one-sheet survey I handed out to 20 local non-baseball athletes:

SINHA POLL: Athlete Attitudes Towards Baseball

NAME: PRIMARY SPORT(S):

TEAM/SCHOOL: E-Mail/Phone # (optional):

RACE (circle all that apply): African-American Caucasian Latino Asian Other:

1. Did you ever play baseball growing up? (circle at least one)

a) Never b) No organized, but played recreationally c) Little League

d) Up to junior high e) Some high school f) Four years of high school

g) College

2. Did you have a baseball mitt as a child?

a) Never b) For a few years c) Most of my childhood d) Always

3. Did you ever dream of becoming a Major League Baseball Player?

a) Never b) Briefly c) Much of my childhood d) My entire childhood

4. If you don't/didn't play, what keeps/kept you from playing baseball? Circle ALL that apply.

a)Wasn't good enough b)Game is too slow c)Loved my sport much better d)Played my sport much better e)Had no opportunity to play

f)No one to play catch with g)Too expensive

h)Saw it as White Man's game i)Poor facilities in area

j)Didn't attract girls as much

OTHER:

5. If you didn't play the sport you are playing now (or played at highest level), would you have tried to play another collegiately/professionally? Which one and why?

6. Do you ever watch Baseball?

a) Never b) Rarely c) A few games a month on TV or in person

d) A few games a week on TV or in person e) A lot, almost every day

7. Was your father (or primary father figure) particularly interested in baseball? How?

8. Do you think you have/had the athletic ability to become a Major League Baseball player had you played the sport all along? Why or why not?

9. How much more interested would you have been in Baseball had there been as many Black players as there are in the NBA or NFL?

a)A lot more interested b)A little more interested c)No difference
d)Less interested

10. If you have a son, do you plan to introduce him to baseball at a young age? Why or why not?

11. What do you think is the biggest barrier for Black men to play baseball?

Further Comments:

Thank you!

Appendix H: Number of African-American All-Stars 1947-1979

Data was provided by the National Baseball Hall of Fame Library in Cooperstown, New York, and slightly modified as pertinent to this book.

1947 (0)

1948 (0)

1949: American League = 1, National League = 3

1950: AL=1, NL=3

1951: AL=1, NL=2

1952: AL=2, NL=2

1953: AL=2, NL-2

1954: AL=1, NL=3

1955: AL=2, NL=5

1956: AL=1, NL=6

1957: AL=1, NL=4

1958: AL=1, NL=5

1959: AL=1, NL=9

1960: AL=2, NL=6

1961: AL=1, NL=8

1962: AL=3, NL=9

1963: AL=4, NL=6

1964: AL=2, NL=6

1965: AL=4, NL=10

1966: AL=4, NL=11

1967: AL=3, NL=8

1968: AL=2, NL=6

1969: AL=8, NL=8

1970: AL=6, NL=8

1971: AL=5, NL=12

1972: AL=5, NL=11

1973: AL=9, NL=9

1974: AL=5, NL=8

1975: AL=7, NL=8

1976: AL=5, NL=6

1977: AL=7, NL=7

1978: AL=6, NL=6

1979: AL=7, NL=6

Appendix I: Letter to Darrell Miller Regarding Miami Urban Youth Academy Site

(Sent September 8th, 2009)

Re: Visited Proposed Site

From **nupester** nupester@aol.com
To **darrell.miller** darrell.miller@mlb.com

Hi Darrell,

I'll give you my feedback via e-mail, since I know you're busy and this should be easier to digest. We can talk later on.

First, I'm assuming the proposed site is the one listed in the Miami paper, an area in northwest Hialeah between I-75 and the Florida Turnpike.

I personally have a number of concerns about that site. My primary concern is simply that I don't believe it is a convenient location in order to achieve the objectives of the Urban Youth Academy.

At the present time, the area is swampy and undeveloped, and it takes a dirt road to get there. While I understand they are building roads and such around it, the academy would still be very difficult to get to for the kids the UYA aims to serve. There are no residences in the immediate area and even kids from Hialeah would have difficulty finding transportation to the proposed location.

From my knowledge of Miami and from speaking with others in the area, I feel the the areas that are richest in untapped baseball talent are in the northwest Miami corridor off of I-95, including areas like Carol City, Miami Lakes, Opa-Locka, Liberty Center etc. It is an area that is largely working class and predominantly African American. It is, not coincidentally, the nation's most productive area for future NFL football players. In fact, it is #1 by a longshot in the entire nation for football yet I can't name a single present day major league baseball player who has come out of there.

I'm estimating it to be a half hour drive from the midpoint of that corridor to the proposed site in Hialeah, assuming normal traffic. The proposed location make it difficult to attract those kids, from my estimation.

I don't know if you are locked into the proposed site or if there is room for modification, but I wanted to give you my feedback for what it's worth.

If it were completely up to me and there were no extenuating circumstances, I'd emphatically pick Miami-Dade North College as ther perfect site. Like Compton College, they have pre-existing facilities (that need repair) and enough land for the fields the UYA requires. Its location is in the heart of the corridor I described above. In fact, the local high schools' football stadium is on the edge of their campus.

Florida Memorial College, from what I hear, is also in an area of importance on the edge of Hialeah and Miami, with some pre-existing facilities and land. I haven't been there, myself.

I've investigated on my own how the NFL has done so well in that area and what comes up is their Pop Warner programs are outstanding. They really hammer it into kids in that area and get the parents involved. I was surprised to see the junior highs have no football (or baseball) programs. Pop Warner goes ages 6-15 and that's really where they're getting kids hooked.

I can only imagine how great it would be to introduce baseball there, because there is little opportunity in that area. Most of Miami is baseball crazy, but in this corridor it's almost nonexistent and there are some exceptional athletes whose talents go undiscovered.

Just some of my musings, I hope it's helpful. I look forward to talking to you, and seeing you later on.

Sincerely,
Anup Sinha

-----Original Message-----
From: Miller, Darrell <darrell.miller@mlb.com>
To: nupester@aol.com
Sent: Tue, Sep 8, 2009 2:22 pm
Subject: Re: Visited Proposed Site

Yes I have been to the proposed site many times I have been busy with the koshien usa tournament with the japanese all stars

Feel free to give me any input and observations when you have a chance

(phone number)

Darrell

From: nupester@aol.com <nupester@aol.com>
To: Miller, Darrell
Sent: Thu Sep 03 00:44:05 2009
Subject: Visited Proposed Site
Hi Darrell,

I was wondering if you'd had the chance to visit the proposed site for the Miami/Hialeah UYA. I went by there today and would like to share my impressions, if you care to hear them.

Feel free to call me anytime you wish, or I can pass them on via e-mail.

Hope all's well.

-Anup

(c)(phone number erased)
(h)(phone number erased)

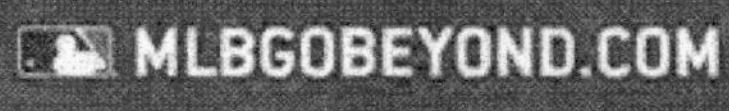

This summer, please join Major League Baseball and the PEOPLE All-Stars Among Us in your community by signing up to volunteer at MLBGoBeyond.com.

Appendix J: Cuban-Born Major League Players as of 2013 All-Star Break (17)

**Attended high school in United States*

Yonder Alonso*, 1B, San Diego Padres

Yuniesky Betancourt, 3B/1B, Milwaukee Brewers

Yoenis Cespedes, CF, Oakland A's

Aroldis Chapman, LHP, Cincinnati Reds

Jose Contreras, RHP, Pittsburgh Pirates

Yunel Escobar, SS, Tampa Bay Rays

Jose Fernandez*, RHP, Miami Marlins

Yasmani Grandal*, C, San Diego Padres

Adeiny Hechavarria, SS, Miami Marlins

Jose Iglesias, SS, Boston Red Sox (traded to Detroit Tigers in late July)

Leonys Martin, CF, Texas Rangers

Yuniesky Maya, RHP, Washington Nationals

Kendrys Morales, 1B, Seattle Mariners

Brayan Pena, C, Detroit Tigers

Yasiel Puig, RF, Los Angeles Dodgers

Alexei Ramirez, SS, Chicago White Sox

Dayan Viciedo, LF, Chicago White Sox

All of these Cuban-born players are Black except for Alonso, Fernandez, Grandal, Iglesias, and Maya (5). Maya is Caucasian whereas the other four are considered mulatto by CIA race classification.

Appendix K: 1st-Round Drafted African-American Players by High School State Since 2000

This includes only the true 1st-round, not the sandwich-compensation picks. College players are assigned to the state where they graduated high school.

The number of Black 1st-round picks is the first number in the parentheses over the number of total 1st-roudners that year.

2000 (1/30): New Jersey-1

2001 (3/30): Georgia-1, Tennessee-1, Texas-1

2002 (5/30): Florida-2, Missouri-1, Texas-1, Virginia-1

2003 (3/30): Florida-2, California-1

2004 (3/30): California-1, Georgia-1, Texas-1

2005 (5/30): Florida-1, Missouri-1*, North Carolina-1, Oklahoma-1, Virginia-1

2006 (1/30): Virginia-1

2007 (4/30): Georgia-1, Kentucky-1, Mississippi-1, Tennessee-1

2008 (3/30): California-1, Connecticut-1, Florida-1

2009 (3/32): Florida-1, Georgia-1, Louisiana-1

2010 (4/32): Georgia-2, New York-1, Texas-1

2011 (1/33): California-1

2012 (7/31): Florida-2, Georgia-1, Michigan-1, Mississippi-1, New York-1, Texas-1

2013 (6/33): Califoria-3, Alabama-2, Georgia-1

*Missouri was represented twice by John Mayberry Jr. He was a 1st-round pick out of high school in 2002 and again out of Stanford University in 2005.

BIBLIOGRAPHY

Aaron, H., & Wheeler, L. (1991). *I Had a Hammer: The Hank Aaron Story.* New York: HarperPaperbacks.

Annie E. Casey Foundation. (2011). *Kids Count: Singe Parent Households.* Baltimore, MD.

Brashler, W. (1978). *Josh Gibson: A Life in the Negro Leagues.* New York: Harper & Row.

Central Intelligence Agency . (2013). *CIA World Factbook.*

Dawson, A., & Maimon, A. (2012). *If You Love This Game... An MVP's Life in Baseball.* Chicago: Triumph Books.

Dorish, J. (2011, November 12th). *Yahoo!Sports*. Retrieved from Average Salary in the NBA, NFL, MLB, NHL: www.yahoosports.com

Doyel, G. (2010, December 23rd). *NFL is Killing its Players*. Retrieved from CBS Sports: www.cbssports.com

Gaines, C. (2011, March 14th). After Five Years, MLB's Urban Youth Academy is a Resounding Success. *Business Insider*.

Glassey, C. (2010, June 16th). MLB Urban Youth Academy Sees 25 Drafted. *Baseball America*.

Harris Interactive. (2010). *Harris Interactive Poll: Favorite Sport.* Rochester, NY.

Hirsch, J. S. (2012). *Willie Mays: The Life, The Legend.* New York: Scribner.

Hochman, S. (2011, May 18th). Why Are Plans for Urban Youth Academy Stalled? *Philadelphia Inquirer*.

Lapchick, R., Aristeguieta, F., Clark, W., Cloud, C., Florzak, A., Frazier, D., et al. (2011). *The 2011 Racial and Gender Report Card: National Basketball Association.* The Institute for Diversity and Ethics in Sport (TIDES), Orlando, FL.

Lapchick, R., Calderon, A. D., Harless, C., & Turner, A. (2010). *The 2009 Racial and Gender Report Card: College Sport.* The Institute for Diversity and Ethics in Sport (TIDES), Orlando, FL.

Lapchick, R., Clark, W., Frazier, D., & Sarpy, C. D. (2011). *The 2011 Racial and Gender Report Card: National Football League.* The Institute for Diversity and Ethics in Sport (TIDES), Orlando, FL.

Lapchick, R., Kaiser, C., Caudy, D., & Wang, W. (2010). *The 2010 Racial and Gender Report Card: Major League Baseball.* The Institute for Diversity and Ethics in Sport (TIDES), Orlando, FL.

Lavigne, P. (2012, February 1st). *Top Football Talent Shifts to the South*. Retrieved from ESPN.com: www.ESPN.com

Lewis, M. (2003). *Moneyball: The Art of Winning an Unfair Game.* New York: WW Norton.

MLB Advanced Media, L.P. (2001-2013). Retrieved from Official Site of Major League Baseball: www.MLB.com

National Collegiate Athletic Association. (2013). *NCAA Official Website*. Retrieved from www.NCAA.org

NBA Media Ventures, L.L.C. (2013). Retrieved from NBA Official Website: www.NBA.com

Newton, C., & Thompson, C. (2013, June 13th). *My Path to the Pros*. Retrieved from ESPN The Magazine (ESPN.com): www.ESPN.com

NFL Enterprises LLC. (2012). Retrieved from Official Site of the National Football League: www.NFL.com

NHL Enterprises, L.P. (2012). Retrieved from Official Website of the National Hockey League: www.NHL.com

O'Neil, B., Wulf, S., & Conrads, D. (1996). *I Was Right On Time: My Journey From the Negro Leagues to the Majors.* New York: Simon and Schuster Paperbacks.

Pop Warner Little Scholars, Inc. (2013). *Greater Miami South Florida Pop Warner Football.* Retrieved from www.miamipopwarner.org

Puckett, K. (1993). *I Love This Game! My Life and Baseball.* New York: HarperCollins.

Rickey, B. (1995). *Branch Rickey's Little Blue Book: Wit and Strategy from Baseball's Last Wise Man.* New York: Macmillan.

Rickey, B., & Riger, R. (1965). *The American Diamond: A Documentary of the Game of Baseball.* New York: Simon and Schuster.

Ruck, R. (2011). *Raceball: How the Major Leagues Colonized the Black and Latin Game.* Boston: Beacon Press.

Ruggles, S. (1994, February). The Origins of African-American Family Structure. *American Sociological Review*, 136-151.

Saint Onge, J. M., Krueger, P. M., & Rogers, R. G. (2008, December). Historical trends in height, weight, and body mass: Data from U.S. Major League Baseball players, 1869–1983. *Economics and Human Biology*, 482-488.

Simmons, B. (2009). *The Book of Basketball.* New York: ESPN books.

Sokolove, M. (2004). *The Ticket Out: Darryl Strawberry and the Boys of Crenshaw.* New York: Simon & Schuster.

Sports Reference, LLC. (2000-2013). *Baseball-Reference.com.* Sports.

Sports Reference, LLC. (2000-2013). *Basketball-Reference.com.*

Sports Reference, LLC. (2000-2013). *Hockey-Reference.com.*

Sports Reference, LLC. (2000-2013). *Pro-Football-Reference.com.*

Statistics Canada. (1971). *Canada 1971 Census.*

Statistics Canada. (2011). *Canada 2011 Census.*

Thrift, S., & Shapiro, B. (1990). *The Game According to Syd: The Theories and Teachings of Baseball's Leading Innovator.* New York: Simon and Schuster.

United States Census Bureau. (2001). *2000 Census.*

United States Census Bureau. (2011). *2010 Census.*

USA Football. (2011). *2011 Opening Day and Hometowns.* New York: NFL Media.

Weiner, J. (2010, June 7th). Youth Baseball Academy Pitched in Stadium Deal Sits on Bench. *Miami Today.*

Weiner, J. (2011, September 8th). Major League Baseball's Youth Academy in Florida Marlins Stadium Deal Still Just a Dream. *Miami Today.*

White, F., & Althaus, B. (2012). *One Man's Dream: My Town, My Team, My Time.* Olathe, KS: Ascend Books.

Wilczynski, M. (2011, November 22nd). *Average NBA Career Length for Players*. Retrieved from Weak Side Awareness: www.weaksideawareness.blogspot.com

INDEX

Aaron, Hank, 6, 7, 16, 35, 158, 184, 187, 201, 235
Abdul-Jabbar, Kareem, 34, 35, 79
Acres Homes (Houston, TX), 145, 146
Alabama State University, 123
Alexander, Jay, 123
All-Black lineup in the NBA, 30
Allegheny Cemetery, 11
Alley, Gene, 30
All-Star Games in the 1950s, 32
Alma College, 153
Alomar, Roberto, 193
Alonso, Yonder, 158, 233
American Basketball Association (ABA), 117
American League, 31, 32, 33, 68, 71, 148, 150, 153, 225, 229
Amite High School (Amite City, LA), 116
Anaheim, CA, 28
Anderson, Tim, 185
Andrus, Elvis, 159
Andujar, Joaquin, 12
Annie E. Casey Foundation, 126, 182, 235
Appling County High School (GA), 181
Arizona Diamondbacks, 134, 155, 156
Arocho, Steve, 37
Atlanta: inner city, 182
Atlanta Blue Jays, 179, 183
Atlanta Braves, 48, 107, 140, 152, 156, 175, 180
Atlanta, GA, 16
Atlantic Coast Conference (ACC), 118, 119
Auburn University, 72, 177, 185
Austin, Jay, 179, 181, 182
Avery, Xavier, 179, 182
Baerga, Carlos, 194
Baez, Danys, 108
Baker, Lejon, 140, 141
Baldwin, Guerry, 178
Baltimore Orioles, 67, 85, 91, 92, 93, 148, 224
Barney, Lem, 118
Baseball America, 74, 75, 91, 140, 235
Baseball Hall of Fame, 32, 36, 37, 229
Baseball Writers Association of America (BBWAA), 64
Baseball-Reference.com, 45, 49, 237
Basketball, 5, 6, 13, 14, 18, 20, 21, 22, 27, 34, 35, 36, 40, 41, 45, 46, 47, 48, 62, 63, 68, 77, 80, 82, 95, 99, 100, 103, 105, 107, 108, 109, 111, 113, 114, 115, 117, 118, 120, 121, 122, 123, 124, 125, 126, 127, 128, 129, 130, 132, 144, 145, 146, 149, 153, 155, 156, 157, 158, 160, 161, 166, 168, 171, 177, 178, 179, 181, 183, 185, 186, 189, 190, 192, 193, 195, 196, 197, 199, 210, 235, 236, 237
Basketball Association of America (BAA), 117, 152
Basketball Hall of Fame, 153
Batista, Riley, 129
Battier, Shane, 199, 215
Baxley, Georgia, 178
Baylor University, 195
Beane, Billy, 59, 80, 84
Beaumont, Texas, 119
Beckham Jeremy, 183
Beckham, Tim, 179, 182, 183, 185
Belanger, Mark, 58
Bell, Buddy, 58
Bell, Cool Papa, 10, 189
Bell, George, 12
Bell, Raja, 168
Belle Isle, 47, 115
Bellflower, California, 141
Beltre, Adrian, 159
Bench, Johnny, 117
Berrien High School (Nashville, GA), 181
Berwanger, Jay, 116
Bethune Cookman University, 123
Big-10 Conference, 119
Big-12 Conference, 118
Bird, Larry, 63, 64
Birmingham Black Barons, 184
Birmingham, AL, 16, 46, 184
Black Bambino, The, 2, 8, 9, 40
Blackburn, Wayne, 68
Blanks, Kyle, 104, 105, 106
Blomberg, Ron, 117
Bloomfield Hills, Michigan, 96
Blount, Mel, 119
Blue, Vida, 71, 74, 201
Bol, Manute, 48
Bonds, Barry, 75, 87, 162
Boomer Babies, 7
Boras, Scott, 56
Boros, Steve, 149
Boston Celtics, 30, 63, 153
Boston Red Sox, 27, 31, 59, 84, 177, 224, 233
Bourgeois, Jason, 25, 145, 146
Bourn, Michael, 25, 145
Bowden, Bobby, 156
Boys and Girls Club, 24
Bradley, Bill, 153

Brashler, William, 10, 40, 235
Brasuell, Thomas, 29, 131, 132
Braun, Ryan, 64
Brett, George, 150
Brooklyn Dodgers, 10, 33
Brooks, Hubie, 13
Brown, Chris, 18
Brown, Domonic, 77, 78, 89, 176, 177, 192
Brown, Hubie, 18
Brown, Jim (NFL Hall of Famer), 35
Brown, Willie (former NFL player), 119
Buchanan, Buck (former NFL player), 119
Bullington. Bryan, 156
Burleson, Rick, 17, 58
Business Insider, 141, 235
Butler, Tommy, 12, 142
Butzel Field (Detroit, MI), 115
Buxton, Byron, 178, 181, 186
Byrd, Marlon, 178
Cabell, Enos, 13, 17, 201
Cabrera, Miguel, 46
Cador, Roger, 123, 125, 160
Cal State-Fullerton, 140, 170
California Angels, 41, 117, 132
Campbell, Jim, 49
Campbell, Luther, 128
Canada, 6, 27, 128, 129, 130, 152, 237
Canadian census, 129
Cano, Robinson, 12, 159
Canyon Springs High School (Moreno Valley, CA), 54
Cardinal Newman High School, 111
Carew, Rod, 7, 22, 201
Carlton, Steve, 133
Carmichael, Harold, 119
Carol City (Miami, FL), 133, 134, 167, 220, 231
Cash, Dave, 30, 201
Castlemont High School, 22
Castro, Fidel, 158
Caudill, Bill, 56
CBSsports.com, 162
Cedeno, Cesar, 126
Centennial High School, 13
Centennial High School (Compton, CA), 143
Central Intelligence Agency Factbook, 158
Cerone, Rick, 66
Cespedes, Yoenis, 159, 187, 233
Chamberlain, Wilt, 34, 35, 153
Chapman College, 15, 17
Chapman, Aroldis, 159, 187, 233
Character is Not a Statistic, by Bill Lajoie and Anup Sinha, 55, 67
Charleston, Oscar, 10, 36, 187, 189
Chen, Albert, 63
Chicago Bears, 69, 116, 182, 197
Chicago Bulls, 63
Chicago Cubs, 15, 66, 69, 224
Chicago White Sox, 12, 66, 117, 142, 159, 224, 233
Chicago, IL, 23
Chigbogu, Justin, 83
Choo, Shin-Soo, 46
Cincinnati RBI program, 27
Cincinnati Reds, 13, 84, 88, 90, 152, 159, 173, 187, 224, 233
Cincinnati Royals, 152, 153
Cincinnati, OH, 22, 27
Clairton, Pennsylvania, 41
Clark, Will, 16, 17
Clarke, Chevy, 179, 181
Clemente, Roberto, 30, 187
Cleveland Indians, 46, 224
Clines, Gene, 30, 201
Cobb, Ty, 44
Cochrane, Mickey, 9, 189
Cole, Alex, 53
Coleman, Len, 37, 38, 172
Coleman, Vince, 52, 53
College Scholarship Plan (CSP), 124, 164
College World Series, 170
Colombia, 113
Colorado Rockies, 74, 90
Comerica Park, 190
Compton Baseball Academy Teams (CBAT), 143
Compton Connie Mack League, 17
Compton High School, 13
Contreras, Jose, 159, 233
Cooper, Cecil, 58, 201
Copperas Cove High School (TX), 195, 198
Courter Technological High School (OH), 92
Cowens, Al, 13
Cows and chickens playing baseball, 132
Crawford, Carl, 25, 26, 79, 145, 159
Crawford, Willie, 131, 201
Creighton University, 46
Crenshaw High School (Los Angeles, CA),13, 14, 140
Cressy Park, 17
Cretin-Derham High School, 111
Crisp, Coco, 19
Cromartie, Warren, 22, 133
Crosby, Sidney, 63
Cruz, Nelson, 159
Cuba, 7, 108, 112, 113, 158, 159
Cy Young Award, 64, 76, 159

Dallas Mavericks, 196, 197
Dallas, TX, 23
Davis High School (Houston, TX), 26
Davis, Eric, 14, 18, 131, 143
Davis, Willie (former NFL player), 119
Dawson, Andre, 7, 22, 56, 57, 69, 70, 73, 74, 75, 133, 150, 195
Dead Ball Era, 43, 44
DeBuscherre, Dave, 115
DeBusschere, Dave, 153
Decker, Fred, 49
Del City High School (OK), 81
Delaware State University, 123
Dempsey, Rick, 58
Denby High School (Detroit, MI), 71
Dent, Bucky, 133
Denver Broncos, 196
DePodesta, Paul, 84
DeShields Jr., Delino, 179, 182
Detroit Austin Catholic Preparatory School, 153
Detroit Country Day School, 115, 199
Detroit Free Press, 95
Detroit Lions, 91, 101, 160, 181, 190, 191, 192
Detroit News, 95
Detroit Pistons, 25, 153
Detroit Public School League, 47, 115
Detroit Tigers, 4, 15, 16, 41, 47, 49, 60, 63, 68, 69, 70, 71, 72, 84, 94, 96, 153, 160, 190, 192, 224, 233
Detroit Wheels, 49
Detroit, MI, 23, 27
Detroit, Michigan, 4, 115
Dickerson, Eric, 79
Dickey, Bill, 9, 189
DiMaggio, Joe, 10, 189
Doby, Larry, 10, 45, 123
Dominguez High School, 13
Dominican Republic, 7, 19, 108, 112, 113, 114, 126, 127, 133, 151, 152, 158
Dorish, Joe, 161, 235
Dorsett, Tony, 54, 55, 162
Dorsey High School, 13
Doyel, Gregg, 162
Drexler, Clyde, 189
Duke University, 117
Dunedin High School, 80
Dunn, Adam, 90
DuPont High School (WV), 190
Durham, Leon, 22
Durst, Nathan, 160
Dye, Anthony, 179, 181
East Coast Showcase, 179
East Cobb Baseball, 178, 179
Eastern Michigan University, 96, 123
Ebony Magazine, 37
Economics and Human Biology, 43, 236
Eisenhower High School (Houston, TX), 145
Ellis, Dock, 17, 30, 202
Elway, John, 63
Emory University, 180
Encarnacion, Edwin, 159
Ervin, Phillip, 185
Esasky, Nick, 133
Espinosa, Luis, 136
ESPN, 35, 75, 182, 186, 236
ESPN The Magazine, 193
Ewing, Patrick, 79
Fairfield Industrial High School, 46
Fantasy baseball, 5
Feliz, Neftali, 159
Feller, Bob, 189
Fernandez, Jose, 158, 233
Fernandez, Lionel (former Dominican Republic president), 126
Fielder, Cecil, 74
Fielder, Prince, 74, 76, 77, 87, 158
Flagler Development, 138
Flood, Curt, 115
Florida A&M University, 69, 70, 123, 151
Florida Marlins, 76, 135, 138, 194, 237
Florida Memorial University, 134, 167
Flowers, Burnell, 92
Football, 2, 5, 6, 13, 14, 20, 21, 23, 34, 35, 36, 39, 40, 41, 42, 45, 47, 48, 49, 50, 51, 54, 55, 62, 63, 72, 77, 78, 80, 88, 89, 90, 93, 94, 95, 96, 97, 99, 100, 101, 103, 105, 107, 108, 109, 110, 111, 112, 113, 114, 116, 118, 119, 120, 121, 122, 123, 124, 125, 126, 127, 128, 129, 130, 133, 134, 136, 144, 145, 146, 149, 155, 156, 157, 158, 159, 160, 161, 162, 163, 164, 166, 167, 168, 169, 171, 173, 175, 177, 179, 181, 182, 183, 184, 185, 186, 189, 190, 192, 193, 194, 195, 196, 197, 198, 200, 220, 231, 232, 235, 236, 237
Forbes Field, 43
Ford, Dan, 13, 131, 201
Ford, Dave, 67
Forest Brook High School (Houston, TX), 146
Foster, George, 12, 201
Fowler, Dexter, 74, 178
Freehan, Bill, 115, 153
Fremont High School, 12, 13, 14, 16, 20, 131
Frierson, Jarred, 140
Fulton County Stadium, 180

Gaines, Cork, 141
Galileo High School, 34
Gammons, Peter, 63
Garces, Rich, 131
Garcon, Pierre (NFL player), 114
Gardena High School, 13
Gault, Willie, 183
Gaye, Marvin (singer), 75
Gayo, Rene, 108, 126, 158
Georgia: Black baseball revival in, 175
Georgia Tech, 88, 91, 129, 192, 212, 213, 215, 216, 218
Giamatti, Bart, 37, 124
Gibson, Bob (Hall of Fame pitcher), 35, 45, 46, 65, 79, 117, 187, 202
Gibson, Josh, 9, 10, 11, 36, 39, 40, 41, 42, 65, 187, 188, 189, 235
Gillick, Pat, 52, 60
Gipp, George, 189
Gonzalez, Adrian, 46
Gonzalez, Alden (MLB.com), 148
Gonzalez, Alex, 133
Gooden, Dwight, 2, 66, 67, 74, 76
Goodrich, Gail, 153
Goodwin, Danny, 66, 71
Goodwin, Greg, 176, 178
Gordon, Dee, 81
Gordon, Tom, 74, 75
Gorman, Lou, 151
Gose, Anthony, 141
Grambling State University, 119, 123
Grand Rapids, MI, 12
Grandal, Yasmani, 158, 233
Greenberg, Hank, 117
Greene, Joe (NFL Hall of Famer), 163
Greene, Larry (minor leaguer), 181, 185
Gretzky, Wayne, 63
Grich, Bobby, 193
Griffey Jr., Ken, 24, 27, 87, 190
Griffin High School (GA), 182
Griffin III, Robert, 188, 190, 195, 198
Griffin, Alfredo, 58
Griffin, Trey, 182
Guerrero, Pedro, 12
Guzik, Rob, 190
Gwynn, Tony, 123
Haiti, 114
Halas, George, 189
Hall, Irvin, 25, 147
Hampton, Ike, 142
Hamptons, Rodney and Robert, 49
Hanson, Jason (former NFL player), 160
Harlem (New York, NY), 172
Harlem Globetrotters, 46
Harlem RBI, 22, 24
Harris Interactive Polls, 107
Harris, Lenny, 76, 133
Harrison, Bill, 149
Harvard University, 116, 146, 162, 211
Harvey, Ryan, 80
Haslem, Udonis, 168, 212
Hazzard, Walt, 153
Heinsohn, Tommy, 153
Heisman Trophy, 116, 194
Henderson, Rickey, 7, 22, 57, 199
Hendrick, George, 12, 13, 17, 131, 201
Hendrix, Jimi (singer), 75
Hernandez, Carlos (mayor of Hialeah, FL), 139
Hernandez, Felix, 64, 159
Hernandez, Jackie, 30, 33
Hernandez, Keith, 58
Hernandez, Livan, 159
Hernandez, Orlando, 159
Herzog, Whitey, 53
Heyward, Jason, 175, 178, 186
Hialeah, Florida, 133, 135, 136, 137, 138, 139, 167, 231, 232
Hill, Grant (former NBA player), 161
Hiroshima, Japan, 19
Historically Black Colleges and Universities (HBCU), 118, 119, 123, 142
Hochman, Stan, 137, 148
Hockey, 5, 6, 96, 128, 129, 130, 171, 194, 195, 198
Hoffman, Trevor, 67
Holy Cross College, 153
Homeplate Chili Dogs, 179
Homestead Grays, 40, 42
Horton, Willie, 72, 115, 153, 201
Hough, Charlie, 133
Houston Astros, 52
Houston Police Department, 146
Houston, inner city, 133
Houston, TX, 25
Houston's RBI program, 25
Howard, Dwight, 47, 79, 186
Howard, Juwan, 161
Howard, Ryan, 44
Hurricane Katrina, 147
I Had a Hammer, by Hank Aaron and Lonnie Wheeler, 35, 235
I Love This Game, by Kirby Puckett, 110

If You Love This Game, by Andre Dawson and Alan Maimon), 151, 235
Iginla, Jarome, 129
Indianapolis, IN, 23, 28
Inkster High School (MI), 71
Iverson, Allen, 96, 189
Jackson State University, 118
Jackson, Bo, 14, 40
Jackson, Desean, 199
Jackson, MS, 16
Jackson, Muzzy, 36, 90, 125, 134, 155, 173, 189
Jacobs, Brandon (minor leaguer), 177
Jacobs, David, 163
James Madison High School (Houston, TX), 146
James, Bill, 59
James, LeBron, 47, 188, 199
Jennings, Desmond, 184
Jesuit High School (New Orleans), 16
Jeter, Derek, 63
Johnson, Alex, 115, 201
Johnson, Calvin, 88, 89, 90, 91, 93, 94, 181, 190, 191, 192, 196
Johnson, Charles, 74
Johnson, Jervenski, 51, 116
Johnson, Magic, 9, 36, 63, 64, 189
Joiner, Charlie (former NFL player), 119
Jones, Adam, 87
Jones, Darryl (former minor leaguer), 131
Jones, James (NBA player), 168
Jupiter, FL, 132
Jurges, Billy, 68
Kaepernick, Colin, 190, 200
Kaiser, Bobby, 95, 101
Kaiser, Cecil, 95
Kansas City Royals, 36, 107, 148, 150, 151, 167, 173, 189
Kansas City Royals Academy, 148, 150, 151
Kansas State University, 149, 215, 218
Kauffman Stadium, 107
Kauffman, Ewing, 148, 151
Kazmaier, Dick, 116
Kemp, Matt, 64, 65, 80, 81, 82, 83, 86, 87, 159, 187, 192
Kidd, Jason, 161
Kids Count, 126, 182, 235
Kirkland, Willie, 71
Koufax, Sandy, 117
Kring, Steve, 88
L.A. City Section, 131
Lachemann, Marcel, 17
Lachemann, Rene, 17
Lajoie, Bill, 15, 16, 49, 50, 55, 67, 68, 69, 70, 71
Lake Howell High School (FL), 196
Landis, Kennesaw Mountain, 10
Landreaux, Ken, 13, 142
Lapchick, Dr. Richard (TIDES), 45, 121, 235
Larkin, Barry, 27, 63, 197
Larkin, Shane, 197
Larkins, Bruce, 122, 127
Latino, Benny, 51, 116
Lavigne, Paula, 182, 186
Lawrence, Chip, 78, 89, 175, 192
LeFlore, Ron, 49, 50, 54, 55, 201, 204
Lemming, Tom, 186
Lemon, Chet, 13, 56, 95, 131
Leuzinger High School, 13
Leuzinger, Mike, 81
Liberty City (Miami, FL), 133, 167, 173
Lincoln High School (Kansas City, MO), 149
Locke High School, 12, 20
Logan. Joe, 127, 197
London, Ontario, 198
Loney, James, 81
Long Beach Poly High School (CA), 199
Long Beach State University, 119, 140, 170
Long Beach Wilson High School, 141
Los Angeles Angels, 178
Los Angeles Clippers, 14
Los Angeles Dodgers, 47, 81
Los Angeles Lakers, 153
Los Angeles, CA, 12, 13, 14, 15, 17, 18, 19, 21, 22, 23, 27, 29, 52, 64, 83, 84, 86, 89, 115, 131, 133, 140, 141, 142, 143, 144, 145, 146, 153, 168, 169, 172, 173, 177, 191, 192, 193, 203, 204, 205, 206, 207, 208, 210, 211, 220, 224, 233
Lucas, Jerry, 153
Lucas, Ray, 71
Luhnow, Jeff, 53
MacGregor Park (Houston, TX), 145, 146
Maddox, Garry, 59
Maddox, Gary, 56
Major League Baseball (MLB), 2, 3, 5, 6, 7, 8, 18, 19, 20, 21, 23, 24, 25, 28, 29, 31, 35, 36, 37, 41, 42, 43, 45, 52, 56, 57, 62, 63, 66, 68, 71, 80, 84, 85, 87, 91, 92, 111, 112, 113, 117, 121, 123, 124, 128, 129, 131, 132, 133, 134, 135, 136, 137, 138, 139, 140, 141, 142, 144, 145, 146, 147, 148, 152, 153, 154, 155, 161, 162, 163, 166, 167, 168, 169, 170, 171, 172, 173, 174, 175, 177, 185, 188, 191, 192, 193, 194, 195, 196, 197, 198, 201, 203, 205, 207, 208, 224, 226, 227, 232, 235, 236, 237
Major League Scouting Bureau (MLSB), 68

Malone, Moses, 79
Manno, Bruce, 53
Manual Arts High School (Los Angeles, CA), 115
Manz Field (Detroit, MI), 115
Marichal, Juan, 126
Marino, Dan, 63
Marist Academy (GA), 176
Markakis, Nick, 178
Marlins Ballpark, 135, 136, 138
Marlins RBI program, 134
Marshall, Brandon, 196
Martin Luther King High School (Atlanta, GA), 182
Martin, Al, 48, 49
Martin, Mike (baseball coach, Florida State), 156
Martin, Russell, 40, 81
Martinez, Pedro, 112
Martinsville, Virginia, 68
Martz, Jim, 92, 93, 94
Mattingly, Don, 194
Matumbo, Dikembe, 79
Mauer, Joe, 154
Maxpreps.com, 145
Maxwell, Jim, 93
Mayberry Sr., John, 27, 115, 201
Mays, Willie, 6, 7, 9, 16, 45, 46, 64, 65, 82, 95, 158, 184, 235
McAlister, Fred, 53
McAlpin, Chris, 89, 178, 180, 186, 191, 192
McCann, Brian, 178
McClymonds High School (Oakland, CA), 115
McCovey, Willie, 117, 184, 201
McCutchen, Andrew, 89, 158, 187
McDonald Jr., James, 48, 81
McDonald Sr., James, 48
McGee, Willie, 52
McGwire, Mark, 162
McIlvaine, Joe, 55, 67, 109, 113, 120, 121, 122, 164
McKeon, Jack, 149
McNabb, Donovan, 39
McNamee, Brian, 163
Melbourne, Florida, 77
Mendoza, Mario, 58
Mentoring Viable Prospects (MVP), 177
Merrill Lynch, 125
Miami Dade College, 167
Miami Dade-North College, 134, 136
Miami Gardens, FL, 133
Miami Heat, 168, 196, 199
Miami Jackson High School, 133
Miami Lakes, FL, 133, 220, 231
Miami Marlins, 144, 154, 158, 233
Miami Northwestern High School, 133
Miami Southridge High School, 133
Miami Today, 136, 138, 237
Miami, FL, 23, 132
Miami-Dade County Department of Environmental Resources Management, 136
Michigan State University, 119
Midwest City High School (OK), 81
Miller, Cheryl, 132
Miller, Darrell, 3, 132, 133, 136, 137, 141, 143, 147, 231
Miller, Reggie, 132
Miller, Ron, 144
Milloy, Lawyer, 190
Milwaukee Brewers, 64
Minnesota Twins, 150, 154, 181
Mississippi State University, 17
Mobile, AL, 16
Mobile, Alabama, 35, 184, 203, 210, 223
Monahan, Mark, 96
Moneyball, 59, 80, 81, 84, 236; *The Art of Winning an Unfair Game,* by Michael Lewis, 59
Monk, Art, 162
Montreal Canadiens, 194
Montreal Expos, 69, 77, 127
Moore, Matt, 104
Moose, Bob, 31
Morgan, Joe, 22, 201
Moriarty High School (NM), 104
Moseby, Lloyd, 22, 56
Moss, Randy, 189, 190
Mount Carmel High School, 15
Murphy, Dale, 56, 80
Murphy, Dwayne, 56, 57
Murray, Eddie, 12, 13, 58
Murtaugh, Danny, 30
Myers, D'Arby, 141
Naismith, James, 117
Nash, Telvin, 183
Nathaniel “Traz” Powell Stadium, 167
National Basketball Association (NBA), 2, 5, 6, 8, 14, 20, 21, 22, 23, 27, 30, 33, 34, 35, 45, 46, 47, 48, 60, 65, 79, 103, 107, 109, 114, 117, 132, 145, 147, 152, 153, 154, 158, 160, 161, 164, 166, 168, 170, 185, 187, 188, 189, 190, 191, 192, 193, 196, 197, 198, 199, 210, 227, 235, 236, 237
National Collegiate Athletic Association (NCAA), 17, 95, 117, 118, 119, 120, 121, 122, 124, 142, 153, 158, 160, 166, 185, 194, 236
National Football League (NFL), 3, 5, 6, 8, 20, 21, 23, 27, 30, 34, 35, 40, 41, 42, 45, 46, 47, 48, 49, 55, 60,

61, 65, 69, 79, 88, 89, 90, 91, 94, 102, 107, 110, 114, 116, 117, 118, 119, 128, 133, 134, 145, 146, 147, 157, 158, 160, 161, 162, 163, 164, 166, 167, 168, 169, 170, 173, 174, 181, 182, 184, 185, 187, 188, 189, 190, 191, 193, 194, 195, 196, 197, 198, 199, 200, 220, 227, 231, 232, 235, 236, 237
National Hockey League (NHL), 6, 30, 60, 128, 129, 161, 170, 194, 198, 235, 236
National League, 12, 31, 32, 33, 37, 71, 76, 92, 224, 229
NBA Finals, 5, 193, 196
Negro league, 9, 10, 36, 39, 95, 126, 184, 189
Nelms, Chris, 24, 27
Nelson, Chris, 176, 178
Nettles, Graig, 58
New Orleans, LA, 16
New Orleans, Louisiana, 145, 147, 148, 150, 169, 193, 204, 205, 208
New York Giants (NFL), 190
New York Knicks, 153
New York Mets, 14, 67, 116
New York Yankees, 27, 33, 150, 154, 225
New York, NY, 25, 34, 139, 223
Newcombe, Don, 10, 45
Newton, Cam, 186, 190, 193
NFL Players Association (NFLPA), 162
Nicaragua, 113
Nike Combine (football), 156, 157
Norris, Mike, 22
North Carolina AT&T University, 123
North Carolina Central University, 123
North Shore High School (Houston, TX), 146
Northrup, Jim, 153
Northwestern High School (Detroit, MI), 27, 71, 115
Notre Dame High School (Sherman Oaks, CA), 194
Nuss, Melvin, 100
O'Neil, Buck, 36, 67, 189
Oakland A's, 20, 59, 84, 148, 159, 187, 233
Oakland High School, 22
Oakland Tech High School, 22, 223
Oakland, CA, 22
Ogando, Alexi, 159
Ogden, Dr. David, 80, 125
Oglivie, Ben, 22, 201, 203
Okoye, Christian, 48
Olajuwan, Hakeem, 48, 79
Oliver, Al, 30, 201
Omaha Technical High School, 46
One Man's Dream, by Frank White, 149
O'Neal, Shaquille, 35, 36, 79, 189
Opa-Locka, FL, 133, 231
Orlando Reds, 127, 197
Orlando, Florida, 196
Orlando, Frank, 115
Ortiz, David, 159
Otis, Amos, 57, 201
Ottawa Hills High School (Grand Rapids, MI), 153
Overbrook High School (Philadelphia, PA), 153
Owens, Malcolm, 53, 54
Pacheco, Jordan, 104
Page, Mitchell, 13
Page, Ted, 9
Paige, Satchel, 10, 36, 184, 189
Palermo, Steve, 170
Panama, 113
Parker, Dave, 7, 22, 27, 91, 92, 93, 94, 201
Parkview High School (Lilburn, GA), 177
Parr, James, 104
Parrish, Lance, 41, 84
Paul, Chris, 87, 189, 192, 193
Paul, Mike, 17
Paul, Xavier, 81
Payton, Walter, 118, 119, 162
PerfectGame.org, 75
Perkin, Dave, 31, 32, 119, 140, 224
Peterson, Adrian, 39, 87
Philadelphia Eagles, 199
Philadelphia Flyers, 198
Philadelphia Phillies, 52, 77, 131, 150, 181, 224
Philadelphia Warriors, 153
Phillips Baseball Center, 177
Phillips, Brandon, 175, 176, 177, 186, 190
Phillips, James, 177, 178
Phillips, P.J., 178
Phillips, Porsha, 178
Pickens, Gerald, 143
Pierre, Erwin, 112
Pinson, Vada, 115, 201
Pittsburgh Crawfords, 40, 42
Pittsburgh Pirates, 30, 33, 41, 48, 71, 84, 93, 108, 148, 156, 158, 224, 233
Pittsburgh Steelers, 40
Pittsburgh, PA, 9, 11
Plano, Texas, 163
PNC Park, 187
Polo Grounds, The, 43, 95
Ponchartrain Park, 147
Pontiac Central High School, 99
Pontiac Central High School (MI), 94
Pontiac, MI, 25, 94
Pop Warner Football, 128, 134, 168, 232, 236
Posey, Buster, 178

Pote, Phil, 16, 20, 91, 94, 131, 193
Potterson, John, 104
Price, David, 64
Princeton University, 153
ProspectWire.com, 56
Pruitt, Marvin, 176
Puckett, Kirby, 110
Puerto Rico, 113, 152
Puig, Yasiel, 159, 187, 233
Pujols, Albert, 46
Raines, Tim, 57
Ramirez, Alexei, 159, 233
Ramirez, Hanley, 159
Rancho Cucamonga, CA, 131, 210, 211
Randle, Lenny, 13, 17, 201
Randolph, Willie, 22
Range factor (RF), 59
RBI World Series, 29
Redan High School, 77, 176
Reviving Baseball in the Inner Cities (RBI), 18, 19, 23, 24, 37, 172
Reynolds, Terry, 89
Rice, Jim, 7, 71, 201
Richard, J.R., 71, 201
Rickey, Branch, 10, 43, 44, 128, 190, 236
Rivera, Mariano, 46
Rivers, Mickey, 22, 133, 134, 167, 168, 201
Robaina, Julio, 135, 136, 138, 139
Robertson, Bob, 30
Robertson, Donte, 94, 95, 99, 101, 102, 103, 106, 191
Robertson, Oscar, 152, 153
Robinson, David (basketball Hall of Famer), 79
Robinson, Eddie (college football coach), 119
Robinson, Frank, 45, 115, 139, 201
Robinson, Jackie, 10, 31, 39, 43, 45, 118, 128
Robinson, Trayvon, 19, 81, 141
Rodon, Rafael (Flagler Development), 138
Rodriguez, Alex, 46, 133, 154, 162
Rogers, Michael, 81
Rowland High School (CA), 48
Rudolph, Travis, 111
Ruggles, Steven, 126
Russell, Campy, 103
Russell, Frank, 103
Russell, Walker, 103
Russell. Bill (Hall of Fame basketball player), 34, 35
Ruth, Babe, 9, 11, 43, 44
Saban, Nick, 184
Sabathia, C.C., 64, 74, 75, 87
Sabermetric fans, 63
Sabermetrics, 32
San Bernardino Community College, 53
San Diego Padres, 55, 104, 106, 131, 158, 175, 190, 233
San Diego State University, 75, 123, 211
San Francisco 49ers, 200
San Francisco Giants, 17, 71, 224
San Francisco, CA, 22
San Pedro de Macoris, DR, 12
Sanchez, Gaby, 133
Sandberg, Ryne, 193
Sanders, Barry (NFL Hall of Famer), 36, 189
Sandy Creek High School, 88, 192
Santa Fe College, 127
Santa Margarita Catholic High School (CA), 141
Santaluces Baseball Complex (Lantana, FL), 76
Santee, Wes, 149
Scarborough, Ontario, 198
Schmidt, Mike, 58
Schulte, Frank, 43
Scott, Tony, 22, 201
Scouting director, first African-American, 15
Seattle Mariners, 20, 64, 120, 159, 164, 233
Selig, Bud, 60, 61, 135, 139, 163, 164, 170, 171, 172
Serling, Rod (Twilight Zone host), 16
Shannon, Walter, 92
Sheehan, Joe, 63
Simmonds, Wayne (NHL player), 129, 198
Simmons Market Research, 107, 180
Simmons Market Research Bureau, 107
Simmons, Ted, 53
Simms, Chris, 90
Simpson, O.J., 34, 35, 93
Simpson, Wayne, 17
Slow pace of baseball, 6
Smith Jr., Dwight, 182
Smith, Bubba (former NFL player), 119
Smith, Darryl, 27
Smith, Dominic, 144
Smith, Lee, 66, 67, 68, 69
Smith, Lonnie, 13
Smith, Myles, 27
Smith, Ozzie, 7, 12, 13, 52, 58
Smith, Reggie, 13, 17, 201
Smokey Jasper Park (Houston, TX), 145, 146
Snider, Duke, 17
Society for American Baseball Research (SABR), 59
Solomon, Jimmie Lee, 29, 37, 131, 132, 135, 137, 138, 139, 144, 146, 147, 168, 174
Soper, Taylor, 141
Soriano, Alfonso, 159
Sosa, Sammy, 12, 112, 159, 162

Southeastern Conference (SEC), 118, 119, 181
Southeastern Louisiana University, 51
Southern University, 66, 119, 123, 160
Southwest Miami High School, 150
Speaks, Irv, 95
Spelman, Jeff, 152
Spielman, Rick, 101
Sports Illustrated, 31, 63, 119, 140, 191, 224
Springfield, Massachusetts, 117, 153
St. Augustine, Florida, 127
St. Elizabeth School (Oakland, CA), 22
St. Louis Cardinals, 5, 13, 52, 76, 102, 132, 224
St. Louis High School (MI), 153
St. Paul, Minnesota, 111
St. Petersburg, Florida, 153
Stallworth, John, 55
Stanley Cup, 5
Stanley, Mickey, 153
Stanton, Giancarlo, 194
Stargell, Willie, 30, 201, 205
Stennett, Rennie, 30
Stewart, Art, 149
Stewart, Dave, 22
Stewart, Shannon, 133
Stobbs, Chuck, 149
Stone Mountain, Georgia, 182, 212
Stone, Ron, 31
Strawberry, Darryl, 14, 18, 74, 131, 143, 237
Stringer, Martin, 25, 145, 147, 151, 152
Stringtown High School (OK), 150
Subban, P.K., 194
Summer Olympics, 1984, 18
Super Bowl, 5, 169
Sutherland, Dale, 58, 64, 82
Suzuki, Ichiro, 46
Syler, Pop, 17
Sylvester Turner Park, 145
Tallis, Cedric, 151
Tampa Bay Devil Rays, 51, 156
Tampa Bay Rays, 73, 104, 183, 184, 233
Tanana, Frank, 117
Tanner, Joe, 149
Tartabull, Danny, 133
Taylor, Lawrence, 39, 189, 190
Team Elite, 179
Team Georgia, 179
Teixeira, Mark, 24
Television ratings for Major League Baseball, 5
Templeton, Gary, 58
Terry, Joe, 140
Texas Rangers, 5, 17, 147, 154, 159, 233
The American Diamond, by Branch Rickey and Robert Riger, 44, 236
The Palace (of Auburn Hills), 25
Thomas, Derrel, 13, 17, 201
Thompson, Carmen, 193
Thompson, Jacob, 140
Thompson, Mitch, 195
Thompson, Trayce, 141
Thorpe, Jim, 189
Three Rivers Stadium, 30
Thrift, Jim, 85, 88, 94, 148, 149, 192
Thrift, Syd, 85, 148, 149
Tiger Stadium, 95
Tillman, Charles, 197
Toronto Blue Jays, 52, 159
Toronto, Ontario, 195
Trammell, Alan, 58, 63, 84
Trammell, Greg, 104
Trout, Mike, 192
Tuggle, Jesse, 183
Tulowitzki, Troy, 59
Turner Network Television (TNT), 132
Turner, Sylvester, 145, 146
Tuskegee University, 72
U.S. Census, 105, 157, 175
UCLA, 41, 117, 118, 142, 153, 170, 210, 211, 214, 217
Ueberroth, Peter, 18, 37
Ultimate zone rating (UZR), 59
Under Armour All-American Game, 179
Underwood, Pat, 60
Underwood, Tom, 60
University of Alabama, 184
University of Chicago, 116
University of Cincinnati, 152
University of Colorado, 161
University of Detroit, 153
University of Miami, 111, 197
University of Minnesota, 126
University of Nebraska-Omaha, 80, 125
University of New Mexico, 104, 105
University of North Carolina, 190
University of Notre Dame, 189
University of Southern California, 194
University of Texas, 90
University of Wisconsin, 151
Upton, B.J., 87, 109, 156
Upton, Justin, 23, 87, 109, 156
Upton, Manny, 87, 109, 155, 156, 180
Upton, Yvonne, 157
Urban Youth Academy: Compton, CA, 139; Houston, 136, 147

Urban Youth Academy, MLB, 2, 3, 37, 130, 131, 132, 134, 135, 136, 137, 139, 140, 141, 142, 144, 145, 146, 147, 152, 167, 173, 231, 235
USA Football, 128
Valentine, Ellis, 13
Value Over Replacement Player (VORP), 65
Veale, Bob, 31
Venezuela, 113, 151
Verducci, Tom, 63
Vick, Michael, 90, 189
Vickers, Lawrence, 146
Vincent, Fay, 37, 62, 123, 155, 172
Virginia Beach, VA, 24, 109, 156, 207
Virginia Tech, 90
Wade, Daryl, 147
Wade, Dwyane, 196, 199
Wagner, Honus, 44
Wagner, Leon, 71
Walnut High School (CA), 41
Walsh, Steve, 111, 119, 125, 128
Waltrip High School (Houston, TX), 145, 147
Ward, Gary, 13
Ward, Joel (NHL player), 129
Washington Nationals, 107, 233
Washington Redskins, 114, 195
Washington, Gene (former NFL player), 119
Washington, Ron, 147, 150, 151
Washington, U.L., 150, 151
Watson, Bob, 13, 131, 201
Watts riots, 15
Weakside Awareness (website), 161
Weaver, Brent, 81
Weiner, Jacquelyn, 136, 137, 138, 148
Wesley Barrow Stadium, 147
West Bloomfield High School (MI), 94
Westchester High School (Los Angeles, CA), 131
Western Pennsylvania: *as breeding ground for football*, 40
WGN (television network), 69
Whitaker, Lou, 58, 68, 69, 84, 190
White, Frank, 58, 149, 150, 151, 190, 193, 201
White, Logan, 47, 81, 82, 83, 86, 108, 121, 160, 173, 190
White, Roy, 17, 201
Wieters, Matt, 91
Williams, Andy (LADPR), 19
Williams, Billy, 16, 184, 201
Williams, Doug (former NFL player), 119
Williams, Jason (former NBA player from WV), 190
Williams, Jermaine (former minor leaguer), 131
Williams, Reggie (former minor leaguer from Bellflower, A), 141
Williams, Ted, 149, 189
Wills, Bump, 87
Wills, Maury, 87
Wilson, Don, 17
Wilson, Jake, 73, 104, 105, 106
Wilson, Russell, 190
Wilson, Willie, 57
Winfield, Dave, 7, 191, 192, 201
WJLB (Detroit radio station), 97
Wooden, John, 117
World Series, 5, 27, 46, 52, 53, 61, 76, 93, 150, 159, 170; television ratings, 170
World Series, 1971, 30
World Series, 1981, 13
World Series, 1982, 13
Wright, David, 89
Wright, Rayfield, 183
Wright, Wesley, 184, 211, 217, 218, 223
Yahoo! Sports, 161
Yavapai College, 105
Yeager, Steve, 58
YMCA, 117, 152
Young, Chris, 25, 145
Young, Delmon, 80
Young, John, 15, 16, 17, 18, 20, 26, 29, 37, 64, 71, 172
Yount. Robin, 58
Ypsilanti, Michigan, 96, 97

www.ingramcontent.com/pod-product-compliance
Lightning Source LLC
Chambersburg PA
CBHW071955040426
42447CB00009B/1345

* 9 7 8 0 6 1 5 9 0 0 1 4 8 *